Romantic Outlaws, Beloved Prisons

Romantic Outlaws, Beloved Prisons

The Unconscious Meanings of Crime and Punishment

Martha Grace Duncan

NEW YORK UNIVERSITY PRESS
New York and London

NEW YORK UNIVERSITY PRESS
New York and London

© 1996 by New York University
ALL RIGHTS RESERVED

Library of Congress Cataloging-in-Publication Data
Duncan, Martha Grace, 1945–
Romantic outlaws, beloved prisons : the unconscious meanings of
crime and punishment / Martha Grace Duncan.
p.   cm.
Includes bibliographical references and index.
ISBN 0-8147-1880-9 (alk. paper)   ISBN 0-8147-1881-7 pbk. (alk. paper)
1. Prison psychology.   2. Criminal psychology.   3. Prisons in
literature.   4. Criminals in literature.   I. Title.
HV6089.D84   1996
364.3—dc20   96-10124
                  CIP

Sections of Part One were originally published, in different form, in
the *California Law Review*, © 1988 by *California Law Review*, Inc. Reprinted from *California Law Review*, Vol. 76, No. 6, Dec. 1988, pp.
1201–48, by permission.

Sections of Part Two were originally published, in different form, in
Volume 1991 of the *University of Illinois Law Review*.

Sections of Part Three were originally published, in different form,
in 68 *Tulane Law Review*, © 1994, the *Tulane Law Review* Association.
All rights reserved.

New York University Press books are printed on acid-free paper,
and their binding materials are chosen for strength and durability.

Manufactured in the United States of America

10 9 8 7 6 5 4 3 2

This book is dedicated to the memory of

DONALD W. FYR.

For without friends, no one would choose to live,
though he had all other goods.

ARISTOTLE

Contents

Preface and Acknowledgments

> The web of our life is of a mingled yarn, good and ill together.
> —Shakespeare

This is a book about paradoxes and mingled yarns—about the bright sides of dark events, the silver linings of sable clouds. The book portrays law-abiding citizens who harbor a "strange liking" for criminal deeds, and criminals who find an "extraordinary beauty" in their prison yards. Thus, the book describes a nonutopian world in which criminals and noncriminals—while injuring each other in ways plain for all to see—nonetheless live together in a symbiotic as well as an adversarial relationship, needing each other, serving each other, living *for* as well as *off* each other, enriching each other's lives in profound and surprising ways.

This book has its roots in my doctoral training in the Political Science Department of Columbia University. There, in the 1970s, I became fascinated by individuals and groups who reject the legitimacy of the state and oppose its right to govern their lives. In papers with such titles as "Consciousness versus Spontaneity" and "Utopian Fury," I explored the socioeconomic and political matrices of Spanish anarchism, Brazilian peasant movements, and the Colombian "violencia." Throughout these endeavors, I benefited from the wise counsel of four scholars: Professors Douglas Chalmers, Mark Kesselman, Arnold Rogow, and Allan Silver.

During my years in graduate school, my interest gradually shifted from the objective conditions fostering radical and revolutionary movements to the idiosyncratic meanings of the movements for the participants themselves. In my search for better tools to investigate these subjective meanings, I decided, upon completion of my doctorate, to seek training as a research candidate at the Psychoanalytic Institute at the State University of New York, Downstate School of Medicine (now the NYU Psychoanalytic Institute at New York University Medical Center). Through a training analysis, classes, and clinical experience, I studied the complex vicissitudes of the human mind and the genesis of mental associations in childhood. From the beginning of my psychoanalytic training until the present time, I have received sustaining encouragement from the faculty of the Psychoanalytic Institute. I especially wish to thank my advisers, Drs. Marvin Nierenberg and Martin Silverman, and the former director of the Institute, Dr. Austin Silber.

In the fall of 1980, my ongoing preoccupation with issues centering on authority and interpretation led me to matriculate as a J.D. candidate at Yale Law School. Not surprisingly, I soon found myself drawn to Criminal Law as the arena where the state and the individual confront each other in the most dramatic fashion. It was my good fortune to study Criminal Law with Professor Abraham Goldstein, who fostered wonderful class discussions ranging far beyond the elements of crimes. Professor (now Dean) Anthony Kronman encouraged me to bring my previous training to bear on the law and gave generously of his time to help me obtain a position as a law professor.

In addition to these long-term intellectual debts, I am obligated in more immediate ways to the Emory University School of Law and its Dean, Howard O. Hunter, for summer research grants and a sabbatical leave to work on this project. I am also grateful to the following colleagues at Emory University, who took time from their own work to comment on previous drafts of this book: Professors David Bederman, Harriet King, Andrew Kull, Marc Miller, John Sitter, Gary Smith, and John Witte, Jr. I owe a word of special appreciation to Professors Thomas Arthur and Colleen Murphy, who not only read early drafts, but also served as my first audience for many of the ideas and much of the language in the book. My gratitude goes as well to Professor Sheridan Baker; the Reverend Richard Duncan; Professor Michael Hoffheimer; Professor James Kincaid; Richard Levin, Esquire; Professor Norval Morris; Dr. Ralph Roughton; C. G. Schoenfeld, Esquire; Professor J. Allen Smith; and Professor Walter O. Weyrauch—all of whom gave me the benefit of their thoughtful criticism.

Professors James Boyd White and Howard Kushner extended themselves far beyond the call of duty to help me find a suitable publisher; I am extremely grateful for their efforts. My secretaries, Radine Robinson and Rosalind Wiggins, took an active interest in the substance of the book while typing draft after draft with patience and good humor. The staff of the Emory Law Library provided indispensable research support.

I owe my greatest debt to my late friend and colleague, Donald W. Fyr. His overflowing love of books and ideas gladdened many an hour; his belief in me and my project helped to keep me on a steady course.

Introduction

> This was sometime a paradox, but now the time gives it proof.
> — Shakespeare

While Morton Sobell was serving a thirty-year prison sentence as a co-conspirator of the Rosenbergs, his wife, Helen, observed that the two of them were actually happier than many couples living in freedom. Sobell agreed, but cautioned his wife against expressing such an idea to others, lest it be misunderstood. People, he thought, "would say we were nuts, or even worse. Anyway, happiness is never as easy to explain as unhappiness." [1]

Recognizing that his and his wife's response to his imprisonment was paradoxical, Sobell feared that other people would reject their experience as invalid—a theme we see again in Erica Wallach's prison memoir, *Light at Midnight.* Describing the five years she served in Soviet camps and prisons, Wallach wrote that the great beauty of the Siberian landscape often awed her and her fellow prisoners; at times, they could not help stopping their work to admire the scenery. Yet, she reflected, "we did not dare admit it openly to each other: how could we possibly enjoy anything in the inferno!" Instead, they kept telling each other how much they *would* have admired the majestic views if they had gone there as tourists. [2]

In these vignettes, a complex, differentiated reality defeats the stereotyped expectation that penal confinement will prove an unequivocal evil. For certain positive aspects of experience—among them, love and beauty—the dichotomy of confinement and freedom is simply irrelevant. Yet, if Sobell's and Wallach's experiences strike us as paradoxical, still more deeply so are situations where the prisoner's happiness is not merely unaffected, but actually enhanced, by incarceration. In such cases, prison, because of its symbolic resonance, may come to stand for a nurturing mother or a matrix of spiritual rebirth. Here we see clearly the truth of Northrop Frye's remark: "Man lives, not directly or nakedly in nature like the animals, but within a mythological universe, a body of assumptions and beliefs developed from his existential concerns. Most of this is held unconsciously."[3]

This book will endeavor to explore two adjoining regions of this unconscious mythological universe: (1) positive images of penal confinement, and (2) romantic visions of criminals and their illegal deeds. Thus far, I have touched on only the first of these regions, but the second, likewise, is rich in paradox, inner conflict, and reluctant admission of painful truths. Consider, for example, the following passage from Sir Walter Scott's novel *Rob Roy*. Here, Nicol Jarvie, a prudent Scots businessman, muses over his attraction to a violent outlaw who extorts fees from his countrymen in exchange for protection:

> It's a queer thing o' me, gentlemen, that am a man o' peace mysell, and a peacefu' man's son, for the deacon my father quarrelled wi' nane out o' the town-council—it's a queer thing I say, but I think the Hieland blude o' me warms at thae daft tales [of Rob Roy], and whiles I like better to hear them than a word o' profit, Gude forgie me! But they are vanities—sinfu' vanities, and moreover, again the statute law—again the statute and gospel law.[4]

Honestly acknowledging that Rob's criminal adventures appeal to him more than "a word o' profit," Jarvie recognizes that this fascination is surprising in someone of his character. At the end of his statement, he endeavors to appease his inner moral voice by roundly condemning Rob's acts.

A book such as this one, which seeks to examine the labyrinthine chains of meanings that we associate with crime and punishment, cries out for an interdisciplinary approach. Specifically, it demands a source that can reveal our unconscious as well as our conscious associations. Such a source is literature. With its allusiveness, its internal cross-references, and its richness of metaphor and symbol, literature is especially well-suited to convey unconscious meaning. Therefore, throughout this book, I employ literary classics, supplemented by prison memoirs, films, and legal history, to demonstrate the paradoxical symbiotic relationship between criminals and law-abiding people. My approach to these texts is informed by psychoanalytic theory. I thus take for granted such basic psychoanalytic tenets as the existence of the unconscious, the meaningfulness of all mental manifestations, and the profound causal significance of early life.

This book is divided into three distinct, yet closely related, parts. Part One, "Cradled on the Sea: Positive Images of Prison and Theories of Punishment," seeks to show that alongside the negative vision of prison as a living hell, an island of the damned, or a place where men rot under their rocks and yearn for freedom, many prisoners and nonprisoners exhibit powerful positive associations to incarceration. In particular, I will present evidence to suggest that prison is viewed as a refuge from life's trivia, a "cradle on the sea," an academy, and a place where time stands still. Besides setting forth the affirmative images of prison, I endeavor to explain them. The sources discussed range from psychological processes (such as institutional transference and oral fixation), to cultural archetypes (such as the dialectically related polarities of death and rebirth, suffering and redemption), to sociopolitical factors (such as the actual negative aspects of life in freedom). At the end of Part One, I draw implications from the positive meanings of confinement for the classical theories of punishment: retribution, deterrence, and rehabilitation.

Part Two, "A Strange Liking: Our Admiration for Criminals," makes a shift from lawbreakers looking at punishment to law-abiding people looking at criminals. Drawing on criminal-noncriminal dyads in such works as *The Grapes of Wrath, Heart of Darkness,* and *Les Miserables,* I examine the paradox of our wondering esteem for those who break the law. I begin by showing both the pervasiveness of admiration for criminals and the simultaneous resistance to that admiration. Inner division is painful; therefore, noncriminals develop strategies for minimizing this mental conflict. One such strategy is what I call "Rationalized Admiration:

Overt Delight in the Camouflaged Criminal." Noncriminals adopting this approach openly admire criminals but believe that they do so because of the lawbreakers' virtues—for example, their embodiment of justice (Robin Hood, Tom Joad in *The Grapes of Wrath*); freedom (Carmen, Moll Flanders); greatness (Kurtz in *Heart of Darkness*, Raskolnikov in *Crime and Punishment*); or glamor (Alan Breck in *Kidnapped*, Jay Gatsby in *The Great Gatsby*).

The second strategy for coping with the inner conflict over criminals is repression. By this mechanism, noncriminals energetically bar from consciousness their admiration for criminals, thereby alleviating their guilt. Often, these noncriminals replace their buried esteem for lawbreakers with conscious loathing and repudiation. To illustrate this dynamic, I analyze the travelers' rejection of the prostitute in de Maupassant's story "Ball-of-Fat" and Pip's disgust for Magwitch in *Great Expectations*.

In defending against their admiration for criminals, some non-criminals go beyond disgust and loathing to persecution—a stance that enables them to associate with criminals and even imitate their ways while maintaining an inner conviction that they are upholding the law. To portray this vicissitude, I draw on the villagers' treatment of Christy in Synge's drama *The Playboy of the Western World* and Javert's shifting attitudes toward Jean Valjean in Hugo's *Les Miserables*.

Part Three, "In Slime and Darkness: The Metaphor of Filth in Criminal Justice," builds on the foundation laid in Part Two, in particular, the discussion of loathing, disgust, and repudiation as vicissitudes of admiration for criminals. At the outset, I trace the association between slime and criminality in such works as *Macbeth*, *The Hound of the Baskervilles*, and *Jamaica Inn*. In the course of this analysis, I adduce psychoanalytic theory and child observations to demonstrate that soft, wet dirt is as deeply attractive to us as it is repulsive. I suggest that slime's unconscious and forbidden allure helps to explain its popularity as a metaphor for criminals.

Criminals are seen not only as slimy, but as *ineradicably* slimy. For this reason, they are viewed as worthless objects that may be thrown away. Thus, the static metaphor of the criminal as slime leads to a dynamic allegory in which criminals commit a bad act, become indelibly stained, and are cast out. This allegory found a resonance in eighteenth- and nineteenth-century Britain, when the British government elected to solve its penal crisis by banishing hundreds of thousands of criminals to Australia. The history of Australia is replete with descriptions of convicts as "sewage" and their island-prison as a "dunghill," a "cesspool," and a "sink of wickedness." In even more graphic terms, Jeremy Bentham described the policy of transporting criminals to Australia as projecting an "excrementitious mass." Notwithstanding the richness of these expressions, it was not for its language that I elected to analyze the Botany Bay experiment, but because this episode represents a remarkable effort by noncriminals—an effort to eliminate the very relationship with criminals, to repudiate convicts utterly and treat them as if they were on another planet, or a distant star.

Ironically, the Australian penal colony soon acquired a positive significance as a new promised land where criminals could rebuild their lives. It was not only a place East of Eden to which they were banished, but also a new Jerusalem to which they came. Thus, this "prison of infinite space," like the traditional prisons and penitentiaries depicted in "Cradled on the Sea," became, in the eyes of some convicts, a beloved prison. Much later, idealization also replaced contempt with regard to the original transported convicts, the First Fleeters; today, they are seen as romantic outlaws. And so we come full circle.

In the book's Conclusion, I suggest that the prisoners' exalted conception of their prison and the noncriminals' glamorous vision of lawbreakers are both manifestations of a romantic yearning. Specifically, these portrayals reflect a desire to escape from the mundane world-as-it-is into a nobler and more meaningful time and place. Such romanticism serves to defend against the narcissistic wound of our relative puniness and mortality.

PART ONE

Cradled on the Sea: Positive Images of Prison and Theories of Punishment

My good, my gentle friend, my cell! My sweet retreat, mine alone, I love you so! If I had to live in all freedom in another city, I would first go to prison to acknowledge my own, those of my race.

—Jean Genet, *Our Lady of the Flowers*

CHAPTER I

A Thousand Leagues Above: Prison As a Refuge from the Prosaic

> By "world" I mean the whole complex of incidents, demands, compulsions, solicitations, of every kind and degree of urgency, . . . which overtake the mind without offering it any inner illumination.
>
> —Paul Valéry

Toward the end of Aleksandr Solzhenitsyn's novel *The Cancer Ward*, Oleg Kostoglotov is released from the hospital where he has been confined and goes to buy a shirt in a department store. While looking over the shirts, he hears a man ask the clerk, "Do you have a size twenty-five shirt like this one, with a size fifteen collar?" Oleg reacts with horror and righteous indignation to the small-mindedness that he feels this question reflects:

> It staggered Oleg like an electric shock. He turned in amazement and looked at this clean-shaven, smooth man in the good felt hat, wearing a white shirt and tie, stared at him as though the man had struck him.
>
> Men had endured the agony of the trenches, bodies had been heaped in mass graves, others had been buried in shallow pits in the icy Arctic, people had been arrested time and again and sent to camps, they had frozen in barred railroad cars, men had broken their backs working with pick and shovel to earn the price of a tattered padded jacket, and this sniveling fop remembered not only his shirt size, but his collar size?
>
> This last fact shattered Oleg. He could not have imagined that a collar had its own separate size. Suppressing a groan, he turned his back on the shirt counter. A collar size, no less! Why such a refined life? *Why return to this life? If you had to remember your collar size, you'd have to forget something. Something more important!*[1]

The cancer ward as depicted by Solzhenitsyn is not, of course, a prison, but it resembles one in important respects. Solzhenitsyn himself calls attention to the parallel, for he describes Oleg as thinking: "Emerging from these hospital gates—how did this differ from emerging from prison?"[2]

The incident of the collar size illustrates the former captive's rejection of the trivial preoccupations that he finds in freedom. We see a similar reaction in a book by a very different kind of prisoner: an American who spent more than thirteen years in a Florida state penitentiary for breaking and entering, petit larceny, and burglary. During an interval of freedom, James Blake writes to a friend:

> Another kind of nostalgia I've been fighting is the Brotherhood-Of-The-Doomed feeling I had in the penitentiary and no longer have, with nothing to put in its place. I've been trying hard to isolate and name this virus, and think I have. *Thing is, it's better than many things the world of electric toothbrushes has given me.*[3]

In an earlier letter, written inside prison, he attempts to explain what attracts him to a life of confinement. Again, the words resonate with those of Oleg Kostoglotov: "Life has indeed been reduced to its simplest terms, a state of affairs not completely unpleasant. So many of the trimmings that go with life outside have often been merely confusing to me. The food here is simple but entirely adequate, as are the pleasures."[4] Blake's words suggest a parallel between the allure of imprisonment and that of monastic life—a point that others have made explicitly.[5]

In a letter written just after returning to prison for another crime, Blake elaborates his vision of life outside prison as meaningless, frenetic activity:

> Your concern over my welfare is indeed gratifying, . . . but the basic misconception of most civilians about convicts is that they suffer, when actually they are comparatively blithe and carefree. *Certainly they're not as harried as the gnomes I see on New York streets, scuttling and scurrying into subways like apprehensive White Rabbits.*[6]

By contrast with this negative image of life in freedom, Blake names prison with a symbol of the eternal: "I'm still trying to make it here and resisting the awful temptation to go back to the peace and quiet of the Rock."[7]

The image of prison as an island of calm amidst the hurly-burly also appears in Shakespeare's *King Lear.* Here too we see a variation on this theme: prison as a place of endurance amidst ephemerae. Toward the end of the play, just after Lear and Cordelia are reunited, Cordelia asks: "Shall we not see these daughters and these sisters?" Lear's reply constitutes one of the loveliest carceral fantasies in literature. It suggests that he, who has been greatly troubled by possessions, and who suffers from guilt over his treatment of his youngest daughter, can look forward with rapture to an austere existence.

> No, no, no, no! Come let's away to prison.
> We two alone will sing like birds i'th cage.
> When thou dost ask me blessing, I'll kneel down
> And ask of thee forgiveness. So we'll live,
> And pray, and sing, and tell old tales, and laugh
> At gilded butterflies, and hear poor rogues
> Talk of court news; and we'll talk with them too—
> Who loses and who wins, who's in, who's out—
> And take upon 's the mystery of things,
> As if we were God's spies: *and we'll wear out,*
> *In a wall'd prison, packs and sects of*
> *great ones,*
> *That ebb and flow by'th moon.*[8]

The prisoners are still and endure, while those in freedom come and go.

Like James Blake and Shakespeare, Solzhenitsyn imagines prison as a calm place in the midst of motion. In *The First Circle,* he depicts the *sharashka* (a special prison for intellectuals) as an ark resting on the water. He suggests that by virtue of their seclusion and relative stillness, the prisoners enjoy a truer perspective on life than they could attain from the outside world, which is rushing by: "From here, from the ark, . . . the whole tortuous flow of accursed history could easily be surveyed, as if from an enormous height, and yet at the same time one could see every detail, every pebble on the river bed, as if one were immersed in the stream."[9]

Elaborating on his metaphor, Solzhenitsyn conceives of the prisoners as floating on the river, hence "weightless" in that they are free of prosaic concerns:

> Those who floated in the ark were weightless and had weightless thoughts. They were neither hungry nor satiated. They had no happiness and no fear of losing it. Their heads were not filled with petty official calculations, intrigues, promotions, and their shoulders were not burdened with concerns about housing, fuel, bread, and clothes for their children. Love, which from time immemorial has been the delight and torment of humanity, was powerless to communicate to them its thrill or its agony.[10]

Whereas this excerpt depicts prison as a calm but passionless abode, elsewhere Solzhenitsyn portrays prison as the place where one can engage life at its most profound level. In the following passage he describes the thoughts of the prisoner Gleb Nerzhin on the occasion of his wife's visit to the prison:

> Seen from the outside [his life] appeared an unhappy one, but Nerzhin was secretly happy in that unhappiness. He drank it down like spring water. Here he got to know people and events about which he could learn nowhere else on earth, certainly not in the quiet, well-fed seclusion of the domestic hearth. From his youth on, Gleb Nerzhin had dreaded more than anything else wallowing in daily living. As the proverb says, *"It's not the sea that drowns you, it's the puddle."*[11]

The broadening experience of imprisonment is contrasted with the narrow "seclusion of the domestic hearth," with wallowing in the quotidian, with drowning in a puddle.

In addition to the symbol of calm amidst motion, another image used to express the theme of prison as a refuge from the prosaic is that of a high place. Thus, in Stendhal's novel *The Charterhouse of Parma*, the prison is constructed so far above the ground that Fabrizio refers to "this airy solitude."[12] On the first night of his incarceration, Fabrizio spends hours at the window, "admiring this horizon which spoke to his soul."[13] In prison, he finds the happiness that had eluded him in freedom: "By a paradox to which he gave no thought, a secret joy was reigning in the depths of his heart."[14] Endeavoring to account for this paradox, Fabrizio reflects: "[H]ere one is a thousand leagues above the pettinesses and wickednesses which occupy us down there."[15]

We see the same theme of prison as a cloister in Solzhenitsyn's depiction of the meek Baptist, Alyoshka, in *One Day in the Life of Ivan Denisovich*. When the protagonist, Shukhov, tells him that prayer is ineffectual, since it cannot shorten one's sentence, Alyoshka remonstrates: " 'You mustn't pray for that.' Alyoshka was horror-struck. *'What d'you want your freedom for?* What faith you have left will be choked in thorns. Rejoice that you are in prison. *Here you can think of your soul.'* "[16] Shukhov reflects: "Alyoshka was talking the truth. You could tell by his voice and his eyes he was glad to be in prison."[17]

A variation on the theme of prison as a refuge from the commonplace appears in Graham Greene's novel *The Power and the Glory*, which concerns a Mexican priest imprisoned during a period of religious persecution. The following passage occurs following the priest's release from prison, while he is hearing confessions in relative safety:

> The old woman prattled on and on, . . . prattled of abstinence days broken, of evening prayers curtailed. Suddenly, without warning, with an odd sense of homesickness, he thought of the hostages in the prison yard, waiting at the water-tap, not looking at him — the suffering and the endurance which went on everywhere the other side of the mountains. He interrupted the woman savagely, "Why don't you confess properly to me? *I'm not interested in your fish supply or in how sleepy you are at night . . . remember your real sins.*"[18]

Here we see the priest's nostalgia for prison as a place where serious things happen, where people suffer and acknowledge grave sins. To the trivial preoccupations of his civilian penitent, he opposes prison as an embodiment of what is "real."

I have said that prison is often pictured as a refuge from the trivial or prosaic. But what is it a refuge *for?* Two principal themes emerge from the literature: prison as the quintessential academy and prison as a catalyst of intense friendship. The image of prison as an academy appears in Solzhenitsyn's novel *The First Circle*.

Early in the book, Gleb Nerzhin elaborates on the ways that prison has developed his understanding of life. He says that as a free man he read books on the meaning of life or the nature of happiness but understood those works only superficially. "Thank God for prison!" he exclaims. "It gave me the chance to think."[19]

Nerzhin goes on to tell a fellow prisoner that an understanding of happiness comes from recognizing that it does not depend on external blessings: "Remember that thin, watery barley or the oatmeal porridge without a single drop of fat? Can you say that you *eat* it? No. You commune with it, you take it like a sacrament. . . . [I]t spreads through your body like nectar. . . . Can you really compare the crude devouring of a steak with this?"[20] Compare the similar insight that Tolstoy attributes to Pierre in *War and Peace:* "While imprisoned in the shed Pierre had learned not with his intellect but with his whole being, by life itself, that man is created for happiness, that happiness is within him, in the satisfaction of simple human needs, and that all unhappiness arises not from privation but from superfluity."[21]

The black American prisoner Samuel Melville perceives what he has learned in prison in much the same light:

> for the first time since i was a small boy i have no money and no keys in my pockets. you can't imagine the rehabilitating effect of that! from the muslims i am learning to fast and control my own body. from reading thoreau and some of the eastern teachings i can live on much less than even prison allows . . . . and i am tripping all the time. not with the frenzy of acid but with the confidence of my liberation from superficialities.[22]

Whereas these prisoners regard prison as a place where they have gained wisdom, Malcolm X portrays his confinement as a catalyst of learning in a more concrete sense. In a chapter of his autobiography entitled "Saved," he describes how he taught himself to read with understanding while in prison and how this ability opened up a new world to him. He believes that prison enabled him to study more intensively than would have been possible in college, where there are "too many distractions, too much panty-raiding, fraternities, and boola-boola and all of that."

He asks: "Where else but in a prison could I have attacked my ignorance by being able to study intensely sometimes as much as fifteen hours a day?"[23]

Malcolm X views prison as a catalyst of learning in that it provides an environment free from worldly concerns. Other prisoners have pictured prison as a matrix of intense friendship because it forces prisoners to live together in isolation from the world. Thus, throughout *The First Circle* Solzhenitsyn contrasts the isolation and mistrust that characterize relationships among the civilians with the camaraderie and profound friendship that pervade the prisoners' lives. In the following passage Solzhenitsyn describes friendship in the *sharashka* in the language of ecstasy:

> In these Sunday evening hours solid matter and flesh no longer reminded people of their earthly existence. The spirit of male friendship and philosophy filled the sail-like arches overhead.
>
> Perhaps this was, indeed, that bliss which all the philosophers of antiquity tried in vain to define and teach to others.[24]

Solzhenitsyn is not alone in portraying prison friendships as unusually passionate. For example, Eugenia Ginzburg, imprisoned by Stalin for eighteen years, declares simply: "There are no more fervent friendships than those made in prison."[25] So too Vera Figner, confined by the tsars, writes that upon her release from prison she experienced despair at losing the people with whom she had spent twenty years "in close communion, under the most exceptional circumstances."[26]

Beyond describing the intensity of friendship in prison, many prisoners have attempted to explain why friendships tend to flourish under conditions of penal confinement more than in freedom. Figner and Solzhenitsyn cite the absence, in prison, of those relationships that tend to compete with friendship in the outside world. Thus, Figner explains that the "whole world was closed to [her], all human ties broken," and her fellow prisoners substituted for "family and society, . . . party, homeland, and all humanity."[27] Incarceration imposes an isolation from the world, but those who share this isolation see themselves as forming relationships of an emotional power unequaled in the world outside. Solzhenitsyn theorizes in a similar vein: "Men with exceptional intellect, education, and experience, but too devoted to their families to have much of themselves left over for their friends, here belonged only to friends."[28] He reiterates this point in a later scene:

> They drank to friendship. They drank to love. Rubin praised it: "I have never had any doubts about love. But to tell you the truth, until the front and prison I didn't believe in friendship, especially the 'give-up-your-life-for-your-friend' kind. *In ordinary life you have your family, and somehow there's no place for friendship, is there?*"[29]

Other prisoners have explained the passion of prison friendships by the frankness that characterizes carceral relationships[30] or the unusually close living. As Blake writes: "Locking together in a joint is like no other association I know of, a constant proximity and ubiquity comparable only to that of Siamese twins. A profound attachment can ensue."[31] Finally, Eugenia Ginzburg offers an explanation centering on the sharing of a unique experience, which imparts a knowledge available only to initiates:

> Oh, the feeling of prison kinship! It is perhaps the strongest of all human relationships. Even now, many years later, as I am writing these memoirs, all of us who have tasted the blood of the lamb are members of one family. Even the stranger whom you meet on your travels, or at a health spa, or at someone else's house, immediately becomes near and dear to you when you learn he was *there*. In other words, he knows things that are beyond the comprehension of people who have not been there, even the most noble and kind-hearted among them.[32]

Three ideas serve to explain the image of prison as a refuge from the trivial and mundane. This image may reflect (1) actual negative characteristics of life in freedom; (2) personality growth that sometimes occurs under conditions of penal confinement; and (3) impulse neurosis, which causes some people to experience as gratifying a situation where they are controlled.

Let us consider first the theory that this pleasant carceral image, prison as an escape from the commonplace, is in part a reaction to the unattractive aspects of life in freedom.[33] James Blake repeatedly denigrates life outside prison, characterizing it as the "world of electric toothbrushes" and describing the people as scurrying like white rabbits or gnomes. While his remarks may be attributable in part to a "sour grapes" reaction, many civilians would agree with Blake that materialism and careerism impoverish contemporary life. Blake's observation that the "trimmings that go with life outside . . . [had] often been merely confusing" to him parallels the feelings expressed by men studied in a noncarceral setting, men whose perceptions of life in freedom cannot be explained away as a disparagement of what they cannot have. Thus, in Robert Lane's study of working-class American men, we find the following wistful passage in a chapter entitled "The Burden of Freedom." The speaker, a wholesale-shoe salesman, is responding to the question: "What does the word *freedom* mean to you?"

> What it makes me think of is a pastoral scene—I don't know why—being soothed by a nice balmy breeze, green pastures, and a girl and a boy romping through the fields. That's what freedom means to me. . . . It would suggest to me a closeness to God. . . . There are times, I'll say that "What the heck" to my existence, rather that or crying. You're bombarded by so much—ah, pressure in the present day, pressures of business, pressures of actual day-to-day living—cost of living. . . . *There are so many things that you are bombarded with—tiny messages the people are trying to get across to you in their effort to sell you.* It's a tough life. *I think the recluse has probably got something. And every so often you get a little bit tired; you sort of wish you could get some place and just lead that kind of existence.*[34]

Commenting on this passage, Lane recalls Freud's observation that "[p]rotection against stimuli is an almost more important function for the living organism than *reception* of stimuli."[35] Some forms of penal confinement may afford such protection.

The idea that positive images of prison reflect actual negative aspects of life in freedom finds further confirmation in Russian and Soviet prison memoirs. For example, in *Notes from a Dead House*, a novel based on his own experiences in a Siberian prison, Dostoevsky writes that some people committed crimes deliberately "to get into hard labor and thus escape liberty, which is harder for them than imprisonment."[36] The context makes clear that Dostoevsky is referring not to any psychological longing to "escape from freedom" but rather to the fact that in Siberian prisons—even in hard labor—the work was easier and the bread more plentiful.[37]

Echoing *Notes from a Dead House* a little over a century later, Erica Wallach writes that many women prisoners in Vorkuta dreaded the day of release more than another ten-year sentence. She reports that often they had to be thrust out of the camps by the soldiers. At least in the camps the women enjoyed shelter, food, and security. Once released, unable to return to their original homes, the women had no choice but to stay "in liberty" in the Vorkuta area. Consequently, "[f]reedom for most of the women meant prostitution," that is, becoming the wife of the first man who could offer them protection and material support.[38]

Finally, in thinking about objective sources of the idea that prisoners live life on a higher plane, let us consider the dissimilar descriptions of friendship inside and outside prison walls. In totalitarian societies, where governmental control penetrates even intimate relationships, suspicion and atomization characterize social life. For example, in her memoir of life under Stalin, Nadezhda Mandelstam describes how many Soviet civilians found their friendships pervaded by mistrust, because "friends" sometimes betrayed people for whom they had professed affection and loyalty.[39] Likewise, in his autobiographical work, *Prisoner of Mao*, Bao Ruo-Wang reports that friendship blossomed more in prison than in the suspicion-riddled society outside:

> "A living hell" is the popular image inevitably conjured up by the idea of Communist labor camps. There is truth in the image, of course, but it is distorted because it is incomplete. The reality, the most exquisite irony that I discovered as the years slipped by, was the same that had already been testified to by the survivors of Stalinist camps: Not only is the society within the camps in many ways purer than the larger one outside but it is also freer. *It is in the prisons and camps that the notions of friendship and personal freedom are the most highly developed in China.*[40]

In democratic societies, as well, the image of prison as a catalyst of friendship can be explained partly by the loneliness that permeates civilian society. Thus, anthropologist Robert Brain writes:

To me it is the strangest thing that in Western Christian society, founded on the love of God and the fellowship of mankind, loneliness has become one of the hallmarks. . . . [S]o many of us eke out an existence as loveless and unloved atoms—free individuals in an open society, condemned to form part of the great grey subculture of the lonely.[41]

Brain offers an explanation for this isolation in the culture of chronic change: "Friendship is a basic need but in our swift turnover of jobs, homes, and even marriages we are constantly starting off to look for a new 'community' of friends."[42] In contrast to civilians, prisoners are immobilized and, to that extent, are better situated to form lasting relationships characterized by affection and trust. Moreover, instead of going through life as modern man does—having an essentially unique and individual pattern of experiences—prisoners share most aspects of their lives and experience a more collective existence.

A second explanation for the image of prison as a refuge from the quotidian is that, in some persons, incarceration fosters intellectuality and spirituality. A study by the late psychoanalyst Edith Jacobson supports this conclusion. She observed one hundred female political prisoners during her two years' confinement in the state prisons of Nazi Germany.[43] With respect to strong and intelligent persons, Jacobson found that prison often set in motion a constructive development. For example, nearly all the political prisoners felt impelled to do artistic work, such as writing poetry, and many embarked on a systematic study of natural science, history, or languages. Some who had never before felt any interest in the classics began to learn the ancient poets by heart.

Analyzing this behavior, Jacobson posits that the experience of imprisonment causes a regression of the ego to a state of adolescent dissolution. As in adolescence, so in prison, a strong id confronts a relatively weak ego. The deprivation and frustration of confinement produce aggression, but discharge of this aggression is impossible in the prison situation. Similarly, in prison a normal sex life is precluded. To cope with this impasse, the prisoner develops reaction formations and sublimations.[44]

As an example of this process, Jacobson recounts the story of a thirty-two-year-old woman who had lived as a prostitute prior to her arrest. In prison "for the first time in her life, the prisoner met with outward barriers against those impulses which had ruled her so far."[45] Living among people who were well-controlled and intellectual, she changed greatly. Not only did she grow to love poetry, but she also arranged for courses in anatomy and first aid. In addition, she began to question the spiritual basis of her existence. While still in prison she obtained a divorce from the procurer on whom she had been dependent and found work and lodgings for herself in another region.[46]

By contrast with this example, Jacobson stresses that for most common criminals, imprisonment tends to have harmful effects, aggravating an already infantile personality.[47] Moreover, she believes that even where sublimations are formed in prison, they will not endure once the situation of extreme privation comes to an end.[48]

Robert Jay Lifton's book *Thought Reform and the Psychology of Totalism* provides an extension and partial confirmation of Jacobson's findings. On the basis of interviews with people imprisoned for years in the People's Republic of China, Lifton finds that the Western subjects, long after their release from prison, "consistently reported a sense of having been benefitted and emotionally strengthened, of having become more sensitive to their own and others' inner feelings, and more flexible and confident in human relationships."[49]

While acknowledging the difficulty of explaining this reaction, Lifton believes it has to do with the prisoners having explored their emotional limits, of having "hit rock bottom" in their negative view of themselves, and having then reacquired some degree of self-respect. He analogizes this to the feeling of well-being that people exhibit after subjection to severe stress. In contrast to the limited rebound euphoria that occurs after a brief stress,

> after an experience as totally disintegrating as prison thought reform, the relief at being put together again is more basic and enduring. In the experience itself, and in the process of recovery and

renewal which followed it, these men and women gained access to parts of themselves they had never known existed.[50]

Finally, a third explanation for the image of prison as a refuge from the prosaic lies in the concept of impulse neurosis. Impulse neurosis is a form of severe character pathology characterized by "chronic, repetitive eruption of an impulse." The individual experiences gratification of the impulse as highly pleasurable during the impulsive episode but as unacceptable at other times.[51]

The basic disposition for this disorder is the same as that for addiction and depression: impulse neurotics are fixated on the earliest, oral, phase of development. Hence, any tension is experienced as a dangerous trauma, and sexual gratification and the sense of security are not differentiated from each other. Because they cannot tolerate tension, impulse neurotics direct their actions not so much toward "the positive aim of achieving a goal but rather more toward the negative aim of getting rid of tension."[52] More specifically, the unconscious purpose of most impulsive acts is to avoid depression.[53] Typical examples of impulse neurosis are alcoholism, drug addiction, kleptomania, and impulsive running away.

James Blake can be understood as an impulse neurotic who unconsciously—and even to some extent consciously—experiences incarceration as pleasurable, because it affords him the control that his own ego cannot provide. In the following passage Blake expresses his awareness that in prison he is able to concentrate and sublimate in a way he finds impossible outside: "I wrote Dr. Algren about a week ago and as yet no reply. I hope he isn't displeased with me. . . . Certainly the book will be finished in a shorter time than it would if I were out, *with all the distractions I manage to find.*"[54]

Although here and elsewhere Blake displays considerable insight into his attraction to imprisonment, he falls short of understanding the deepest sources of this fascination. The true nature of the distractions against which Blake feels he needs protection is suggested by the juxtaposition of his descriptions of homosexual love affairs and his expressions of nostalgia for prison. Immediately after describing an affair he regards as demeaning, he writes: "How many times I have wished myself back in the joint, *the perfect peace I had* and did not value."[55] Again, after being seduced in a way he considers humiliating, he declares: "I wish now I'd never left the Rock in Florida, but this maniac [his lover] didn't come on like a maniac at first."[56] Significantly, it is not when he is in prison, but when he is involved with a sadistic lover outside that Blake writes: "So here I am—trapped, beset, lonely, bored, frightened, and confused."[57] In contrast, Blake describes his homosexual affairs in prison less in terms of self-abasement and more in terms of either pragmatism or genuine passion.[58]

As additional evidence of the impulse-controlling function that prison performs for Blake, I would cite the contrast between the letters Blake writes from inside and outside prison. In prison, he writes more about music, books, and writing, whereas outside he writes predominantly about his obsessive infatuations with one man after another—and about his longing to return to prison.

The Irish playwright Brendan Behan, who described his prison experiences in *Borstal Boy*, provides another example of the impulse neurotic who unconsciously feels the need to be controlled by an external force. A writer reviewing a biography of Behan sums up the benefits Behan derived from incarceration:

> He seemed at home in prison. Most of his formative reading was done in Borstal, and it was in Dublin jail that he learned to read Gaelic and began to write.
>
> Prison gave him material for "The Quare Fellow," the gallows-humor play which brought him world fame. It inspired "Borstal Boy," which will outlive a swarm of "Papillons." And, what is important, it kept him off the drink.[59]

The writer continues: "In retrospect it seems odd that he spent so many of his years in jails, for if there was anything he was not, it was a revolutionary."[60] But it is precisely because of the benefits prison provided him, in terms of freedom from being subject to his alcoholism, that Behan, on some level, sought incarceration.

Consider also the case of Paul Verlaine, for whom prison was "really and objectively, a solution to an untenable situation: his murderous impulses, the alcoholism which stoked them, the torment of his 'bimetallism' made of Mons a refuge into which he threw himself."[61]

The objection may arise that such prisoners as Behan, Verlaine, and Blake are hardly representative; their reactions may not tell us anything about less cultured criminals. However, the notion of prison as a place where one is protected from oneself also finds support in the popular literature about common criminals. A *New York Times* article, for instance, describes an American woman, Terry Broome, imprisoned in Italy on a charge of premeditated homicide. After reporting on the Italian-language lessons and the ceramics workshop in which she was engaging at the prison, Broome is quoted as saying: "Maybe I needed to get away, to be put away, so I could get out of the kind of life I was leading, *so self-destructive,* and change myself. I have changed myself. I am a different person now."[62]

A similar observation appears in a popular magazine article that describes a woman suffering from irresistible impulses to spend money. She was imprisoned for embezzlement after taking money to cover her spending sprees. The author of the article writes that, while in prison, "Sandi felt free for the first time in years," because she did not have to face the temptation to spend.[63]

In the next chapter I continue with the motif of prison as a refuge. The emphasis there, however, will be less on prison as an escape from mundane preoccupations and more on prison as a protective and nurturing abode. Whereas the most salient images in the preceding pages were of prison as high up, or a calm place in the midst of motion, in the next chapter the images will be those of envelopment: being cradled, surrounded, and embosomed.

CHAPTER 2

Cradled on the Sea: Prison As a Mother Who Provides and Protects

The student of prison memoirs cannot fail to be startled by the repeated characterizations of prison as a peaceful and safe place. In some instances the idea can be understood by reference to the relative quietude of life inside, but the theme is equally salient where there is no such basis in reality. Thus, notwithstanding that he had earlier listened in anguish to the sounds of a gang rape, during an interval outside of prison Blake writes to a friend:

> You know what's in my mind? The joint. I thought I was getting off free from that experience. I thought they hadn't managed to touch me, but it colors every moment and every action of my life. *I think always of the peace that I had there*—this working to survive and surviving to work seems increasingly like an arrangement I would not have chosen, were it up to me. *Those gates, man, they're inviting.*[1]

Blake resists his attraction to prison, but in the very passage where he announces his determination to stay outside, his choice of metaphors reveals his image of freedom as a battlefield and prison as a place of safety: "It's too easy to crawl back inside the gates. I want to stay out and do battle—but I need a couple of hammers."[2] Here Blake's use of the word *crawl* underscores the infantile nature of the dependent, passive longings with which he is struggling.

The motif of prison as a uniquely protected place is echoed in the autobiographical account of a British criminal, Diana Christina. At 47, the age when she wrote her memoir, Diana Christina had spent nearly a third of her adult life incarcerated for burglary, pimping, and prostitution. Reflecting on her attraction to prison, she says: "After a great deal of looking into my past I realized that spending those years in prison was beneficial to me in an important way: it had, I was convinced, saved me from being murdered! I had had so many violent encounters with men, and some very near misses."[3]

Although here Christina writes of safety in a literal sense, elsewhere she provides a glimpse of a deeper vision of prison as a protected abode: "I began to believe that it wasn't thieving that was my natural bent, it was being a gaol-bird that was my natural disposition.... *I began then to have visions of landing in a cell in isolation in prison and of spending the rest of my days there—curled up in a little ball and immersed in dreaming fantasies.*"[4] Much like a fetus in a womb, the prisoner in this image is passive and sheltered. By contrast with the usual stereotype of prison as a jungle, Christina, like Blake, views prison as the peaceful place and life outside as unremitting effort: "I told myself, you've got to stop escaping into gaol to hide away from it all. You've got to go forward into the struggle and come out on the other side."[5]

Christina does not appear to recognize that the struggle is, at least in part, with herself. By her own admission, she had been attracted to violent men and had initiated or acquiesced in her relationships with them. It was her own self-destructive impulses against which she needed protection. We see this still more clearly in Christina's decision, during an interlude of freedom, to take a job and residence in a nurses' home, where no men were allowed. Of this decision she observes that it would "make life far easier" for her: "I could still carry on meeting men socially but I could also withdraw from them into my nurse's room—my own little cell-in-the-world—whenever I felt the need to."[6]

Malcolm Braly's autobiography, *False Starts: A Memoir of San Quentin and Other Prisons*, provides another variation on the theme of prison as the quintessential safe place. Braly had been raised on the West Coast in a family that moved frequently. "The only continuity of our lives," he writes, "was that we had none."[7] Abandoned by his mother at age seven, Braly remembers her as a cold person who had expeditiously disabused him of his early beliefs in Santa, the Easter Bunny, and God. He cannot recall ever

feeling love for her, whom he often imagines as "an angry Medea
who murdered the normal lives" they might have had.[8]

Braly does remember loving his father, a used-car salesman and
embezzler who "always tried to laugh and joke his way through
. . . misfortunes."[9] However, the father, too, abandoned him seven
years after his mother did. In a passage lacking in his usual keen
insight, Braly writes that he "didn't care," as he had "spent most
of . . . [his] life trying to avoid him."[10]

After his stepmother turned him over to the county probation
officer, Braly was well-treated by the community. He attended
school, worked part-time as a reporter for the local paper, and
received an offer of a college scholarship. Nevertheless, partly out
of an identification with his father, Braly began to engage in
regular stealing. He later realized that he must have wanted to be
caught, because he stole clothes from a dry-cleaning establishment
in a small town, then proceeded to wear the garments publicly. In
and out of prison for most of his early adulthood, Braly served
eighteen years for burglary and other theft crimes.

Toward the end of his autobiography Braly relates an epiphany
he had about the years he spent behind bars. He had just been
released from prison and had decided to steal when a patrol car
happened along, and he ran in a panic. Of this moment he writes:
"I sensed then in some clarity how that part of me which had
always been fearful was once again trying to return me to *the safest
place I had ever found.* Some primitive center, some ur-self, who
still refused to recognize that life is always a gamble."[11] To Braly,
prison seemed safe not because he encountered no physical danger
there, but rather because it entailed no risk that he would fail to
meet his own standards. Thus, he describes his feelings immediately after his release in this way: "I was discharged. Finally free.
Free to be lonely. Free to go broke. Free to fail. Free to deal with
the still ominous mysteries of my own most intimate nature. Still
I was free."[12] Through irony, Braly expresses his insight that
leaving prison forces the relinquishment of a childlike status.

Elsewhere he notes a more concrete similarity between the
conditions of prisoner and child: "[H]owever harshly, the joint

mothered us—fed us, kept us warm, treated our ailments—and now, away from home, I could hardly remember to pay the rent and the gas bill and the phone bill, let alone take proper care of my teeth."[13] In the same vein, J. D. Bing, a character in one of Braly's novels, expresses his appreciation for the "twenty years of free food," the "clean socks every night," and the "clean clothes three times a week" that he received in prison.[14]

The point, of course, is not the material benefits that prison provides; rather, it is the unconscious *meaning* of having them provided, and provided unconditionally. Tamsin Fitzgerald, a nineteen-year-old woman imprisoned for her role in hijacking an airplane, makes this meaning explicit: "In a way, the less free you are, the more freedom you have. With every rule and locked door you have one less responsibility. . . . No worries, no job hassle, no bother about when or what to eat, what to wear. *Free of responsibility, returned to a form of infancy.*"[15]

If one similarity between prison and idealized infancy is the dependence on others for food and shelter, still another resemblance is the perception of life as timeless. Dylan Thomas has lyrically rendered the child's obliviousness to the passage of time in these lines:

> Oh as I was young and easy in the mercy of his means,
> Time held me green and dying,
> Though I sang in my chains like the seas.[16]

James Blake writes wistfully of prison as a place where time is virtually infinite: "So much lovely time stretches out before you, time to read, to write, to play, to practice, to speculate, contemplate."[17] Similarly, Malcolm Braly experiences imprisonment as being outside of time. Upon returning to San Quentin after a period of freedom, he associates timelessness with lack of responsibility: "In some ways it wasn't awful to be back. . . . *This was not our real life, our real lives were once again projected into the future. . . .* We could neither succeed nor fail here, *we were in stasis,* and preserved against failure and loss until once again, we were set free."[18]

The associations between imprisonment, timelessness, and childhood are elevated to a symbolic level in Mary Renault's novel, *The King Must Die*. Here she describes Theseus's thoughts as he is being taken in captivity to Crete:

> We victims lived on the afterdeck, and had an awning to sleep under, just as if we had paid our passage. We belonged to the god, and had to be brought unspoiled. . . .
>   It was a time of pause with me. I had passed from my own keeping. I lay in the god's hand, as once in boyhood, cradled on the sea. Dolphins raced along with us, diving under the waves, and blowing 'Phoo!' through their foreheads. I lay and watched them. *My life was still.*[19]

Though a particularly idyllic fantasy, this description resembles the other fictional portrayals and the realistic prison memoirs in equating imprisonment with a pleasant sense that one is no longer responsible for one's life. The image of the child borne up by the waves is reminiscent of Solzhenitsyn's prisoners floating in the ark on the water. And the sea is a common symbol of the mother, as in Swinburne's lines:

> I will go back to the great sweet mother,
> Mother and lover of men, the sea.[20]

In the memoirs and novels quoted above, prison is described as a place that is uniquely safe, as an unconditional provider of food and shelter, and as a timeless space. Because these qualities are also identified with home or, more exactly, with being a child in a nurturing and protective home, prison becomes assimilated to this powerfully charged symbol. In psychoanalytic terms, some people develop toward prison an institutional transference—unconsciously displacing onto prison the feelings they originally experienced toward the significant figures of their childhood.

More specifically, as we have already seen in the proliferation of water imagery, prison is associated with the mother—the one who provides and protects. An unusually clear portrayal of this meaning appears in *Little Dorrit*, when Dickens describes the relationship between Little Dorrit and the debtors' prison where her family dwells: "The Marshalsea walls, during a portion of every day, again embraced her in their shadows as their child."[21] That the yearning for prison is unconsciously a yearning for a nurturing mother comes through in the last entry in Blake's book, *The Joint*. Here Blake describes his abortive attempt to hold up a gourmet food counter and his subsequent realization that he wants to return to prison:

> [T]hen at the cash register I showed the piece to the fat lady in charge and told her in menacing tones to put all the bread in the bag.
>
> Well. She sagged, a deflating dirigible, slowly toward the floor and lay there like a beached whale, out cold, of no fucking use to anybody, especially me. I couldn't understand the mechanism of the cash register, and so the money remained out of my reach. There was nothing to do but walk out into the warm Florida evening, into jingle bells jingle all the way.
>
> I think it was then I realized I wanted to go back to the tribe, to my people, in the joint. And I said to myself, home is where, when you go there, they can't turn you away.
>
> Homesick, how about that? And homesick is where, when you go home, they make you sick.
>
> No, Virginia, there is no Santa Claus. So dummy up and drink your beer.[22]

Blake immediately reacts to a woman's failure to give to him by experiencing an impulse to run away, back to the penitentiary. For him prison is a place where love, or the material goods symbolic of love, are provided unconditionally. To be sure, he quickly scoffs at his "homesickness," expressing the other side of his ambivalence toward prison. But his penultimate comment reflects his profound disillusionment with, and repudiation of, the outside world where "there is no Santa Claus," where one is *not* "cradled on the sea" — where one must earn one's keep.

Prior to the events described above, Blake had attempted to stay outside, for a time taking a job in a sanitarium for mental patients in the Westchester countryside. Like the nurses' home of Diana Christina, the sanitarium represented the total institution that Blake unconsciously sought.[23] In the end, however, Blake's attraction to prison proved more powerful than his good intentions. On the same day that he wrote the letter just quoted, Blake was arrested outside a medical building after an attempted burglary there. He was sentenced to five years in the state prison.[24]

As I discussed in the preceding chapter, Blake, an impulse-neurotic and drug addict, exhibits a fixation on the oral level of development. Like all other such orally fixated people, he desperately needs external supplies, in the form of love and approval, to maintain his self-esteem. If the vital supplies are lacking, we can surmise that he will go into a severe depression. However, Blake acts impulsively to ward off depression by returning to a place where he can perceive himself as a loved and cared-for child.

Clinical findings suggest that oral fixation characterizes many chronic thieves like Blake, Christina, and Braly. In their classic study, *Roots of Crime*, Franz Alexander and William Healy concluded that thieves exhibit a regressive longing to be in a passive, dependent condition—a longing that is inadmissible to their conscious minds.[25] Within this context, stealing functions as a compromise formation. On the one hand, by symbolizing aggressiveness and independence, it defends against the unconscious dependent longings. On the other, by allowing the thief to get something without working for it, stealing gratifies his passive yearnings.[26]

If thieves typically display an oral fixation, it follows that they may find imprisonment deeply gratifying—gratifying enough that they would even in some cases commit crimes to be incarcerated. For such orally dependent people, the risk of imprisonment constitutes, not a deterrent, but an incentive, to commit crimes.

We may not all evince an oral fixation to this degree, but we do all manifest less pronounced regressive yearnings. As Norman O. Brown has pointed out, our deep childhood fixation reflects a nostalgia for the illusion that time does not pass and, hence, that we do not die. This wish to avoid death is related to dependency, for separation from the mother is the first step toward individual life, which in turn must lead to death.[27]

Our unconscious feelings toward imprisonment are affected by this desire to return to a period before we came to terms with the reality principle, to the womb, to the fantasy of paradise. Hence, on an unconscious level, we can never regard penal confinement as an unequivocal evil. Hence, too, the ill-disguised envy that some civilians express toward prisoners, who, it is felt, are "coddled" when they are merely deprived of their freedom. Thus, the universal oral fixation may help to explain why our prisons remain places of great brutality: to the degree that the civilian population unconsciously associates imprisonment with a peaceful womb or a timeless Arcadia, it finds the mere deprivation of liberty an insufficient punishment. The word, *paradise*, after all, is derived from the Middle Iranian word for enclosure.

In the next chapter I examine a different kind of positive fantasy about incarceration—one in which prison is associated not with a static image but rather with a drama or allegory, with a journey during which the traveler undergoes profound change.

CHAPTER 3

To Die and Become: Prison As a Matrix of Spiritual Rebirth

> Except a corn of wheat fall into the ground and die, it abideth
> alone: but if it die, it bringeth forth much fruit.
>
> —John 12:24

In *The Gulag Archipelago*, Solzhenitsyn writes of prison: "[T]he day when I deliberately let myself *sink to the bottom and felt it firm under my feet—the hard, rocky bottom which is the same for all*—was the beginning of the most important years in my life, the years which put the finishing touches to my character."[1] Solzhenitsyn thus describes in positive terms the condition of having lost everything: the appeal of having something firm under one's feet, as one can fall no farther, and the state of equality with one's fellow man.

This passage illustrates the association between prison and the *downward*, or *chthonic*, spatial dimension.[2] Prison is thereby also linked with earth and earth's two principal mythic roles: as the recipient of the dead, and as the mother of all life.[3] The connections between prison, descent, and resurrection are made explicit by Bill Sands in his autobiography, *My Shadow Ran Fast*:

> All I can say for sure is that Warden Duffy was looking into my eyes with an expression that few men are privileged to see. The thief on the other cross, the one who repented, must have seen a Face like that when he cried out in his agony. When he spoke, *I knew at last that my long descent had ended.* My life was not over. It was just beginning.[4]

John Cheever's fictional work *Falconer* also depicts prison as the site of a drama based on the Christian story. This novel concerns a professor named Farragut, who is serving time for killing his brother with a fire iron. At the end of the novel Farragut escapes from prison by taking the place of a dead inmate in a burial sack, which he refers to as "his grave." Farragut experiences himself as someone in an infantile, even embryonic, state:

> He had never, that he remembered, been carried before. . . . The sensation of being carried belonged to the past, since it gave him an unlikely feeling of innocence and purity. How strange to be carried so late in life and toward nothing that he truly knew, freed, it seemed, from his erotic crudeness, his facile scorn and his chagrined laugh. . . . How strange to be living and to be grown and to be carried.[5]

While the guards are busy elsewhere, Farragut slits the burial sack with a razor and makes his exit into the free world. A stranger he meets at a bus stop befriends him, offering to share an apartment with him and making him a gift of a raincoat. Farragut then walks to the front of the bus and gets off at the next stop. Cheever concludes the book with these words: "Stepping from the bus onto the street, [Farragut] saw that he had lost his fear of falling and all other fears of that nature. He held his head high, his back straight, and walked along nicely. Rejoice, he thought, rejoice."[6]

These passages portray prison as the set for a drama of falling and rising, dying and being reborn. A different image links prison with rebirth in the following passage by Malcolm X:

> For the next years, I was the nearest thing to a hermit in the Norfolk Prison Colony. . . . I still marvel at how swiftly my previous life's thinking pattern slid away from me, like snow off a roof. It is as though someone else I knew of had lived by hustling and crime. I would be startled to catch myself thinking in a remote way of my earlier self as another person.[7]

The metaphor of snow falling off a roof captures Malcolm X's perception of the ease and naturalness with which the transformation occurred. In a similar example, Watergate convict Charles Colson asserts his belief that prison is a price he has to pay "to complete the shedding of [his] . . . old life and to be free to live the new."[8]

Why do these authors view prison as a vehicle for rebirth? The answer seems to be that, for them, imprisonment offers an opportunity to renounce arrogance and separateness. We have already seen an example of this view when Lear happily envisioned prison as a place where he would kneel down and ask Cordelia for forgiveness. Another illustration appears in Diana Christina's memoir. There, she writes that, during a period in solitary confinement, she forgave her mother. She reports: "Magic happened to me then. . . . I was completely transformed. I had a feeling of complete harmony and bliss with the whole of creation."[9] Similarly, in *Kiss of the Spider Woman*, Manuel Puig associates the relinquishment of separateness and superiority with prison life. The revolutionary Valentin, who at first despises homosexuals and considers personal relationships inferior to the revolutionary cause, comes to embrace a fuller vision of life through his love for his cellmate, Molina.[10]

The acceptance of equality with others is also linked to imprisonment, death, and personal transformation in Graham Greene's novel *The Power and the Glory*. Greene's priest protagonist, traveling incognito in Mexico during an era of religious persecution, is thrown into jail for bootlegging when he tries to buy wine for Mass. While in jail, he tells the other prisoners that he is a priest and fully expects them to betray him to the authorities. When one of the prisoners declares roughly, "Nobody . . . here wants their blood money," the priest is "touched by an extraordinary affection. He [is] just one criminal among a herd of criminals" and has "a sense of companionship which he had never received in the old days when pious people came kissing his black cotton glove."[11]

The priest, who had previously held himself above and apart from others, while they "kissed his black cotton glove," now accepts his commonality with them—as "just one criminal among a herd of criminals." So strong is his sense of fellowship that in the morning, when no one betrays him, "[i]n an odd way he [feels] abandoned because they have shown no sign of recognition."[12] The guilt-ridden priest comes to see the night in prison as a turning point in his life: "It was the oddest thing that ever since that hot and crowded night in the cell he had passed into a region of abandonment—almost as if he had died there . . . and now wandered in a kind of limbo."[13]

Since prison is often imagined as a matrix of spiritual rebirth, it should not surprise us that some people aspire to experience imprisonment, embracing the opportunity joyfully when it arrives. Thus, Russian political prisoner Vera Figner describes the calm and radiance of the prisoner who realizes that the moment of her test has come.[14] And Jawaharlal Nehru writes of his wife Kamala's arrest in 1931: "I was pleased, for she had so longed to follow many of her comrades to prison."[15] In the contemporary United States, street youths often want to go to prison to prove their toughness. For the same reason, some of them prefer a prison such as Attica or Stateville to a "softer" facility.[16]

A particularly interesting example of prison as a rite of passage appears in John Edgar Wideman's nonfictional book, *Brothers and Keepers*.[17] Wideman, a professor and successful author, sets out to understand the divergence between his fate and the fate of his brother Robby, who is serving a life term for felony murder. Toward the end of his book, Wideman comments on the prisoner's grace—a grace he attributes to his brother's suffering behind the walls:

> In prison Robby had achieved an inner calm, a degree of self-sufficiency and self-reliance never apparent when he was running the streets. I didn't know many people, inside or out, who carried themselves the way he did now. *Like my mother, he'd grown accustomed to what was unbearable, had named it, tamed it. He'd fallen, but he'd found the strength to rise again. Inch by inch, hand over hand, he'd pulled himself up on a vine he'd never known was there, a vine still invisible to me.* . . . To discover the source of my brother's strength I found myself comparing what I'd accomplished outside the walls with what he'd managed inside. The comparison made me uncomfortable.[18]

Here, the successful civilian feels threatened by what he perceives to be the prisoner's achievement. The vine, which Wideman imagines his convict-brother climbing, is a symbol of Christianity; specifically, in the Gospel of John, the vine becomes a metaphor for Christ.[19]

Insofar as it is perceived as a rite of passage, incarceration confers a status on those who experience it. Imprisonment is thought to afford a special insight, attainable only to the initiated.

Thus, Irina Ratushinskaya, the poet and political activist released from a Soviet prison in the autumn of 1986, reports that prison taught her to "discriminate among people's souls." She adds: "I have seen the reverse side of humanity."[20] Her remark evokes the myth of Orpheus, whose ordeal is not a trial of strength, requiring an effort of will, but rather an act of submission, a descent into a fearful realm, an exposure of self to the darkness.[21]

The affiliation between incarceration and death stems in part from the significance of imprisonment as a withdrawal from life in the world. Because it is imagined as an inward movement, an entrance into a great container, being incarcerated may unconsciously signify an entry into the mother's womb, which, in turn, implies the possibility of being reborn.[22]

The dialectical relationship between death and rebirth has religious origins as well. It is a salient theme of the Old Testament, expressed especially in the books of *Job* and *Psalms*, that one must be humbled through suffering in order to appreciate one's dependence on God. Christianity teaches that suffering enables man to put away the corruption of the flesh and to embrace the Kingdom of Heaven.[23] Moreover, the central symbol of Christianity, the Cross, means not only death, but also resurrection.

From a psychoanalytic perspective, the connection between imprisonment and rebirth derives from the universal sense of guilt and the consequent feeling that one deserves to be punished. Since all persons fail to live up to the requirements of the superego, everyone experiences guilt. Like anxiety, guilt feelings create a tension that craves release. The primary means of alleviating this tension, this burden of guilt, is through punishment. Thus, all people experience, to some degree, a need to be punished—not as a good in itself, but rather as a lesser evil, a means to the goal of absolution. This largely unconscious belief that through suffering one can placate a threatening superego is a very archaic one.[24]

Clear documentation of this psychological dynamic in the prison context is hard to obtain; most prisoners either do not consciously feel guilt or do not write about these feelings. An exception is the Communist Party member and history professor Eugenia Ginzburg, who spent eighteen years in Soviet prisons and camps during the Stalinist era. Since, prior to her incarceration, she had been an ardent Bolshevik, she felt responsible for the Party's murder and imprisonment of her fellow citizens, even though she had not taken part in such actions directly. "*Mea culpa*," she writes, "and it occurs to me more and more frequently that even eighteen years of hell on earth is insufficient expiation for the guilt."[25]

In the preceding chapters I have attempted to delineate images of prison as a place better than the outside world. The chapter that follows, by contrast, sets forth a view of imprisonment as merely no worse than life in freedom. The reader may question just how positive such a perspective is. But compared with the common perception of penal confinement as horrific, the notion that prison is the same as any other place can be considered positive.

CHAPTER 4

Flowers Are Flowers: Prison As a Place Like Any Other

> Lately, I've seen . . . [my prison] as an English garden because of the flowers that grow in abundance along the walks. . . . Flowers are flowers. Walls and fences have no real power over them.
>
> —Busby Crockett, "The Prison Trip"

> You are still in jail, in the hole or out of the hole. You are in jail in the street or behind bars. It is the same thing.
>
> —Claude Brown and Arthur Dunmeyer, "A Way of Life in the Ghetto"

While serving time on death row, Edgar Smith was often asked to explain why he read and made other efforts to improve himself. In his prison memoir, he answers this question as follows: "There is perhaps nothing more frightening to me than the prospect of finding myself stuck for the rest of my life in some dreary small town, working in some gas station or hardware store for sixty dollars a week. *That would be going from one prison to another, from a cell to a cage, and I have had enough of prisons and cages.*"[1] For nonprisoners, the defining characteristic of prison is the deprivation of liberty. But the protean character of the concept *liberty* permits Smith to equate being behind iron bars with being stuck in a small town, working at a gasoline station for sixty dollars a week. In equating the two situations, Smith may be drawing on either the positive or negative sense of liberty. On the one hand, he may be viewing his imagined life in a dreary small town as prisonlike because he believes that others have prevented him from obtaining the education and financial resources to leave. This reasoning would place his remark within the classical liberal understanding of freedom, that is, negative liberty, or freedom from constraint. On the other hand, he may be drawing this equation because liberty to him means not merely the absence of coercion but also the capacity for self-realization. In the latter case, his observation would draw upon the concept of positive liberty best exemplified in the works of T. H. Green and Jean Jacques Rousseau.[2]

I began with an example of someone who imagines prison and the world outside (or some parts of it) to be equally bad, equally unfree. This same theme often appears in prisoners' reflections on the similarity between their plight and that of the guards. Note, for instance, how former prisoner Thomas Flynn empathically describes the constrained life of a prison guard nicknamed "Absurdo": "Absurdo hasn't had much freedom, no time to explore, just school, the service, marriage, children, and the first government job that required nothing more than a high school diploma. Two weeks off a year, three after another five on the job, Absurdo knows about being institutionalized, he knows about time."[3]

Albie Sachs, a prisoner in South Africa, also recognizes an important similarity between his situation and that of the guard who repeatedly seeks him out: "It occurs to me that the station commander may be almost as lonely for company as I am."[4] And Charles Colson, in *Born Again*, describes his fellow inmate's "conclusion . . . that some of the guards seemed more imprisoned than the inmates themselves."[5] Finally, an anonymous prisoner states: "You have to realize that the guards are there doing time just like the inmates." He elaborates with this vignette:

> I remember asking a guard how long he had been in Sandstone. "Twelve years." "Do you think that you will be doing all your TIME [*sic*] here?" "No, I'll finish up in Leavenworth." It blew my mind. He was talking about the next twelve years, which he has to serve in order to be eligible for retirement. I thought to myself— Wow, I am going home in a year, and this guy has twelve more years of this stuff."[6]

In these examples it is unclear whether the guards perceive themselves as unfree. Colson's observation, in particular, seems to draw upon a concept of freedom as the absence of even *unperceived* restraints on behavior. This sense of the word *liberty* implies the possibility of false consciousness, of being unfree while thinking one is free. Another inmate, Julian Beck, makes his analogy between prison and the world outside clearly dependent on this sense of the word *freedom:* "I often think that if the people on the street would realize that the world we live in is a prison, they'd do more yelling and railing too. The sad, perhaps tragic, thing is that people do not realize they're not free."[7]

This concept of false consciousness is also expressed in a passage by the nineteenth-century revolutionary Vera Figner. Soon after learning that she will be released in twenty months, Figner writes the following indictment of the characters in Chekhov's play *The Three Sisters:*

> "The Three Sisters" aimlessly wander through life, expecting salvation from moving to Moscow. *But it is within himself that man bears corroding melancholy, or the buoyant spirit of creative life;* and the "sisters" will wither as fruitlessly in Moscow, as they withered in the provinces. . . . *If such was life, then what difference did it make whether one languished in prison or out of it? One would simply come out from behind the walls of the Fortress to find himself in a larger prison.*[8]

To this ardent activist, a dull and languid life, which she fearfully anticipates finding outside prison, is not worth living. In comparing an apathetic life in freedom to a larger prison she, like Edgar Smith, draws upon a concept of positive liberty—not the absence of coercion, but the full realization of one's potential.

If one way of perceiving prison as a place like any other is to emphasize the coercive forces in the outside world, another is to affirm the capacity to transcend one's physical environment, to be free even in prison. The imperviousness of one's essential self to incarceration comes through in the following passage from *War and Peace.* The scene occurs when the French are holding Pierre as a prisoner-of-war.

> "Ha-ha-ha!" laughed Pierre. And he said aloud to himself: "The soldier did not let me pass. They took me and shut me up. They hold me captive. What, me? Me? My immortal soul? Ha-ha-ha! Ha-ha-ha! . . ." and he laughed till tears started to his eyes. . . .

Pierre glanced up at the sky and the twinkling stars in its far-away depths. "And all that is me, all that is within me, and it is all I!" thought Pierre. "And they caught all that and put it in a shed boarded up with planks!" He smiled, and went and lay down to sleep beside his companions.[9]

Pierre is a character in a work of fiction, but his reflections resemble those of Tamsin Fitzgerald, the young woman imprisoned for hijacking a plane. She writes that there are two kinds of freedom: the "outer" and the "inner." Consequently, one can "be in prison and yet be free." It is futile and absurd, she concludes, to imagine that one can take away a person's freedom.[10]

A similar observation occurs in Robert Bolt's play, *A Man for All Seasons*. When Thomas More is imprisoned in the Tower and his family comes to visit him, the following dialogue ensues:

ROPER: This is an awful place!

MORE: Except it's keeping me from you, my dears, it's not so bad.

Then he adds, in a mild tone, one fancies, and with a twinkle in his eye:

Remarkably like any other place.[11]

For More, who had wanted to be a monk, prison and life in freedom were essentially the same, because neither was the Kingdom of God. Besides, as a scholar, he probably believed it was the life of the mind, the inner life, that mattered.

One explanation for the image of prison as a place like any other place is that this perception constitutes a "sour grapes" reaction: the disparagement of what one cannot have. This theory could explain not only remarks made by prisoners while they are confined—as a means of easing the trauma of incarceration—but also observations made by ex-prisoners, after the fact—as a way of justifying the wasted years.

From a psychoanalytic point of view, the notion that the "grapes are sour anyway"—that civilians too are entrapped, or that one can be freer in prison because the real life is the life of the mind—represents the use of a primitive defense mechanism: denial. In denial, the ego avoids becoming aware of a painful aspect of reality by creating a fantasy that obliterates the unpleasant fact.[12] Thus, the reasoning would go, "I am not confined; I am free," or alternatively, "I may be confined, but nonprisoners are also incarcerated in a different way."

Doubtless there is some truth in this theory. As a complete explanation of this positive image, however, it is inadequate. The sour-grapes theory does not explain, for example, the numerous instances of ex-prisoners committing crimes in order to return to prison. Recidivism, of course, has many dimensions, but one explanation may be the positive images of prison I have identified.

Another approach to explaining the image of prison as a place like any other lies in recognizing that people care not only about negative liberty, or freedom from constraints, but also about positive liberty, or the capacity for self-mastery and self-realization. As Isaiah Berlin discusses in his classic essay, throughout history it has proved impossible to limit the concept *liberty* to its Western sense of "an area within which the subject . . . is or should be left to do what he is able to do or be, without interference by other persons."[13] Rather, the positive, or idealist, notion of liberty has persisted—reflecting the idea that a person may be divided against himself, or may suffer from false consciousness. We have seen numerous instances of this perspective on liberty in the prisoners' writings.

Still another source of the idea that imprisonment represents a difference only in degree from normal life lies in the inevitable gap between man's efforts to conceptualize reality and the complex, differentiated nature of reality itself. Dostoevsky makes this point in his prison memoir, *Notes from a Dead House:* "Reality is infinitely varied compared with even the subtlest workings of abstract thought and does not tolerate broad, clear-cut distinctions. Reality strives for infinite graduation. We too had a life of our own, poor though it may have been. By this I mean not the outward, but the inner life."[14]

Erica Wallach provides another commentary on the same theme in her memoir of her five years in Soviet prisons and camps. She describes a dialogue with a friend in a camp in Vorkuta, at the beginning of their working day. As they watch their black-clad fellow-prisoners march ahead of them through the snow, the two women remark on what a moving scene it would make in a film. Wallach and her friend agree that anyone watching the film would feel terribly sorry for them, whereas they, the prisoners, would be "laughing and joking or just thinking about taking the next step, protecting . . . [their] faces, keeping the circulation going."[15] Wallach goes on to tell her friend that when she read Dostoevsky's description of the conditions he lived in as a prisoner, she had thought she could never stand it. Yet there she is, in conditions she deems much worse than those of Dostoevsky's time, tolerating and even joking about them.[16]

In the Introduction, I quoted another remarkable passage from this memoir—a passage showing the contrast between the stereotyped view of imprisonment and the prisoners' joyous response to Siberia's great beauty. Beauty, I suggested, is a positive aspect of life that is unaffected by penal confinement. And here I may expand the point to summarize one thesis of this book—that happiness itself bears no necessary correlation to either confinement or freedom.

CHAPTER 5

Methodological Issues

Before considering the implications of the foregoing analysis for criminal law, it is important to discuss two questions: (1) given the elusive relationship between text and meaning, how can we be sure that the interpretations presented here are legitimate? and (2) are the authors whose works we have examined representative— either of criminals or of people generally?

The Problematic Relationship between Text and Meaning

There is, of course, some risk in assuming that a writer means what he says in any straightforward sense. When he writes, for example, "Those gates, man, they're inviting," or "[H]ere one is a thousand leagues above the pettinesses and wickednesses which occupy us down there," there is always the possibility that the writer is speaking ironically, or merely expressing a nostalgia that would never lead to action.[1]

Without denying that irony and nostalgia may partly underlie the positive images delineated above, I submit that these images represent something more significant than such explanations would suggest. Several of the prison memoirists quoted in the preceding pages appear to have committed crimes, or bungled their escapes, in order to go to prison. I have already referred to this pattern in the case of Blake, who realized he wanted to return to prison after his failure to hold up the gourmet food counter, and later that day was arrested outside a medical building he had attempted to burglarize.

Similarly, Malcolm Braly reports several incidents which suggest that a yearning for prison may have motivated his criminal acts. In one such incident, he was walking along the street, searching for a place to burglarize, when what he calls "his voice" spoke to him, saying: "When you're back in Quentin, you'll have time to paint."[2]

Braly's intuition warned him another time just after he committed a burglary with his friend George. He and George had gone through a suite of medical and dental offices, which they left carrying a stolen briefcase filled with money, drugs, and dental gold. Once out on the street, Braly became anxious because, in their dirty, unshaven state, they were conspicuous in the college town. Braly urged George to hide with him somewhere until morning, when it would be safe to travel, but George insisted on going home. On their way to the edge of town, George spotted an all-night coffee shop. Braly recounts what happened then as follows:

> George said, "Let's get some coffee. It'll pick us up."
> "It's not a good idea."
> "I don't care if I have to do ten years in San Quentin, I want a cup of coffee."
> That should have told me what forces were at work here, but I didn't hear precisely. I said, "Okay, but maybe we should leave the briefcase outside."
> George looked at me sharply. "What's the matter with you?"
> My intuition was screaming, but I was so easily led I simply followed him into the shop and we ordered coffee and bearclaws.

Soon after they left the coffee shop, police officers stopped for their own break at the same shop and heard that "two strangers had just been there with an expensive briefcase." Shortly afterward, they picked up George and Braly. Considering these kinds of "mistakes" it is no wonder that, as Braly later observes, he "served more time for a handful of inept burglaries than most men would have served for killing a police officer."[3]

These examples are not atypical; prison memoirs are replete with instances of criminals deliberately acting in a way that leads to their arrest and incarceration.[4] Often it is apparent, to the criminals themselves or to fellow inmates, that they not only wanted to be caught after committing the crime, but also committed the crime in order to be caught. For example, Thomas Flynn, author of *Tales for My Brothers' Keepers*, describes his friend Al's ill-fated interlude in freedom: "As time passed he continued to find too subtle the world he had yearned to join when within the walls. Wearied by repeated gaffes, judging himself unfit for freedom, he committed a small and forlornly unsuccessful burglary and was returned inside."[5] Or again, the British woman Josie O'Dwyer, unsure of how to cope with life outside, describes herself as "actually . . . breaking and entering with the full intention of getting . . . [herself] nicked."[6] Examples such as these serve to confirm the real feeling behind the textual passages.

THE PROBLEM OF REPRESENTATIVENESS

We turn now to the second question raised above: whether the writers of these texts are representative of prisoners in general. Most of the prisoners cited here are gifted and articulate. Many of them are not common criminals but rather political prisoners.[7] Some, such as Tolstoy, Stendhal, and Graham Greene, did not experience incarceration. Moreover, many of the works quoted were written in other cultures and eras. What relevance can these writings have for penal policy or criminal law in twentieth-century America? Impressionistic evidence on this point comes from Kenneth Lamott, author of *Chronicles of San Quentin* and a teacher at that prison. In reviewing Braly's book, *False Starts: A Memoir of San Quentin and Other Prisons*, Lamott comments on the typicality of Braly's attraction to imprisonment: "Our prisons are full of men who (whatever they may tell the parole board) are in fact in headlong flight from the uncertainties and outright terrors — women and jobs, for instance — of life outside. I've listened to dozens of them and, *mutatis mutandis*, Braly's story is, up to a point, their story."[8]

Lamott's impressions are supported by clinical findings suggesting that certain kinds of criminals typically exhibit a personality syndrome such that one would expect them to find imprisonment gratifying. I am referring again to the classic study, *Roots of Crime*, by Franz Alexander and William Healy. Based on seven detailed case studies of young criminals, all but one of them men, the book presents the results of an unusual enterprise: the individual psychoanalytic treatment of criminal offenders. The study does not claim to represent a scientific sample of adolescent offenders; rather, the authors deliberately excluded mildly psychotic people as well as those exhibiting pronounced neurotic or psychotic symptoms. They also selected offenders whose criminal behavior seemed to flow from inner conflicts, rather than external circumstances. Most of the people they studied were habitual thieves.

What is most fascinating for our purposes is the finding that chronic thieves exhibit a regressive longing to be in a passive, dependent state—a longing that is inadmissible to their conscious minds. As I mentioned earlier, the act of stealing functions as a compromise formation, simultaneously gratifying the passive longings and defending against them.

We would expect that individuals with the characteristics Alexander and Healy describe would unconsciously enjoy being incarcerated. And, indeed, to the extent that their study treats this topic, it bears out these expectations.[9] I therefore conclude that chronic thieves, at least those who steal because of internal conflicts and not external forces, are particularly likely to experience imprisonment as gratifying.[10]

In addition to impressionistic and clinical evidence, there is at least one other reason to believe that the writers considered here represent many people besides themselves. In the preceding pages, I have adduced positive images from a wide spectrum of times and places—tsarist Russia and 1950s Florida, Elizabethan England and modern-day South Africa, exemplary federal penitentiaries and notorious state prisons. That we find the same themes recurring across such a range of cultures and institutional settings suggests that the positive meanings of incarceration do not depend on particular conditions but rather express something deep-seated about the way human beings experience the world.

CHAPTER 6

Positive Images of Prison and Theories of Punishment

This study, which thus far has focused on the prisoner's subjective experience of imprisonment, will now undergo a shift of perspective. It endeavors to explore some implications of the preceding analysis for the three traditional theories of punishment: deterrence, retribution, and rehabilitation.[1] These theories, which are really justifications for punishment, are necessarily advanced from the viewpoint of society rather than the prisoner.[2]

DETERRENCE THEORIES AND THE POSITIVE IMAGES

Deterrence theories are based on the idea that fear of a threatened punishment may dissuade a person from committing a crime. Legal theorists customarily distinguish between specific deterrence, which is the effect of a punishment on the person being punished, and general deterrence, which refers to the effect of a punishment on everyone else.[3]

The positive meanings of incarceration bear on both types of prevention, not merely, as it might seem at first blush, on specific deterrence. If the favorable images of penal confinement were solely the result of institutionalization, then we might infer that the positive meanings applied only to individuals who had previously been incarcerated.[4] But we have no reason to take for granted that this is the case. Rather, people with a longing to perceive themselves in a cared-for, controlled situation might recognize the affinity between their needs and incarceration prior to experiencing prison. For example, before he had any experience in prison, Malcolm Braly attempted to join the navy. Announcing his decision to his favorite teacher, he explained: "I need to be somewhere where I am made to do things."[5] He was consciously looking for a place where he would be controlled. It makes sense, then, to assume that the attraction to prison might apply both to those who have been penally confined and to those who have not. In those individuals for whom the attraction to prison overrides the aversion to it, the risk of incarceration is not a deterrent, but an incentive, to engage in criminal acts.

This is not to say that the unconscious yearning for prison is the *only* motive for antisocial behavior, even in those individuals for whom it is *a* motive. That is, even for chronic thieves—people with a personality type that may incline them to find prison gratifying—we can isolate several other reasons for stealing. In some cases, theft has come to have a masturbatory meaning and is associated with intense sexual excitement.[6] Stealing may also signify an identification with a beloved criminal parent, or revenge against a parent who is hated.[7] Given the multidetermined nature of any criminal act, it is impossible to say precisely to what extent that act is caused by the desire to go to prison. What we *can* say is this: for the subgroup of criminals who conform to my model, the risk of imprisonment constitutes one incentive to commit crimes.

The possibility that incarceration might function as a motive to commit crimes has received little attention from modern legal scholars.[8] Although the deterrent theory of punishment has generated a large, conflicting body of literature, the controversy has centered on whether criminals are rational in the sense that they tend to engage in cost/benefit analysis. Scholars have assumed that if criminals are rational, and hence capable of being dissuaded by the threat of a sanction, they will be dissuaded by imprisonment. My analysis makes plain that the orthodox economists and others who adopt a choice-analysis paradigm are confounding two questions: (1) are criminals deterrable at all? and (2) which measures do criminals regard as punitive?[9] Nothing in my study points to a finding that criminals are undeterrable. My analysis does suggest the need to adopt a more complex view of criminal motivation, a view that takes into account the existence of inner conflict and of prison's sometimes potent allure.

Could this allure be diminished if prisons were made even more horrible than they already are? A few readers of earlier versions of my work have drawn such an inference. But this idea is based on a misunderstanding of my findings. For it is not the *objectively* positive character of prison that produces the positive images delineated above. As we have seen, James Blake remembered prison as a peaceful place even though he had painfully listened to a gang rape one night in his cell. Similarly, Brendan Behan experienced prison in a predominantly favorable way although his chums had to serve as his bodyguards, and a fellow inmate had his buttocks razored until they were rivers of blood, as a punishment for stealing cigarette butts. The images of prison as an attractive abode are by no means unmediated reflections of external circumstances. Rather, there is an affinity between prisons and previous love objects, or current psychological needs, and that partial resemblance leads the individual to perceive prison in a positive light.

Retributivist Theories and the Positive Images

The retributivist theory of punishment depends upon the idea that a tribute, or price, must be paid to vindicate the law (general retribution) or avenge the victim (special retribution).[10] This view of what justifies society in punishing can be characterized as backward-looking in that it looks back toward the wrongful act rather than forward toward the consequences of the punishment.[11] In H. L. A. Hart's words, the "application to the offender of the pain of punishment is itself a thing of value."[12]

How do our findings on the positive images of prison bear on retributivist theories? On the one hand, the preceding analysis undermines any formulation of retributivist theory which requires that the offender himself experience prison as a privation, evil, or pain.[13] Where the prisoner says, with Solzhenitsyn, "Thank you, prison, for having been in my life," or with San Quentin inmate Fernando Jackson, "I'm almost ready to thank them for sending me to prison,"[14] incarceration may be realizing other purposes, but it is not effecting the goal of retribution in this narrow sense.

On the other hand, other versions of retribution theory may be compatible with the positive meanings of imprisonment. Emile Durkheim, for example, maintained that the primary purpose of punishment was neither intimidation nor cure but rather the maintenance of social cohesion in the civilian population. Social solidarity, he argued, would break down if a violation of the common conscience were not met with a compensatory emotional reaction. Specifically, the common morality must be affirmed by expressing the extreme repulsion which the crime inspires by inflicting suffering upon the criminal.[15]

From this perspective, it does not matter what meanings incarceration has for the inmates, so long as the civilian population believes that the criminals are suffering in proportion to their crimes.[16] This brings us back to the question whether the positive images of prison necessarily apply exclusively, or with special force, to individuals who have already been incarcerated. In the discussion above we answered this question in the negative. It remains to be added, however, that perhaps a disproportionate number of people who are orally fixated or tend to regress to the oral level are to be found in prison. If this is true, then the positive meanings of incarceration may be more evident to inmates than to civilians who have never been incarcerated. That would mean that the Durkheimian function of incarceration could be fulfilled even though some people were committing crimes to go to prison—provided the general public did not learn of the affirmative meanings that penal confinement had for the inmates.

Rehabilitative Theories and the Positive Images

Like deterrence theory, rehabilitative theories view punishment not as an end in itself, but rather as a means to a beneficial result. While there are many definitions of the rehabilitative ideal, its core is the notion that the sanctions of the criminal law should be used to effect a transformation in the offender, with the two-fold aim of protecting society and of enhancing the offender's well-being.[17]

More than deterrence or retribution, the rehabilitative ideal exhibits a consonance with the affirmative meanings of incarceration that we have examined. It is altogether fitting that this should be so, for a positive vision of prison is embedded in the original rehabilitative model, the model espoused by many prison advocates in the late eighteenth and early nineteenth centuries. Images of prison as a refuge from the hurly-burly, an academy, a matrix of spiritual rebirth, even a nurturing mother, all pervade the early prison reform literature. Thus, the following passage from John Brewster's *The Use of Solitude in Prisons* portrays prison as a place of religious retreat: "It has been recommended, both by the practice and precept of holy men, in all ages, sometimes to retire from scenes of public concourse, for the purpose of communing with our own hearts, and meditating on heaven."[18] In its purity and optimism, this passage resonates with the words spoken by Solzhenitsyn's character, Alyoshka: "Rejoice that you are in prison. Here you can think of your soul."[19]

Consider also the following statement, by nineteenth-century prison advocates in Pennsylvania, which presents a mental picture of the prison as an academy and a refuge: "In what manner can man be placed, where the words of the gospel would be more impressive than in their situation sitting alone . . .; nothing to distract their thoughts, or divert them, from the truths delivered to them."[20] Here we see the idea that books carry a heightened emotional impact when encountered in a prison setting—a view that Malcolm X and Eugenia Ginzburg would espouse later, from their perspective as inmates.

A more elaborate conception of the prison as a refuge and academy appears in the following statement by the Inspectors of the Western-Pennsylvania Penitentiary in their Annual Report for 1854:

> If hungry, he is fed; if naked, he is clothed; if destitute of the first rudiments of education, he is taught to read and write. . . . Shut out from a tumultuous world, and separated from those equally guilty with himself, he can indulge his remorse unseen, and find ample opportunity for reflection. . . . [H]e has books to read, and ink and paper to communicate with his friends at stated periods;

and weekly he enjoys the privilege of hearing God's holy word expounded by a faithful and zealous Christian minister.

Thus provided, and anxiously cared for by the officers of the prison, he is in a better condition than many beyond its walls guiltless of crime.[21]

Among the affirmative aspects of penal confinement mentioned here, the image of prison as a catalyst of friendship between prisoners is significantly absent. Many of the early prison advocates, fearing that prisoners would corrupt each other, preached and implemented solitary confinement.[22]

The passage quoted above implies that the prisoner's earlier existence in freedom may have been lacking in some essentials of life. Another report from the same period presents an explicitly negative picture of the typical prisoner's life in the world prior to entering the penitentiary. Note how these Pennsylvania officials' words reverberate with James Blake's vision of the harried gnomes on New York streets, "scuttling and scurrying into subways like apprehensive White Rabbits":

> Let us look for a moment at the condition of the majority of those who become subject to . . . [the prison's] regulation. We find them living a hurried and thoughtless life of hourly excitement, and shuddering at the possibility of a pause which could let in (to them the demon) reflection. We see them wanting the ordinary comforts of clothing and cleanliness, without home save that afforded by chance companionship. We find them in the brothel and the gin-shop, giving up to all manner of excesses, indulging in every extreme of vice, self-degraded and brutal.[23]

By contrast, within the prison walls, the prisoners are restored to dignity: "They are taken to the bath and cleansed of outward pollution, they are new-clad in warm and comfortable garments, . . . they are lifted gently from their state of humiliation; self-degradation is removed, and self-esteem inducted."[24]

Remarkably similar is the vision of a state-prison warden speaking a century and a half later. In a telephone interview in the summer of 1987, I spoke with James Garvey, Jr., the warden of New York City's Correctional Institution for Men ("Rikers Island"). I asked him to elaborate on an observation he had made to the *New York Times* to the effect that people "have to come back to jail to regain their self-respect."[25] Warden Garvey replied that he would answer my question on the basis of his earlier experience at a women's prison; however, he later stated that everything he had said would apply to the men's prison as well.

In prison, he observed, the correctional personnel *must* listen to the prisoners. They must make sure the prisoners get their special diet: Moslem, Kosher, salt-free, or low-calorie. The prisoners have a right to a job and to pick out the commissary they want. They have a right to spend two hours a day in the law library even if they are illiterate. If a woman has a cold, she has the right to go to a doctor, even if she is a hypochondriac. Thus, when they leave prison, the women are clean, their clothes are clean, they have money, they weigh more. Once they hit the streets, they begin selling themselves and they are treated with disrespect by everyone, including the housing authorities and other authorities. The warden then remarked: "*The confusion is that jail to them is freedom and society is the jail. They can't operate in society because society has turned its back on them.*"[26] The point here, of course, is not the objective veracity of Warden Garvey's description, but rather the way he *imagines* the offender and the prison experience.

Like the nineteenth-century prison advocates, Garvey exhibits the typical liberal belief in the environment as causative: a poor environment fosters criminality, a benevolent environment overcomes it. Also like the early prison reformers, he sees the prison as providing a benevolent and transformative environment. But, in Garvey, liberal optimism is alloyed with twentieth-century despair. His words contain no hope of a permanent transformation. The rebirth he envisions for the prisoners is not in the Western, Judeo-Christian mode of a one-time salvation, but rather in the Eastern religious style—a cyclical process of death and rebirth, and then again death and rebirth. "They have to come back to prison to regain their self-respect."

I asked Warden Garvey whether he was implying that people

committed crimes for the purpose of returning to prison. He answered that he thought in some cases this happened. If it does, this is an eventuality that was anticipated by the prison reformers. For so attractive was the prison depicted by the prison advocates that their opponents feared people might commit crimes to gain entry. The prison advocates responded by emphasizing the painfully ascetic and solitary character of carceral existence.[27]

My analysis of the positive images corroborates, from the prisoners' own perspective, the prison advocates' affirmative carceral vision. It thus highlights the tension between the rehabilitative model, on the one hand, and the deterrence and retributive models, on the other. It also suggests that there may be a tension between two goals within the rehabilitative ideal. The rehabilitative ideal aims at both the happiness of the prisoner and the prisoner's ability to live a crime-free life outside of prison.[28] Yet, my analysis of the positive images demonstrates that there are individuals for whom prison is rehabilitative in the former sense but not the latter—people whose newly acquired serenity and happiness is conditional on their remaining in prison.

Epilogue to Part One

> But there is no such thing as a simple response to reality. External reality has to be "acquired." To deny that there is anything other than external reality . . . is a denial of the unconscious.
> —Juliet Mitchell

At one point in her prison memoir, when describing her friendship with "Sunshine," nineteen-year-old hijacker Tamsin Fitzgerald writes: "We talked about a farmhouse with fields and woods and about how strange happiness is. She always says, 'But if I hadn't come to prison, then I never would have met you.' "[1] As this quotation suggests, the positive images of prison are but one manifestation of the strangeness of happiness. And yet, it is not really so strange after all that many have found contentment, even joy, in penal confinement. For "[m]an lives, not nakedly or directly in nature like the animals, but within a mythological universe." The images of prison as a desirable abode derive partly from actual negative aspects of life in the world outside. But much more basically, they are an expression of man's essentially psychological and mythopoeic nature, of his tendency to transcend his immediate circumstances, transforming them in the light of his past experience and of his present needs.

PART TWO

A Strange Liking:
Our Admiration for Criminals

Felony . . . says Maitland, is "as bad a word as you can
give to man or thing."

—*Morissette v. United States*

Prick up your ears, Albert! Here's a bandit for you at
last!

—Alexandre Dumas, *The Count of Monte Cristo*

Prologue to Part Two

From beloved prisons, we turn now to romantic outlaws. As we do, our perspective changes from convicted criminals describing punishment to law-abiding citizens describing criminals. Like the beloved-prisons theme of Part One, the subject of romantic outlaws represents a paradox, for the law regards the felon as ignominious; it assumes the convict will be held in dishonor. Indeed, the stigma that is believed to flow from conviction of a particular offense is one factor courts consider in determining whether *mens rea* (a guilty mind) shall be required for that crime. Yet, criminals—even serious offenders—are not invariably the objects of opprobrium. Noncriminals often enjoy, love, even admire, criminals. They admire them not in spite of their criminality but because of it—or at least because of qualities that are inextricably linked to their criminality. That they sometimes do so wonderingly, against considerable inner resistance, serves only to highlight the strength of the attraction.

From a psychoanalytic perspective, this attraction to criminals is not surprising. On an unconscious level, the law, which exercises authority over the citizen, represents the parent, who exercises authority over the child. The law thus serves as a repository of powerful feelings from early childhood—complex feelings of love and hatred, or ambivalence, and concomitant attitudes of submission and defiance.

The negative side of our ambivalence toward the law finds expression in various ways. Some people become revolutionaries or anarchists, fighting to transform or abolish the law. Still others avoid flagrant criminal conduct themselves, while identifying with criminals and vicariously participating in their illegal deeds. Among this last group are those who watch outlaws and listen to their stories, admiring, repudiating, persecuting, and endeavoring to rescue criminals.

Each chapter in Part Two adopts a different approach to the subject of admiration for criminals. Chapter 7, "Reluctant Admiration," sets the stage by presenting evidence that such admiration, and conflict over it, are pervasive. Chapters 8 and 9 present two quite different strategies that noncriminals employ to cope with their inner conflict over criminality. Thus, chapter 8, "Rationalized Admiration," depicts noncriminals who express undisguised enjoyment in, and reverence for, criminals. These noncriminals justify their attraction to the lawbreaker by attributing it to consciously acceptable values, such as justice or freedom.

By contrast, the noncriminals in chapter 9, "Repressed Admiration," energetically bar from consciousness their admiration for criminals. These noncriminals deal with their esteem for criminals not only by repression but also by other defense mechanisms: converting admiration to loathing, repudiation, and persecution. As persecutors, noncriminals sometimes step over the line and commit crimes themselves. They are then in the psychological position of "having their cake and eating it too," as they imitate criminal behavior in the service of bringing criminals to justice.

Part Two draws on fictional characters rather than actual criminals or psychoanalytic patients to illustrate many of its points about noncriminals' attitudes toward criminals. While not a traditional approach in either psychoanalysis or law, extrapolation from literature to life is a method with ample precedents in both disciplines.[1] Moreover, this approach offers an advantage over the use of patients or a scientific sample of the nonpatient population; namely, readers of this book will recognize many of the literary examples and thus will be able to form their own opinions of the interpretations offered.

THE THEORETICAL LITERATURE ON THE "NOBLE BANDIT"

Nonlegal scholars have appreciated the paradox of admiration for criminals and have offered explanations for it. However, they have limited their analyses to the "noble bandit" or "social bandit" type—a category first identified by the eminent British historian E. J. Hobsbawm. On the basis of his research on protest movements, Hobsbawm argued that what he called "social banditry" is a universal phenomenon in peasant societies.[2] He defined social bandits as "outlaws whom the lord and state regard as criminals, but who remain within peasant society, and are considered by their people as heroes, as champions, avengers, fighters for justice."[3]

Hobsbawm proposed several explanations for the appeal of the noble bandit: "the longing for lost innocence and adventure," and "freedom, heroism, and the dream of justice." Above all, Hobsbawm emphasized the appeal of justice: "Social banditry . . . is little more than endemic peasant protest against oppression and poverty: a cry for vengeance on the rich and the oppressors, a vague dream of some curb upon them, a righting of individual wrongs."[4] In an analysis similar to Hobsbawm's, Paul Angiolillo attributes the noble bandit's appeal to men's longing for freedom, exciting adventures, heroism, and fair treatment.[5]

An interesting variation on the explanations offered by Hobsbawm and Angiolillo appears in Stephen Tatum's book, *Inventing Billy the Kid.*[6] Noting that the Kid and other outlaw heroes ultimately receive punishment from legal authorities, Tatum suggests that stories about noble bandits meet our twofold need: (1) for excitement and unpredictability (through the criminal adventures), and (2) for order and stability (through the criminal's defeat by the law).[7]

There is an element of truth in these analyses, but as a complete explanation of our admiration for criminals, they are inadequate. In the first place, many of the criminals whom noncriminals admire fall outside the genre of "noble bandits." Some of the best-loved outlaws in literature—Moll Flanders and Long John Silver, to name two—do not "steal from the rich and give to the poor" or in any sense behave as instruments of justice. Thus, Hobsbawm's and Angiolillo's central explanation cannot account for their appeal. Furthermore, these criminals do not ultimately succumb to punishment at the hands of the law. Hence, Tatum's emphasis on the need for order and stability cannot explain their attraction.

Second, the same criminals whom these scholars identify as "noble bandits" often were not generous and idealistic, but rather brutal and selfish. Even Hobsbawm admits at one point, "In real life most Robin Hoods were far from noble."[8] This suggests that, in admiring criminals, noncriminals are not merely expressing appreciation for qualities that are objectively present; rather, they are going out of their way to perceive criminals in a positive light.

Third, the previous theories proceed on a very general level, which limits their explanatory power and sometimes renders them misleading. For example, Hobsbawm and Angiolillo offer "the appeal of freedom" as one explanation for our attraction to criminals. Stated in this abstract way, their formulation might lead one to believe that criminals embodied a love of democracy. In fact, as I will show in a later section, the freedom that is most closely associated with criminals appears to be of a more primitive variety—either an anal, oppositional kind of freedom that is freedom *against* the law, not within it, or freedom of movement—a somatic kind of freedom.

Tatum's analysis, too, proceeds on an abstract plane, with its emphasis on man's need for disorder and order, for excitement and stability. From his language, one might easily forget that Tatum is writing, not about Carnival time in Rio, but about *crime*. The moral and legal dimensions of the phenomenon he is explaining are entirely missing.

More generally, all of the standard explanations for our admiration for criminals seem unduly charitable to the noncriminal. They focus on values we can admire without shame, while ignoring less noble features of criminality, such as violence, greed, sadism, and anger. Psychoanalysis teaches us to "pay attention," to "ignore nothing," because all manifestations of the human mind have meaning.[9] From this perspective, the more sordid aspects of criminality are not accidental but essential to its appeal. I am suggesting that in addition to the yearning for freedom and justice, the respect for courage, and the vicarious pleasure in adventure, there is a dark side to our admiration for the criminal.

I will return to the question of why we admire criminals in chapter 8. First, let us examine the strategies that noncriminals unconsciously employ to resist awareness of their esteem for criminals.

CHAPTER 7

Reluctant Admiration: The Forms of Our Conflict over Criminals

> When I thought to know this, it was too painful for me.
> —*Psalms* 73:16

In Wilkie Collins's mystery novel *The Woman in White*, the sober and mature heroine, Marian Halcombe, finds herself deeply attracted to Count Fosco, whom she has known for only a few days. Although she does not yet realize on a conscious level that he is a psychopathic criminal, her unconscious mind may sense his depravity. This would help to explain why she finds her attraction to him perplexing and disturbing. As she writes in her journal: "I am almost afraid to confess it, even to these secret pages. The man has interested me, has attracted me, *has forced me to like him.*"[1] And again: "I can only repeat that I do assuredly feel . . . *a strange, half-willing, half-unwilling liking* for the Count."[2] Thus, in attempting to resolve the paradox of her captivation, Marian Halcombe attributes her "strange liking" to a power beyond her control—a resolution that we see again in Joseph Conrad's classic tale, *Heart of Darkness*.

In this novel of self-discovery, Marlow makes a journey into the Belgian Congo to search for Kurtz, a man with a reputation for uniqueness and greatness. Gradually, Marlow learns that Kurtz's dreams have led him to "step over the edge" into evil and crime, including large-scale theft of ivory and murder of Africans. Yet, even after he has made this discovery, Marlow feels a sympathy for Kurtz and finds himself unable to betray the man. Like Marian Halcombe, he perceives this alliance as something he has not totally chosen: "It is strange" he ponders, "how I accepted this unforeseen partnership, this choice of nightmares *forced upon me* in the tenebrous land invaded by these mean and greedy phantoms."[3]

Marian Halcombe and Marlow are characters in works of fiction who exhibit both admiration for criminals and resistance to their admiration. In real life, too, we see individuals in conflict over their esteem for criminals. Arthur Penn, director of the movie about the notorious bank robbers, *Bonnie and Clyde*, provides one such example in the following excerpt from an interview. Here Penn oscillates between his id's attraction to the lawbreakers and his superego's prohibition on admiring criminals:

> INTERVIEWER: *What was it in Bonnie and Clyde that first intrigued you? Any particular aspects?*

> PENN: I suppose I have always been involved with the outlaw to a pretty large extent; I can't say without admiration for them. *Although I find myself offended at saying it*, because I have a large belief in the law.

Immediately he returns to the theme of admiration, followed by another repudiation:

> The history of laws in this country is one of constant change based upon the fact that individuals either spoke out or acted against the oppressive laws. . . . *Now I know it's absurd to be applying it to Bonnie and Clyde* because I don't think of them as being in any sense the noble outlaw of the breed of Robin Hood or William Tell . . . .

Once more he repeats the cycle:

> I suppose that what intrigued me was the enterprise of Bonnie and Clyde, the bravura with which they decided to assault the system. And I have to say it again and again, *I don't mean to suggest that they had heroic character*, because I don't believe that they did.

Finally, abandoning his attempt to merge the historical reality with his wishes, Penn expresses his yearning for criminals he could admire without guilt: "But if they didn't [have heroic character], *I wish that Bonnie and Clyde had had it*."[4]

Throughout the excerpt quoted above, Penn sequentially appeases his id and his superego by alternately applauding and denouncing the criminal. It may have been a similar unconscious conflict that led *Newsweek* film critic Joseph Morgenstern to publish two reviews of *Bonnie and Clyde* one week apart, the first condemning, the second praising the film and its casual, illicit violence.[5]

Alternating appeasement of the id and the superego can also be seen in the behavior of parents in dealing with their delinquent children. Here, too, we see a most poignant expression of the conflict over admiration for criminals; to wit, parents' unconsciously fostering criminality in their children to gratify their own unacknowledged criminal impulses. In one of many similar cases reported by Dr. Ruth Eissler, she describes her treatment of a twelve-year-old boy, the only child of a widow whose husband had been an embezzler and confidence man.[6] Soon after his father's death, when he was seven, the child had begun to steal, lie, miss school, and engage in rude and aggressive behavior. These symptoms of delinquency were pronounced at the time he entered treatment with Eissler.

As the treatment progressed, it became apparent that whenever the boy showed improvement, some temptation occurred, causing a resurgence of the delinquent behavior. For example, his mother's purse would be left out, or a cabinet containing valuable items would be left unlocked. Hoping to gain understanding into these incidents, Eissler sent the mother to another psychiatrist. This colleague reported that whenever the boy ceased stealing, the mother became depressed and created a situation that would tempt her son to steal again. In surrendering to the temptation, the boy was not merely taking advantage of the opportunity; more importantly, he was also responding to his mother's depression and restoring the psychological balance between them. Both the boy and the mother were unconscious of their own motives.

In cases such as this, the child's criminal behavior serves to satisfy vicariously the parent's unacceptable antisocial impulses. Moreover, the same parents who unwittingly turn their children into criminals in this manner frequently go on to denounce their children to the authorities.[7] At this point they gratify their superego's demand for punishment, again in the vicarious mode.[8]

Besides alternating gratification of the id and the superego, another way of coping with ambivalence toward criminality is through negation. A psychoanalytic concept, *negation* refers to the breakthrough of a repressed idea, but in negative form.[9] For example, a patient's words "I haven't been hating my mother today" might be interpreted as a sign that the patient had, indeed, been feeling hatred for his mother but could consciously admit this unacceptable idea only in the negative. As Norman O. Brown writes, "Negation . . . is a dialectical or ambivalent phenomenon, containing always a distorted affirmation of what is officially denied."[10]

A 1989 television documentary entitled "Gangsters: A Golden Age" provides an example of this technique in the context of the conflict over criminality. At the beginning of the film the words "This is not a tribute" appear on the screen while they are also spoken on the sound track. There follows a detailed auditory and visual statement emphasizing that the gangsters were evil people, who inflicted pain on many. The statement concludes with the words: "But such audacity . . . must be saluted."[11] All the language up to the final sentence functions as a negation.

Fredrich Schiller's play *The Robbers* furnishes another illustration of a negation that implies repressed admiration for criminals. In the preface, Schiller defends himself at length against the anticipated charge that he has made criminals praiseworthy. Other writers, he says, have found it necessary to portray outlaws as laudable in some respects: "The Medea of the old dramatists is, in spite of all her crimes, a great and wondrous woman, and Shakespeare's Richard III is sure to excite the admiration of the reader, much as he would hate the reality."[12] Moreover, he continues, it is necessary to depict the criminal's allure; otherwise the reader may unknowingly succumb to his charms: "If I would warn mankind against the tiger, I must not omit to describe his glossy, beautifully-marked skin, lest, owing to this omission, the ferocious animal should not be recognized till too late."[13] The play itself, with its glamorous portrayal of Charles Moor, the outlaw-hero, suggests that Schiller's explanations are but a "distorted affirmation of what is officially denied."

Prohibitions perform, on a cultural level, the role that negations play on an individual level. That is, interdicts against admiring criminals disclose the presence of the very feelings being enjoined. An early warning of this kind comes from *Proverbs:* "Be not thou envious against evil men, neither desire to be with them. For their heart studieth destruction and their lips talk of mischief."[14]

Prohibitions on "envying evil men" reached a peak in England after the publication of John Gay's *The Beggar's Opera* in 1728. Preachers gave sermons and publicists wrote tracts protesting the play's idealization of the criminal.[15] Among those condemning Gay's glamorous depiction of criminals was Charles Dickens, who observed that in *The Beggar's Opera* thieves lead "a life which is rather to be envied than otherwise," with the criminal protagonist Macheath enjoying "all the captivations of command, and the devotions of the most beautiful girl."[16] Dickens concludes that anyone with a criminal bent will see nothing in the play "but a flowery and pleasant road, conducting an honorable ambition—in course of time—to Tyburn Tree."[17] A more subtle condemnation of the same play for encouraging criminality appears in William Hogarth's series of etchings entitled *A Harlot's Progress.* Plate 3 depicts the protagonist about to be arrested as a whore. Enjoying pride of place on her wall is a portrait of Gay's highwayman-hero Macheath.[18]

Injunctions against admiration for criminals continue in the present era. Consider, for example, a magazine article published in 1967 and ironically entitled "Crooks Are So 'Romantic.' " The author, who had studied criminals' lives as a journalist and biographer, urges his readers to "be adult and say that crime is a dirty, squalid, tragically futile business" engaged in by "fundamentally unhappy people." "The romance, thrill and adventure," he asserts, "are largely fake." Earnestly, he points out that burglars sometimes defecate on the floors of the places they rob in order to relieve tension. Such sordid facts, he believes, are little known because they would not correspond to our romantic image of criminals.[19]

Another modern injunction against admiration for criminals appears in a well-regarded textbook, *The Psychiatric Interview,* by

Roger MacKinnon and Robert Michels. The authors warn that beginning psychiatrists may "experience unconscious admiration or even envy" of psychopathic patients—people whose diagnosis is based partly on a history of immoral or illegal behavior.[20] Although they know that psychopaths lack the capacity for some of life's greatest joys, clinicians may find themselves envying the psychopath's ability to "get away with" behavior that is internally prohibited for normal people. In the absence of self-knowledge, the authors caution, psychiatrists may express this admiration in damaging ways, including inadvertent encouragement of the psychopathic acts.[21] That these writers, like others through the ages, entreat people to desist from their "envy of evil men" shows the continuing pervasiveness of this very attraction.

The conflict over admiration for criminals takes many forms—denial of responsibility for one's attraction to criminals, alternating gratification of the id and the superego, negations, and injunctions against worshipping criminals. The very plethora of mechanisms for struggling against attraction to criminals underscores the depth of the attraction. It also raises the question what are the sources of this profound captivation, this wondering esteem for those who break the law. In the next chapter, we turn to a direct exploration of this topic.

CHAPTER 8

Rationalized Admiration: Overt Delight in Camouflaged Criminals

AN HONORABLE KIND OF THIEVERY: THE CRIMINAL AS AN INSTRUMENT OF JUSTICE

> For the foreigner and the rich . . . the *cangaceiro* is an outlaw who should be punished. For the true Brazilian, he is a man of justice, a liberator.
> —Maria Isaura Pereira de Queiroz

A courageous idealist, an instrument of fairness and right, and at the same time a violent outlaw—such is the type of admired criminal that we will consider first. Unlike the criminals we will examine in later sections, these lawbreakers evoke admiration from people who despise the law, which they view as cruel and oppressive. Under what circumstances are noncriminals likely to perceive the law as illegitimate and, consequently, to experience conscious admiration for the lawbreaker? In the story of the admired criminal par excellence, *The Adventures of Robin Hood*, one condition tending to diminish the law's legitimacy is foreign rule. Set in twelfth-century England, this well-known story depicts an outlaw band that commits crimes against the evil rich and powerful, and uses its ill-gotten gains to help the poor and oppressed. Throughout the tale, Robin and his men associate evil with the Norman conquerors, right and goodness with their Saxon subjects. Our admiration for Robin is rendered all the more acceptable to our consciences because Robin approximates the political revolutionary, fighting against his countrymen's foreign oppressors.[1]

The reader may protest my characterization of Robin Hood as a criminal. For Robin Hood, so this argument would go, was always loyal to the true king, Richard the Lion-hearted, who was away fighting in the Crusades. Robin's crimes were committed, not against the representative of the highest law of the land, but against local authorities, such as the Sheriff of Nottingham, or against the usurper, King John. Thus, Robin was not really fighting the law—only the inauthentic expressions of law.

Armed with a psychoanalytic perspective, one can rebut this objection as follows: when the critic says that Robin is not fighting the true law, he presupposes a psychological state of affairs that is too simple. In fact, Robin's divergent attitudes toward the usurping king and the true king are both aspects of his emotional stance toward law, which is best described as one of ambivalence— love and hate, submission and defiance. As portrayed in the legend, Robin copes with his internal conflict over law by externalizing it; more specifically, he splits the law's representatives into two people and expresses his positive feelings toward one, his negative feelings toward the other. The point may be made clearer if we consider the parallel situation in fairy tales, where it is conventional to split the mother into a hated and feared stepmother and a beloved but absent mother. In fairy tales, this split is thought to reflect the child listener's difficulty in dealing with her negative feelings toward the mother.[2] Similarly, in *Robin Hood*, the outlaw's loyalty to King Richard reflects the reader's difficulty in accepting her negative feelings toward the law. By the same token, the outlaw's loyalty to the "true" King serves to camouflage his criminal status, so that the reader may admire him without guilt.

Robert Louis Stevenson's novel *Kidnapped* provides a variation on the theme of admiration for a criminal resulting from the foreign-ruled state's illegitimacy. The novel is set in the years following the events of 1745, when the Jacobite Scots rebelled against English rule and attempted to restore Stuart rule in Scotland. It portrays the complex relationship between a boy, David Balfour, whose clan is allied with England, and Alan Breck, a Jacobite terrorist. Though initially attracted to the glamorous Breck, David repudiates him after witnessing a murder for which he blames the outlaw: "[M]y only friend in that wild country was blood-guilty in the first degree; I held him in horror; I could not look upon his face; I would rather have lain alone in the rain on my cold isle than in that warm wood beside a murderer."[3]

Notwithstanding these words of deepest rejection, David soon comes to see the criminal in a more favorable light: "Alan's morals were all tail-first; but he was ready to give his life for them, such as they were."[4] Upon reaching this conclusion, David seeks a reconciliation with the terrorist: " 'Alan,' said I, 'I'll not say it's the good Christianity as I understand it, but it's good enough. And here I offer ye my hand for a second time.' "[5] Although David does not share Alan's political views, he can admire the terrorist for his willingness to die fighting what Alan perceives to be an unjust state.

The theme of respect for a criminal's idealistic fight against foreign encroachment on indigenous values appears in real life as well. Consider, for example, a 1989 sentencing opinion by a district judge in Alaska.[6] The defendant, an Inupiat whaling captain named Percy Nusunginya, stands convicted of hunting whales out of season. In explaining why he feels that an appropriate sentence should be at the bottom level of the guidelines, Judge Kleinfeld repeatedly expresses his regard for Nusunginya's courage in the service of principles. For example, he describes Nusunginya as "a man of serious and honest convictions" and one who "is entitled to respect" for having "honestly and forthrightly engaged in civil disobedience."[7] Rejecting an analogy to marijuana and alcohol violations that he had drawn previously, the judge empathically reflects that Nusunginya's illegal action is probably closer to a draft violation during the Vietnam War "in terms of the kind of conviction that Mr. Nusunginya brings to the matter."[8] Finally, addressing the defendant directly in the opinion, he tells him: "I have no doubt . . . that your position is a principled one and that you sincerely believe that you are, by engaging in this civil disobedience, preserving what you believe to be the right of the Inupiat people, since time immemorial, to hunt whales."[9] Like the fictional David Balfour, Judge Kleinfeld respects the lawbreaker because he recognizes that, to this criminal, the law appears unjust, since it is imposed by a foreign power.

John Steinbeck's novel *The Grapes of Wrath* also depicts venera-
tion for the criminal as a function of the law's illegitimacy, but
here the rulers are domestic. The characters in the novel perceive
the law as unjust because it is impossible to obey the law and
survive with any self-respect. The story begins as Tom Joad, just
paroled after serving four years in prison for manslaughter, hitch-
hikes his way home to Depression-ridden Oklahoma. Upon arrival, Tom finds that his family and most of his neighbors have
left, driven off the land by large, faceless, faraway companies
that do not even provide their victims with the satisfaction of
confronting a visible enemy. Only Muley, a man half-crazed from
frustration and poverty, remains behind to tell Tom what has
happened:

> "Well, the guy that came aroun' talked nice as pie. 'You got to get
> off. It ain't my fault.' 'Well,' I says, 'whose fault is it? I'll go an' I'll
> nut the fella.' 'It's the Shawnee Lan' an' Cattle Company. I jus' got
> orders.' 'Who's the Shawnee Lan' an' Cattle Company?' 'It ain't
> nobody. It's a company.' Got a fella crazy. There wasn't nobody
> you could lay for." [10]

While this excerpt does not focus on the evil of the law in particular, it does sound the theme of alienation from a system that is
perceived as remote and unfair. Since the law facilitated the tragedy that has befallen people like Muley, these early events pave
the way for the novel's subsequent attack on the law.

Before elaborating on this theme, Steinbeck establishes the
other motif, that of admiration for criminals—an idea he develops
partly through the reaction of noncriminals to Tom. For example,
as old friends and family members greet the returned convict, they
repeatedly ask Tom whether he has "busted out of jail," sometimes
with the implied gleeful hope that the answer will be affirmative.[11]
Tom's grandfather does not ask but delightedly assumes that Tom
has left prison illegally: " 'Jus' like I said, they ain't a gonna keep
no Joad in jail. I says, 'Tommy'll come a-bustin' outa that jail like
a bull through a corral fence.' An' you done it.' " [12] Tom allows
the old man to keep his exciting fantasy, but when he disabuses
others of their expectation that he is still an outlaw, they cannot
hide their disappointment.

Although he is now a law-abiding citizen, Tom continues to elicit hero-worship because of his criminal past. For instance, here is Tom's brother Al responding to the prisoner's return:

> Cockily, he walked close before he recognized Tom; and when he did, his boasting face changed, and *admiration and veneration shone in his eyes*, and his swagger fell away. His stiff jeans, with the bottoms turned up eight inches to show his heeled boots, his three-inch belt with copper figures on it, *even the red arm bands on his blue shirt and the rakish angle of his Stetson hat could not build him up to his brother's stature; for his brother had killed a man;* and no one would ever forget it.[13]

Such is the awe in which Tom is held that those close to him partake of his glory: "Al knew that even he had inspired some admiration among boys of his own age because his brother had killed a man. He had heard in Sallisaw how he was pointed out: 'That's Al Joad. His brother killed a fella with a shovel.' "[14]

Like Al, the younger Joad children look up to their brother in part because he has been a criminal: "[T]hey stood apart and watched him secretly, the great brother who had killed a man and been in prison. They remembered how they had played prison in the chicken coop and fought for the right to be prisoner."[15] In this phase of the novel, the criminal is admired simply as a larger-than-life figure, but as the story proceeds, Tom will increasingly become a criminal who is admired as an instrument of justice. Before this evolution occurs, Steinbeck enriches the other theme, that of the law's association with injustice and oppression.

The subject of the divergence between the law and fairness first arises when the Joad family is on the road to California to find work. Ma Joad worries aloud about Tom's act of breaking parole by crossing the state line. Attempting to reassure her, Tom says that the authorities will not care as long as he commits no crime, but Ma replies: " 'Well, I'm scairt about it. Sometimes you do a crime, an' you don't even know it's bad. Maybe they got crimes in California we don't even know about. Maybe you gonna do somepin an' it's all right, an' in California it ain't all right.' "[16] Because the law is divorced from morality, one cannot predict what the law requires or be sure of staying within its bounds.

The theme of the law's arbitrariness reappears when Grandpa dies on the journey and the family must decide whether to bury him illegally. If they do what the law requires, they will have to pay forty dollars for a decent burial or let Grandpa be buried a pauper. Mulling over the problem, Pa nostalgically recalls the past, when it was legal to bury your own kin. When Uncle John reminds him that the law has changed, Pa replies:

> "Sometimes the law can't be foller'd no way. . . . Not in decency, anyways. They's lots a times you can't. When Floyd [Pretty Boy Floyd] was loose an' goin' wild, law said we got to give him up— an' nobody give him up. Sometimes a fella got to sift the law. I'm sayin' now I got the right to bury my own pa. Anybody got some-pin to say?"[17]

The preacher, Casy, confirms Pa's judgment: " 'Law changes,' he said, 'but 'got to's' go on. You got the right to do what you got to do.' "[18] The law's prohibition on private burials becomes a symbol of the disparity between the law and morality, for Grandpa's burial is the first of three such illegal deeds that the Joad family will feel compelled to do.

If, thus far in the novel, the law has been portrayed as merely arbitrary and unpredictable, as time goes on, the law is more and more associated with evil and oppression. Thus, after the Joad family has reached California, we see a dishonest labor contractor accompanied and assisted by a police officer. When one of the migrants, Floyd Knowles, speaks up, insisting on fairness and trying to warn the other men, the contractor uses the policeman to suppress him. Lying, the policeman claims to have seen Floyd in the vicinity of a theft and tells Floyd to get in the police car. Tom trips the policeman, and Reverend Casy kicks the officer unconscious, enabling Floyd to escape. Sometime after this inci-dent, Tom's second crime, we learn of Ma Joad's view that this son is special: " 'There's Al,' " she observes, " 'he's jus' a young fella after a girl. You wasn't never like that, Tom. . . . Ever'thing you do is more'n you. When they sent you up to prison I knowed it. You're spoke for.' "[19] Significantly, it was society's act of branding Tom as a criminal that confirmed his mother's belief in Tom's specialness.

Eventually, Tom commits his third and, arguably, his most serious offense: killing a man in retaliation for Casy's murder. As the book ends, Tom is leading the life of a fugitive, and the family has just buried yet another person, a baby, absent the authorization of law.

I have recounted the events of *The Grapes of Wrath* at some length to emphasize the close relationship between admiration for the criminal and contempt for unjust laws. While the causal connection is rarely made explicit, it seems clear that the noncriminals in the book admire Tom's criminality largely because they cannot respect the laws he is breaking.

Like *The Grapes of Wrath*, Sophocles' play *Antigone* portrays a state whose laws are problematic because they are unfair and oppressive. Moreover, Sophocles—again like Steinbeck—employs a conflict over a burial to tell a story about a criminal who is an instrument of justice. Just before the action of this classic tale begins, Antigone's two brothers have been killed. One, Eteocles, has received a state burial, while the other, Polynices, has been declared a traitor and his body left to be torn and devoured by birds and beasts. The ruler, Creon, has ordered that no one may perform burial rites for Polynices, upon pain of death.

As the play opens, Antigone is telling her sister, Ismene, of her plan to defy Creon's mandate, which she believes violates the higher laws of the gods. Ismene entreats Antigone not to embark on her daring enterprise, arguing that she is too weak to go against the mighty. Nevertheless, Antigone twice scatters dust over her brother's body and performs sacred rites over him. After Creon decrees that she must die for disobeying his laws, Creon's son comes forward to tell his father that the people are siding with Antigone:

> . . . but I secretly can
> gather this, how the folk
> mourn this maid,
> 'Who of all women most unmeriting,
> For noblest acts dies by the
> worst of deaths,

Who her own brother battle-slain—
unburied—
Would not allow to perish in the fangs
Of carrion hounds or any bird of prey;
And' (so the whisper darkling
passes round)
'Is she not worthy to be carved in gold?'[20]

"Worthy to be carved in gold": this is high praise indeed for a criminal, even a noble criminal. The noncriminals' admiring reaction to Antigone can be explained not only by her courage, but also by the particular crime she committed, for in the ancient Greeks' religion, the souls of the unburied were doomed to wander forever, without rest. It was, therefore, a sacred duty to bury any dead one encountered, whether strangers or kin.[21] More generally, the phenomenon of death is apt to evoke an awareness that the rulers of this realm have but limited power, limited legitimacy. Not only in fictional portrayals, but also in life, laws infringing on the rights of the dead may foster a consciousness of the positive law's illegitimacy. Thus, in the 1950s, when impoverished sharecroppers formed the first of what would later become the radical Peasant Leagues of Northeast Brazil, their original goal was the right to be buried in a coffin.[22]

If we sometimes admire criminals because the state is tyrannical, at other times we admire them because the state is weak. Insofar as we experience hate as well as love for authority, we derive pleasure from acts that render the state ridiculous or highlight its vulnerability. Interestingly, the very word *outlaw*, which we now use to mean a notorious or habitual criminal, reflects the weakness of the state. In medieval times, an outlaw was one who, because of his bad acts, had been banished from society and placed outside the protection of the law.[23] This original concept of the criminal can also be seen in the word *bandit* which derives from the Italian word for banish.[24] By declaring someone an outlaw, a banished person, the state was acknowledging its inability to punish someone who had violated its laws.[25] The impotence of the state that could cope with its unruly elements only through banishment is conveyed by the light tone of this outlaw song in Robert Louis Stevenson's adventure story, *The Black Arrow:* "Then up and spake the master, the king of the outlaws: 'What make ye here, my merry men, among the greenwood shaws?' And Gamelyn made answer—he looked never adown: 'O, they must need to walk in wood that may not walk in town.' "[26] No wonder that the common people often venerated those who, by their very existence, put the state to shame.

The sentence of outlawry ceased to be used after the end of the Middle Ages, when states became powerful enough to enforce their laws throughout their territories. Nevertheless, admiration for criminals as a function of the state's weakness continues to be a striking feature of some societies. In Sicily, for example, successful bandits are honored and described as men who "make themselves respected."[27] According to historian Anton Blok, the preoccupation with honor, along with its particular meaning centering on forcible control of resources, flows from the weakness of the state in Mediterranean societies: "In the absence of stable central control over the means of violence, *people could not rely for protection on State institutions.* With respect to sheer physical survival, they were largely dependent on their own, or on the protection of more powerful persons. *Successful bandits inspire fear and respect. Hence the fascination they radiate.*"[28]

In highly industrialized societies, as well, admiration for criminals may arise out of contempt for the state's weakness. For example, in 1989 a front-page article in the *Wall Street Journal* described a man charged with murder who became a romantic folk hero to residents of Missouri after he managed to elude the law for fifty-nine days.[29] This, the longest and largest manhunt in Missouri's history, inspired songs, stories, and a line of T-shirts. Explaining the public's reaction, one local resident observed, "Defiance of authority tends to draw admiration in rural places like this."[30]

The public response to subway vigilante Bernhard Goetz is another example of admiration for a criminal that reflects disdain for the law's weakness. The basic facts of this case are well-known:

in 1984, Goetz, a white man, was seated in a subway car in New York City when four black youths approached him and asked for five dollars.[31] There was conflicting testimony as to the subsequent events, but all agree that Goetz drew a pistol and fired at the youths, leaving one paralyzed and brain-damaged for life. Many legal scholars believe that, under the most credible version of the facts, Goetz failed to meet the imminence requirement for self-defense, because a reasonable person would not have thought that the fourth victim posed an immediate danger to Goetz.[32] Nevertheless, the jury acquitted Goetz on all the charges except illegal possession of a handgun.

What is interesting for our purposes is not so much the verdict, which can be explained in a variety of ways, but rather the widespread admiration for Goetz and its meaning.[33] That the positive response to Goetz's crime reflects scorn for the state's ineptitude can be seen in the lyrics of this song recorded by Ronny and the Urban Watchdogs:

> He's the subway vigilante
> The brave subway vigilante
> *Where law and order can't*
> *he showed us how to take a stand*
> He had enough and came out fightin'
> Drove the rats back into hidin'
> Let's cheer the subway vigilante
> He's one special kind of man.[34]

Interpreting the popular celebration of Goetz in a similar vein, George Fletcher writes: "The group that fears finally found its folk hero in Bernhard Goetz. . . . *Goetz demonstrated the impotency of law enforcement.* A single individual, well armed and properly trained, can do a better job of thwarting crime than all the men in blue."[35]

From the perspective I am suggesting, Goetz can be understood as a camouflaged criminal. He is a criminal in that he acted illegally when he fired the shots; however, his criminality is camouflaged in that some can see him as an instrument of legitimate vengeance against evil and dangerous people. This camouflage enables noncriminals to admire Goetz without guilt. Nevertheless, the unconscious source of admiration may be, not that he is an instrument of justice, but rather that he expresses the noncriminals' own hostility to authority and to limitations on their instinctual freedom.

On the basis of the preceding examples, we are now in a position to distinguish between two types of criminals who are admired as instruments of justice: the vigilante and the noble bandit. Those, like Goetz, whom we call vigilantes commit illegal acts against other *criminals* out of contempt for the law's weakness and frustration at its inefficiency. By contrast, those, like Robin Hood, whom we consider noble bandits typically commit illegal offenses against evil *non*criminals—the Sheriff of Nottingham or the greedy vicars and bishops. Unlike the vigilantes, noble bandits act out of opposition to the state's tyranny and its unfairness to the poor. Correlatively, those who admire either type of criminal may do so on a conscious level because they share that type's attitude— whether it be impatience with the slowness of the legal process, or outrage at the cruelty and oppression that the law embodies.

Of course, some may object to my interpretations of noble bandits and vigilantes on the ground that they are criminals in name only. Their stories show moral inversion, where the law represents evil, or inefficiency, and those who break the law stand for virtue, or effective law enforcement. Naturally, we would regard such criminals highly; that we do so says nothing about our esteem for the criminal in more normal situations where the law and morality converge.

The problem with this commonsense view lies in its failure to take into account psychoanalytic findings about human nature— more specifically, the clinical findings that people harbor sadistic trends (sexual pleasure in another's pain) and ambivalence (hate as well as love) toward authority.[36] The existence of these tendencies renders it more plausible than not that noncriminals derive unconscious satisfaction from the cruelty and aggression that characterize criminal exploits.

It is important to stress that, for most noncriminals, the gratification received from the criminal acts is truly *un*conscious; it is not accessible to awareness. Indeed, on a conscious level, noncriminals may strongly object to the idea that criminality has any attraction for them. This objection, too, is consistent with psychoanalytic theory, which emphasizes the universality of repression and of an unwillingness to know the unpleasant truths about ourselves.[37]

In the face of the psychoanalytic evidence—both of unconscious drives and of an aversion to becoming aware of those drives—it seems naive to suppose that we admire criminals for their noble qualities alone. I propose an alternative explanation— an explanation that is already implicit in this chapter's title, "Rationalized Admiration: Overt Delight in Camouflaged Criminals." Briefly, my hypothesis is as follows: we admire criminals on many levels and for many reasons—reasons that we feel comfortable acknowledging to ourselves and reasons that, as the Psalm has it, are "too painful to know." When a given criminal seems to have no redeeming features, we will not consciously honor that person, although we may esteem him unconsciously and express the admiration in a distorted form, such as loathing or persecution.

If, however, as is true of the examples in this section, the criminal has some features we can appreciate without guilt, we may consciously respect him for those features, while unconsciously also enjoying and lauding the greed, sadism, or antiauthoritarian aggression. In this view, the explanations we offer ourselves for being attracted to criminals serve as rationalizations, not in the sense that they play *no* role in our attraction, but that they serve to disguise other, less acceptable reasons.

The remainder of this chapter will examine criminals who are not perceived as instruments of justice and who do not live in societies where the law is viewed as evil; nevertheless, they are greatly admired. I turn now to the first category of such criminals—those whose violent, illegal acts are camouflaged by their embodiment of freedom.

The Highwayman Came Riding: The Criminal As a Symbol of Freedom

> The urge for freedom, therefore, is directed against particular forms and demands of civilization or against civilization altogether.
>
> —Freud, *Civilization And Its Discontents*

> Banditry is freedom, but in a peasant society few can be free.
>
> —Hobsbawm, *Bandits*

The novella *Carmen*, by Prosper Merimee, depicts a criminal whose appeal is that of freedom. Carmen, who belongs to a gang of smugglers, regularly provides information to her fellow thieves about any travelers who would be good prospects for robbery. Overtly, boldly sexual, Carmen is irresistibly attractive. Her lawless ways are a part of her appeal and an essential aspect of her being.[38] We see the central role of freedom in her character in her response to her suitor, Don Jose, when he forbids her to speak to the *picador* Lucas: "Beware!" she retorts. "If any one defies me to do a thing, it's very quickly done."[39] Here we see the anal, oppositional meaning that freedom has for Carmen.[40] She is a rebel rather than a revolutionary; she is still reacting to authority, albeit in a negative way.[41]

Charles Moor, the hero of Schiller's *The Robbers*, embodies a similar notion of freedom. As he talks himself into becoming a criminal, Moor associates criminality with freedom, and freedom with life outside the law: "Am I to squeeze my body into stays, and straightlace my will in the trammels of law? What might have risen to an eagle's flight has been reduced to a snail's pace by law. Never yet has law formed a great man; 'tis liberty that breeds giants and heroes."[42] Thus, law, instead of being the necessary condition for liberty, is seen here as an obstacle to liberty.

In addition to freedom as an oppositional struggle against authority, criminality is often linked with freedom of *movement*. This association appears in the following dialogue from the operatic version of *Carmen*, where the gypsy *femme fatale* tries to convince her suitor that he should be glad to join the band of thieves:

CARMEN: Are you one of us now?

DON JOSE (with resignation): I have to be!

CARMEN: Ah! That's not very complimentary! But what's the difference? Come—you'll get used to it when you see *how fine life on the road is, with the world for your country*; and for law, what you want to do! And most of all what makes you alive: Freedom! Freedom![43]

Freedom of movement also plays an important role in the original story by Merimee. Here Don Jose explains what enticed him to the criminal life: "I had often heard talk of certain smugglers who *travelled about Andalusia each riding a good horse*, with his mistress behind him and his blunderbuss in his fist. Already *I saw myself trotting up and down the world*, with a pretty gypsy behind me."[44] The gypsy, a quintessential symbol of the wandering life, heightens the association here between criminality and a somatic kind of freedom.

The image of the gypsy performs a similar function in Alfred Noyes's poem *The Highwayman*, where the road over which the robber gallops is described as "a gypsy's ribbon." Throughout this poem, rapid movement is expressed in both the content and the rhythm of the lines. Consider, for example, the first stanza:

> The wind was a torrent of
> darkness among the gusty trees.
> The moon was a ghostly galleon
> tossed upon cloudy seas.
> The road was a ribbon of moonlight
> over the purple moor,
> And the highwayman came riding—
> Riding—riding—
> The highwayman came riding,
> up to the old inn door.[45]

As in *Carmen*, here the sensation of speed serves to render the abstract concept *freedom* more immediate and concrete.

A particularly interesting example of admiration for criminals who are associated with speed of movement comes from Harrison Ainsworth, author of the popular nineteenth-century novel *Rookwood*. At one point in the novel, Ainsworth reproduces highwayman Dick Turpin's famed 220–mile ride from London to York. Describing how he wrote this part of the book, a total of one hundred pages, in less than twenty-four hours, Ainsworth stresses his admiring identification with the robber and his swiftness:

> Well do I remember the fever into which I was thrown during the time of composition. My pen literally galloped over the pages. So thoroughly did I identify myself with the highwayman, that, once started I found it impossible to halt. . . . In his company I mounted the hillside, dashed through the bustling village . . . and kept an onward course, without fatigue. With him I shouted, sang, laughed, exulted, wept.[46]

Psychoanalytic theory helps to explain the powerful attraction that rapid movement exerts. Freud suggested that the ego (used here to mean the mental self) originally "includes everything. . . . The ego-feeling we are aware of now is thus only a shrunken vestige of a far more extensive feeling . . . of limitless extension and oneness with the universe—the same feeling as that described . . . as 'oceanic.' "[47] Exemplifying the pleasure that comes from an extension of ego boundaries, another psychoanalyst offers these descriptions of a child:

> I. A little boy of one and a half years was taken to an ocean beach for the first time. His sudden view of the tremendous expanse of sand and water, an almost unlimited or infinite expanse, was met with tremendous excitement, one might almost say intoxication. The moment he got on the beach, he ran and ran as fast as his little legs could carry him, his arms outstretched, shrieking with delight. He did not stop running until he was exhausted. In his running one could see how he tried to encompass this tremendous expanse of what must have appeared to him as limitless space, and how his ego seemed to identify with it.
>
> II. The same boy at the age of four and a half was walking in the woods with his father and others. They came to a kind of clearing where the trees were far apart down a large clear hill. He broke away from the group and ran gleefully down the hill singing, "I'm free, I'm free, I'm free like a bird."[48]

In the same vein, a small boy of my own acquaintance used to exhort me in tones of joy and awe: "Kick the ball so it touches the sky!" Similar to the children in these vignettes, grown-ups may undergo a feeling of ego expansion when they vicariously participate in the rapid journeys of the highwaymen.

If freedom of movement is an important reason for our attraction to the criminal, this would help to explain why highwaymen were extolled more than any other criminals in eighteenth- and nineteenth-century England. Evidence of the highwaymen's popularity comes from the memoirs of the Abbe Le Blanc. During his travels in England in 1737, the Abbe wrote that he was continuously meeting Englishmen "who were not less vain in boasting of the success of their highwaymen than of the bravery of their troops." Everyone, he continued, had a story to tell of the highwaymen's generosity and "cunning" and "a noted thief was a kind of hero."[49] In keeping with Le Blanc's impressionistic account is a historian's conclusion that highway robbery "was a kind of thievery that seems to have been *considered fit for a gentleman.*"[50]

In the nineteenth century, too, outlaw "gentlemen of the road" attracted great interest and admiration. The novel *Rookwood*, which idealized the highwayman Dick Turpin, was immediately successful, while sales of *Jack Sheppard*, a tale about the highwayman of the same name, outnumbered those of *Oliver Twist*.[51] Yet another sign of the enduring glamour associated with this kind of criminal is the use of the term *highwayman* to describe fashionable clothes. For example, in 1901, the *Daily Chronicle* described Sarah Bernhardt as looking "very striking in a wonderful gown . . . half-concealed by a long paletot of white silk, made in the 'highwayman' shape, with a number of natty little capes." Or again, a 1966 issue of *Vogue* contains the caption: "Vogue's adventurers wear . . . highwaymen's coats."[52] That garments should become more appealing by virtue of their connection to highwaymen is remarkable in view of the historical facts about this type of criminal: in reality, many highwaymen were vicious rapists and murderers.[53]

Like the English robbers on fast horses, the famous American outlaws of the 1930s are associated with freedom and, more specifically, with speed of movement. On the modern highways that emerged in the early thirties, bandits such as Bonnie Parker and

Clyde Barrow could rob a bank and be two hundred miles away by nightfall. Cars that were faster than ever before, cars that could travel up to ninety miles per hour, not only contributed to the flourishing of these criminals; they are also an intrinsic part of their illustrious image.[54]

Another variation on the association of criminality with freedom is the motif of the criminal as child. We see this idea embodied in the pirate Long John Silver in Robert Louis Stevenson's novel *Treasure Island*. Like other criminals we have considered, Long John can be understood in relation to at least two admiring noncriminals: the reader and a fictional character, the cabin boy and narrator, Jim Hawkins. Upon first meeting Long John, Jim describes him positively: "I thought I knew what a buccaneer was like—a very different creature, according to me, from this clean and pleasant-tempered landlord."[55] Concluding that Silver is not a pirate, Jim becomes friends with him and finds Silver to be "unweariedly kind" and "the best of men."[56] Later, after learning of Silver's scheme to take over the boat and kill many good men, Jim reacts with revulsion to his former friend: "I had, by this time, taken such a horror of his cruelty, duplicity, and power, that I could scarce conceal a shudder when he laid his hand upon my arm."[57] Upon overhearing Silver knife a man to death, Jim describes the buccaneer as a "monster" and "murderer," obliviously "cleansing his blood-stained knife the while upon a whisp of grass."[58] Jim now resists Silver's charms but cannot help noticing, "He was brave and no mistake."[59]

Stevenson's *Treasure Island* never fully resolves the tension between Jim's attraction to Silver and his disapproval of him. In the movie versions of this story, however, Jim's love for Silver proves stronger than his moral scruples. For example, in the 1934 production directed by Victor Fleming, Jim enables Silver to escape prosecution, accepts his parrot as a parting gift, and weeps upon separating from his pirate friend.[60] The Disney version also suggests that the positive side of Jim's ambivalence toward Silver prevails in the end. Nicely epitomizing Jim's psychological conflict in the final scene, the film depicts Silver sailing away from the honest men, waving good-bye to them. Jim hesitates, then puts his hand up quickly, halfway, meeting Silver's wave.[61]

The typical noncriminal reader's response to Silver can be gauged by the summary on the back cover of the Bantam Classic Edition. In an amusing non sequitur, the editors describe Long John as "the merry unscrupulous buccaneer rogue whose greedy quest for gold cannot help but win the heart of every soul who ever longed for romance, treasure, and adventure."[62] Unscrupulousness and greed are not usually thought of as lovable traits, yet here the editors suggest that they may be the very basis for Silver's appeal. Indeed, the essence of his charm seems to lie in an utter obliviousness to the moral code, together with a childlike assumption that people will not hold him accountable for his evil deeds. The following exchange, which occurs near the end of the book, throws these qualities into relief:

> At the top, the squire met us. . . . At Silver's polite salute he somewhat flushed. "John Silver," he said, "you're a prodigious villain and imposter—a monstrous impostor, sir. I am told I am not to prosecute you. Well, then, I will not. But the dead men, sir, hang about your neck like millstones."
> "Thank you kindly, sir," replied Long John, again saluting.
> "I dare you to thank me!" cried the squire. "It is a gross dereliction of my duty."[63]

Notwithstanding the humorous effect of such passages, it is important to note that Long John is no innocuous outlaw but rather a thoroughly immoral criminal who commits deeds that are heinous by anyone's standards. Yet, such is his appeal that, in addition to the original book and the movies, at least one play and a children's book have been written celebrating Silver and his exploits.[64]

Shakespeare's thief, Sir John Falstaff, exerts an attraction on a similar basis, both for the noncriminal playgoer and for Falstaff's fictional friend Prince Hal. Prince Hal's love for his criminal friend comes through in the speech he makes when he believes Falstaff to be dead. Significantly, he alludes to Falstaff's immorality in the very sentence where he stresses his abiding affection:

"What, old acquaintance! Could not all this flesh keep in a little life? Poor Jack, farewell. I could have better spared a better man."[65] Although some critics have denied that Falstaff's appeal lies in his criminality, Robert Hapgood seems right in saying that this view understates our own guilt, for Falstaff's stealing is central to his personality. More specifically, as Hapgood notes, "his thieving is of a piece with his lying: both are appealingly childlike in their uninhibited expansiveness."[66] Although Falstaff is an old man, he is associated both with childlike qualities and with youth itself. For example, in one scene when he and his cohorts rob some travelers, he exclaims: "Hang ye, gorbellied knaves, are ye undone? No, ye fat chuffs; I would your store were here. On, bacons, on! *What, ye knaves, young men must live.*"[67] Like a child, Falstaff allows other people, specifically Prince Hal and the tavern hostess, to provide for his needs. When the hostess endeavors to collect her debt, Falstaff preemptively charges that someone has picked his pockets. The hostess replies: "No, Sir John, you do not know me, Sir John; I know you, Sir John. You owe me money, Sir John, and now you pick a quarrel to beguile me of it. I bought you a dozen of shirts to your back."[68] She goes on to charge that Falstaff also owes her for food, drink, and money previously loaned to him.[69] Falstaff thus represents freedom in the sense of a childlike irresponsibility. Prince Hal, a noncriminal, is attracted to Falstaff in part because he knows that eventually, when he becomes king, he will have to put away childish things.

Prince Hal's affection for Falstaff has been shared by the play-going public. *Henry IV, Part I* went through six editions in its first twenty-five years. Moreover, contemporary authors referred to Falstaff more than to any other Shakespearean character. According to tradition, Queen Elizabeth herself was so pleased with the rogue that she asked to see Falstaff in love. In response to her request, so the tradition continues, Shakespeare wrote the *Merry Wives of Windsor.*[70]

Yet another dimension of the freedom that the criminal symbolizes is freedom from social pressures. Daniel Defoe's heroine Moll Flanders, in his novel by the same name, attracts our admiration by embodying this kind of freedom.[71] A chronic thief, prostitute, and convicted felon, Moll has been described by one critic as "immoral, shallow, hypocritical, heartless."[72] Yet, the same scholar continues, "Moll is marvellous."[73] This very positive assessment of Moll—and the reasons for it—are widely shared by readers of the novel. Virginia Woolf speaks for many in rejecting Defoe's self-declared purpose in writing the book, which was to provide a negative example to his readers. "Defoe," she asserts, "did not pronounce more than a judgment of the lips upon . . . [the criminals'] failings. But their courage and resource and tenacity delighted him."[74]

Woolf points out that Moll enjoyed "the freedom of the outcast," because she had broken the laws of society very young.[75] Other readers have noted Moll's high valuation of independence. They have confirmed Moll's assessment of the options open to her as an eighteenth-century woman: to be a criminal and maintain her independence, or to be a maidservant and lose all hope of individual freedom and development.[76] Because we sense that these are Moll's only choices, we appreciate her decision to be free as a criminal rather than enslaved as an honest person. In the words of Moll's admirer: "What makes her splendid—a great heroine—is that she wants her independence, to work for herself in freedom. She is . . . determined to be a human being, not a servant, and the feeling of what it means to be a servant is what generates the impulses which carry her through most of the book."[77]

A similar conception of the criminal as a hero who is free from social pressures pervades the detective novels of Patricia Highsmith. Highsmith portrays a society where most people are trapped within families, organizations and other collectivities. Criminals, by contrast, lead lives outside of these structures. Often the criminals are the heroes of her novels: they are not only the central protagonists but also the most likeable characters in the books.[78] Highsmith herself cites their embodiment of freedom to explain the appeal of her criminal-heroes: "Criminals are dramatically interesting, because for a time at least they are active, free in spirit, and they do not knuckle down to anyone." [79] Significantly, in *The Talented Mr. Ripley*, the book that many of Highsmith's readers like best, the protagonist, a murderer and thief, goes free in the end. [80]

In the next section, I turn from the criminal's association with freedom to the criminal's association with greatness. Here I take up the powerful link between criminality and pride, especially overweening pride, or hubris.

A Function of His Virtue: The Criminal As an Embodiment of Greatness

> For I was envious of the arrogant, when I saw the prosperity of the wicked.
> . . . .
> Pride is their necklace; violence covers them as a garment.
> . . . .
> They set their mouths against the heavens, and their tongue struts through the earth. Therefore the people turn and praise them; And find no fault with them.
> —*Psalms* 73:3–10

The criminal as a dreamer of dreams, as one who aspires to immortality, as a character larger than life, albeit with feet of clay—such is the type of admired criminal to be considered first under the rubric of "greatness." Robert Penn Warren's novel *All the King's Men* portrays such a criminal in the character Willie Stark, who commits felonies to retain political power and to realize his sometimes idealistic ends. After he is assassinated, his wife names her grandson for Willie. In a conversation with Jack Burden, Willie's loyal man Friday, she explains that she has done so "because Willie was a great man." [81] She goes on: " 'Oh, I know he made mistakes,' she said, and lifted up her chin as though facing something, 'bad mistakes. Maybe he did bad things like they say. But inside—in here, deep down—' and she laid her hand to her bosom—'he was a great man.' " [82] Jack comments that, in the end, he came to believe that too. [83] For Jack, Lucy, and Willie's other admirers, the magnitude of Willie's deeds and aspirations outweighed the evil of the means he employed. But more than that, perhaps the criminal means were an inseparable part of his greatness and thus an essential basis of his appeal.

This association is clearer in Jack's relationship to another criminal, Judge Irwin. As the story unfolds, Jack discovers that the judge, now an upright citizen, committed a crime many years earlier, covering up a felony to keep his house. Reflecting that he himself would not commit a crime to save the house, Jack observes that perhaps this is merely because he does not love the house as much as the Judge had loved it, "and a man's virtue may be but the defect of his desire, as his crime may be but a function of his virtue."[84]

The paradoxical motif of crime as a "function of one's virtue" also runs through Peter Shaffer's modern play-*cum*-detective-story *Equus*. The play focuses on the relationship between a psychiatrist, Martin Dysart, and his patient, Alan Strang, a seventeen-year-old stableboy who plunged a steel spike into the eyes of six horses. In the following passage, Dysart struggles with his fear that, in treating the boy and rendering him less dangerous, he will deprive Alan of a rare and valued quality:

> Look, . . . to go through life and call it yours—*your life*—you first have to get your own pain. Pain that's unique to you. You can't just dip into the common bin and say, 'That's enough!'
> . . . He's done that. All right he's sick. He's full of misery and fear. He was dangerous and could be again. . . . But that boy has known a passion more ferocious than I have felt in any second of my life. And let me tell you something: I envy it.[85]

By contrast with Alan, who has created a religion centering on horses and characterized by emotional, secret, nighttime rituals, Dysart believes that he himself leads a paltry existence. As he confesses to his friend Hesther: "I shrank my *own* life. No one can do it for you. I settled for being pallid and provincial, out of my own eternal timidity."[86]

The idea that criminal behavior may be entwined with the criminal's greatest qualities also appears in Joseph Conrad's novel *Heart of Darkness*. Like Lucy Stark in relation to her husband, and

Martin Dysart in relation to Alan, Marlow finds himself overlooking Kurtz's crimes because they pale in relation to the man's great gifts: "Hadn't I been told in all the tones of jealousy and admiration that he [Kurtz] had collected, bartered, swindled, or stolen more ivory than all the other agents together? *That was not the point. The point was in his being a gifted creature.*" [87] More important even than the magnitude of his talent is the grandeur of Kurtz's vision: "Better his cry ["The horror!"]—much better. It was an affirmation, a moral victory paid for by abominable terrors, by abominable satisfactions. But it was a victory! That is why I have remained loyal to Kurtz to the last." [88]

Like other noncriminals in relationships with criminals, Marlow acknowledges Kurtz's transgressions: "True, he had made that last stride, he had stepped over the edge." [89] But, for Marlow, Kurtz's "abominable terrors" (including murdering natives and displaying their heads on posts) were outweighed by his profound understanding. Marlow's description of his reaction to Brussels upon returning from the Belgian Congo highlights the nature of Kurtz's appeal:

> I found myself back in the sepulchral city resenting the sight of people hurrying through the streets to filch a little money from each other, to devour their infamous cookery, to gulp their unwholesome beer, to dream their insignificant and silly dreams. . . . I felt so sure they could not possibly know what I knew. Their bearing, which was simply the bearing of commonplace individuals . . . was offensive to me like the outrageous flauntings of folly in the face of a danger it is unable to comprehend. [90]

To these noncriminal but trivial and ignorant lives, Marlow implicitly opposes his own life based on superior knowledge—knowledge he gained from the criminal, Kurtz.

The theme of the criminal as one who sees beyond the obvious, who is in touch with a truer or more significant realm, also runs through Colin MacInnes's novel *Mr. Love and Justice*. The book concerns the evolving relationship between a policeman, Edward Justice, and a pimp, Frankie Love. At one point, while Mr. Justice is still learning his job, an informer endeavors to teach him some fundamental truths:

"The fact is this," the nark[91] continued, . . . "You may not approve of what I say, but you and me have one big thing in common: neither of us is mugs: both of us sees below the surface of how things seem."

"Yeah," Edward said.

"And I'll tell you something more," the nark went on. "It's even the same between you and the criminals, as you'll discover. Neither they nor you belong to the great world of the mugs; you know what I mean: the millions who pay their taxes by the pea-eh-why-ee, read their Sunday papers for the scandals, do their pools on Thursdays, watch the jingles on the telly, travel to and fro to work on tubes and buses in the rush hour, take a fortnight's annual holiday by the sea, and think the world is just like that."[92]

Removed from the routinized and benighted domain of ordinary people, criminals lead elevated lives; to borrow a phrase from another novel about criminals, they belong to the "the Realm."[93]

Like *Heart of Darkness* and *Mr. Love and Justice*, Schiller's play *The Robbers* contrasts criminals' important undertakings with the inglorious activities of their noncriminal contemporaries. Near the beginning of the play, the protagonist, Charles Moor, reflects on the pettiness of men's enterprises in his time: "I am disgusted with this age of puny scribblers when I read of great men in my Plutarch."[94] Significantly, his thoughts fall on the ancient god-thief, Prometheus, who stole fire and gave it to man:

The glowing spark of Prometheus is burnt out, and now they substitute for it the flesh of lycopodium, a stage fire which will not so much as light a pipe. . . .

. . . Fie! Fie upon this weak, effeminate age, fit for nothing but to ponder over the deeds of former times.[95]

In this mood, Charles turns a receptive ear to the exhortations of an acquaintance, Spiegel, who promises greatness if Charles will join in forming a band of robbers:

Cowards, cripples, lame dogs are ye all if you have not courage enough to venture upon something great. . . .

. . . My plan will exalt you the most, and it holds out glory and immortality into the bargain.[96]

The motif of the criminal as an embodiment of greatness also pervades Arthur Conan Doyle's short story "The Adventure of the

Final Problem." Here, too, we see a variation on this motif: the criminal as a worthy opponent. Sherlock Holmes' high esteem for the criminal, Professor Moriarty, comes through in the following passage:

> He is the Napoleon of crime, Watson. He is the organizer of half that is evil and of nearly all that is undetected in this city. He is a genius, a philosopher, an abstract thinker. He has a brain of the first order. He sits motionless, like a spider in the centre of its web, but that web has a thousand radiations, and he knows well every quiver of each of them.[97]

Not only does Holmes take vicarious pleasure in Moriarty's power and ability; more specifically, he delights in having found an enemy he can respect. Speaking to Dr. Watson, he exults: " 'You know my powers, my dear Watson, and yet at the end of three months I was forced to confess that I had at last met an antagonist who was my intellectual equal. My horror at his crimes was lost in my admiration at his skill.' "[98] Elaborating on this theme, Holmes tells of the enjoyment he derived from pursuing the criminal: "I tell you, my friend, that if a detailed account of that silent contest could be written, it would take its place as the most brilliant bit of thrust-and-parry work in the history of detection. Never have I risen to such a height, and never have I been so hard pressed by an opponent."[99] Thus, the magnitude of the criminal's talent made him a match for the hero, enlivening the hero's existence and challenging him to his best efforts. After Holmes and Moriarty meet violent, conjoined deaths, Watson equates the two men, pronouncing that there in the water would "lie for all time the most dangerous criminal and the foremost champion of the law of their generation."[100]

In subsequent stories, after Holmes, but not Moriarty, has been restored to life, Holmes's need of a great criminal becomes even more apparent. In "The Adventure of the Norwood Builder," we find the detective complaining, "London has become a singularly uninteresting city since the death of the late lamented Professor Moriarty."[101] He adds that with Moriarty alive, the morning paper had "presented infinite possibilities," by contrast with its sorry state in the criminal's absence.[102] In a still later story, Holmes wistfully observes to Watson that a certain physician would make a wonderful criminal opponent: " 'Dr. Leslie Armstrong is certainly a man of energy and character,' said he. 'I have not seen a man who if he turned his talents that way, was more calculated to fill the gap left by the illustrious Moriarty.' "[103] Here we have, not the usual mitigation of a criminal's sordid qualities to allow for guiltless admiration, but rather the fantasy that a noncriminal might become a great criminal to allow for the pleasures of pursuing a worthy opponent.

Like Sherlock Holmes, Porfiry Petrovich, the inquisitor in Dostoevsky's *Crime and Punishment* appreciates the greatness of his criminal counterpart, Raskolnikov. Porfiry speaks truthfully as well as manipulatively when he tells the murderer: "I look on you as a most honourable man and one, indeed, with elements of greatness in you."[104] Moreover, Porfiry, again like Holmes, is comfortable acknowledging the similarity between himself and the criminal. In the final dialogue between the two men, Porfiry confesses to Raskolnikov that he too has committed excesses, deeds of questionable morality, in the process of seeking the truth about the murder of the old pawnbroker and her sister. He has covertly searched Raskolnikov's room and has spread false rumors through Raskolnikov's friend in an effort to confuse his prey.[105] Unlike Javert, the persecutive police officer in *Les Misérables*, Porfiry does not need to see the criminal as utterly different from himself to maintain his self-esteem.[106]

We have seen that noncriminals associate criminals with greatness in the following senses: (1) caring with passionate intensity *(All The King's Men* and *Equus)*; (2) knowing things that noncriminals cannot know *(Heart of Darkness* and *Mr. Love And Justice)*; (3) dwelling in a higher, more significant realm than noncriminals *(Mr. Love And Justice* and *The Robbers)*; and (4) serving as gifted adversaries who enrich the lives of their noncriminal opponents (the stories about Sherlock Holmes and *Crime and Punishment*).

It is now time to ask what constitutes the appeal of greatness. Or, to put it more precisely, what needs are noncriminals gratifying when they choose to perceive the criminal as great? The psychoanalytic concept of narcissism throws some light on this question. The theory of narcissism takes as its starting point certain findings based on observations of children during the early years of life. These observations suggest that, as junior toddlers, from the age of about ten or twelve months to sixteen or eighteen months, we believe in our own omnipotence. In their seminal study *The Psychological Birth of The Human Infant*, Margaret Mahler and her co-authors describe this phase as follows: "[T]he child seems intoxicated with his own faculties and with the greatness of his own world. Narcissism is at its peak! . . . He is exhilarated by his own ability, continually delighted with the discoveries he makes in his expanding world and quasi-enamored with the world and his own grandeur and omnipotence."[107] There comes a time, however, later in the second year of life, when we realize that we are not all-powerful but highly vulnerable to the many insults and injuries life has to offer.[108] Along with this discovery comes the acute realization that we are, in fact, separate from our parents— that their wishes are not necessarily ours, and ours are not invariably theirs.[109]

This twofold disappointment, this recognition of our essential helplessness and aloneness, is a blow from which we never fully recover.[110] Throughout life, we may at times defend against this narcissistic wound by the mechanism of denial—by creating a fantasy that obliterates the unpleasant reality. This fantasy may take either of two forms: "I am perfect," or "You are perfect, but you are part of me."[111] It is the latter kind of fantasy, termed "narcissistic investment," that seems to characterize noncriminals' relationships with criminals whom they perceive as great. Thus, when Lucy Stark insists that, in spite of everything, Willie was a "great man," or when Marlow chooses the criminal but godlike Kurtz over the "commonplace" Belgians with their "insignificant and silly dreams," Lucy and Marlow are narcissistically investing Willie and Kurtz, respectively; that is, they are idealizing and identifying with the criminals to deny their own nature as limited, mortal creatures. Similarly, when Sherlock Holmes waxes eloquent about the omnipotence of Professor Moriarty, we can understand this as a technique for "self-aggrandizement and subtle self-delusion that . . . [he, like all people] finds necessary to assuage the insult of his true being."[112] That criminals should serve as narcissistically invested objects for noncriminals is not accidental. Criminals readily lend themselves to the category of greatness because they are, by definition, people who refuse to be limited by the rules and scruples that circumscribe normal lives.

I turn now from the criminal who manifests greatness to the criminal who attracts us by virtue of being different, who represents our yearning for the long ago and far away. I have already anticipated this theme with the examples of the respected adversary—the criminal who is opposite yet the same. The criminal who attracts us by his exotic qualities also embodies an intriguing mix of difference and similarity.

PEOPLE OF A FOREIGN COUNTRY: THE CRIMINAL AS A GLAMOROUS STRANGER

In a beautiful essay, Georg Simmel has defined the stranger as the "potential wanderer," explaining: "Although he has not moved on, he has not quite overcome the freedom of coming and going." Simmel points out that to be a stranger is actually a "very positive relation." The inhabitants of a distant star, by contrast, "are not really strangers to us, at least not in any sociologically relevant sense: they do not exist for us at all; they are beyond far and near. The stranger, like the poor and like sundry 'inner enemies,' is an element of the group itself." More specifically, the stranger represents the "unity of nearness and remoteness," of wandering and fixation: "[I]n the relationship to him, distance means that he, who is close by, is far, and strangeness means that he, who is also far, is actually near."[113]

The association between the criminal and the stranger in Simmel's sense appears near the beginning of Prosper Merimee's novella *Carmen*, when the narrator finds himself traveling with a man who seems to frighten his guide, Antonio: "Antonio's mysterious

signals, his evident anxiety, a few words dropped by the stranger
. . . had already enabled me to form an opinion of the identity of
my fellow-traveller." But the narrator remains unperturbed and
even takes pleasure in the knowledge that he is travelling with an
outlaw:

> I had no doubt at all that I was in the company of a smuggler, and
> possibly a brigand. What cared I? . . . I was very glad to know what
> a brigand was really like. One doesn't come across such gentry ev-
> ery day. And there is a certain charm about *finding oneself in close
> proximity to a dangerous being*, especially when one feels the being
> in question to be gentle and tame.[114]

The narrator views the brigand as representing a "unity of nearness and remoteness," nearness by virtue of being "gentle and
tame" and remoteness by virtue of being "a dangerous being"—
thus epitomizing the qualities of the stranger.

Like the narrator of *Carmen*, the narrator of Stevenson's *Kidnapped* perceives the criminal as a glamorous stranger whose company he seeks. The relevant scene occurs when David Balfour,
who has been abducted and forced to serve aboard the brig *Cove-
nant*, first encounters Alan Breck, the notorious Jacobite terrorist.
David, the narrator of the novel, explains to the reader that "there
were many exiled gentlemen coming back at the peril of their lives
. . . [running] the gauntlet of our great navy" in the aftermath of a
failed Scottish uprising against English rule. He continues:

> All this I had, of course, heard tell of; and now *I had a man under
> my eyes* whose life was forfeit on all those counts and upon one
> more, for *he was not only a smuggler of rents, but had taken service
> with King Louis of France*. And as if all this were not enough, he had
> a belt full of golden guineas round the loins. *Whatever my opinions,
> I could not look on such a man without a lively interest.*

Although Breck represents everything that David has been taught
to abhor, the youth cannot resist a man "under [his own] eyes,"
who is associated with danger, wealth, and a foreign country. In
the next line, his fascination leads to an overture: " 'And so you're
a Jacobite?' said I, as I set meat before him."[115]

F. Scott Fitzgerald's novel *The Great Gatsby* provides another
example of a man who attracts others by his embodiment of

criminality and exoticism. To take up the theme of criminality first, Jay Gatsby's career as a bootlegger, his involvement with a hit and run accident, and his association with other criminals play only a minor role in the plot of the novel. Nevertheless, his connection to crime is an important part of his allure, as we see in the following passage where Gatsby's dinner guests speculate about their host's identity:

> The two girls and Jordan leaned together confidentially.
> "Somebody told me they thought he killed a man once."
> A thrill passed over all of us. The three Mr. Mumbles bent forward and listened eagerly.

After further debate about Gatsby's background, the guests return to the theme of homicide:

> "You look at him sometimes when he thinks nobody's looking at him. I'll bet he's killed a man."
> She narrowed her eyes and shivered. Lucille shivered. We all turned and looked around for Gatsby. It was testimony to the romantic speculation he inspired that there were whispers about him from those who had found little that it was necessary to whisper about in this world.[116]

The fantasy that their host has taken a life arouses these jaundiced guests to an unaccustomed level of excitement.[117]

Gatsby inspires interest not only by being a probable killer but also by being a stranger, an embodiment of nearness and remoteness. In a passage that exemplifies this theme, the narrator, Nick Carraway, refers to "those who accepted Gatsby's hospitality and paid him the subtle tribute of knowing nothing whatever about him." In the following exchange between Nick and his date, we see even more clearly that Gatsby's allure is based on his association with the unknown:

> "Who is he?" I demanded. "Do you know?"
> "He's just a man named Gatsby."
> "Where is he from, I mean? And what does he do?"
> "Now *you're* started on the subject," she answered with a wan smile. . . .
> . . . Something in her tone reminded me of the other girl's "I think he killed a man," and had the effect of stimulating my curios-

ity. . . . [Y]oung men didn't . . . drift cooly out of nowhere and buy a palace on Long Island Sound.[118]

The theme of the criminal as an admired stranger also appears in a memoir entitled *Within Prison Walls*, by Thomas Mott Osborne.[119] The book is an account of Osborne's week-long voluntary incarceration in the state prison at Auburn, New York. Osborne's view of the prisoners is centrally informed by the concept of the criminal as stranger. Consider, for example, this excerpt from a speech he makes to the inmates before becoming a prisoner himself: "When a man wishes to understand as fully as possible the temper and character of the *people of a foreign country*—England or France, . . . he will not be satisfied until he has made a personal visit to the country itself."[120] Later in the same speech, he makes clear that his goal is to attain an intimate understanding of these men who are near and yet far: "I have the feeling that after I have really lived among you . . . and not until then, can I feel the knowledge which will break down the barriers between my soul and the souls of my brothers."[121] Here one senses Osborne's elation at the prospect of intimacy with the very different. Throughout the book, he describes his prison sojourn as a "great adventure."[122]

Osborne is not only attracted to these criminal strangers; he also holds them in high regard, as we see in the following passages:

- Describing a prisoner, he writes: "He himself is a clean-cut, fine-looking fellow, with honest blue eyes and a good face—not a single trace of the 'Criminal' about him."

- Of another inmate he writes: "A pair of honest gray eyes light up with a smile."

- He characterizes the next prisoner as "a slightly built, pleasantly smiling young man."

- And again: "My working partner, Murphy, has a life term. . . . He seems like such a good fellow, and the Chaplain has just spoken of him most highly."

- And yet again: "Marching to breakfast I find myself by the side of a young fellow. . . . He is tall and good-looking, with an air of refinement which is appealing." [123]

Osborne's characterizations of the prisoners are overwhelmingly positive, suggesting idealization. Idealization of inmates may reflect an unconscious hostility toward the authorities who are punishing these men. Indeed, we catch a glimpse of the rebel in Osborne when he comments on the gift of sugar that he has clandestinely received from a prisoner: "I find myself wondering if the sugar I'm eating has been honestly come by. . . . I am quite sure that in my present state of mind I should enjoy it better if I knew it had been stolen." [124] Osborne's admiration for criminals came to play a central role in his life. As chairman of the New York State Prison Reform Commission, he initiated self-government among the inmates of Auburn penitentiary. [125] Later, at the Naval Prison at Portsmouth, he handled some six thousand inmates without using any guards within the prison compound. [126]

Like Osborne, the fictional character Nekliudov in Tolstoy's novel *Resurrection* associates criminals with the strange and far away. Traveling to Siberia in an effort to redeem Maslova, a prostitute convicted of murder, he looks about him at the workers on the train:

> "Yes, this is quite a new and different world," thought Nekliudov. . . .
> . . . And he felt the joy of a traveller discovering a new, unknown and beautiful world. [127]

If noncriminals often admire criminals for their exotic glamor, their free, audacious life, and their pursuit of fairness and right, at other times, noncriminals recoil from criminals with disgust — feeling themselves to be unbearably polluted by the criminals' very nearness. In the next chapter, I examine the feeling of loathing that some noncriminals manifest toward criminals. Specifically, I will suggest that this sense of revulsion represents a defense against unconscious admiration for the criminal.

CHAPTER 9

Repressed Admiration: Loathing As a Vicissitude of Attraction to Criminals

NEWGATE IN MY BREATH: ADMIRATION, LOATHING, AND REPUDIATION

In Guy de Maupassant's novella *Ball-of-Fat*, a group of men and women are traveling by stagecoach through occupied France. Among them is a prostitute nicknamed "Ball-of-Fat."[1] Early in the novella, she wins the other passengers' grudging respect for her ardent patriotism. When the passengers stop for the night, a Prussian army officer threatens to detain them indefinitely unless Ball-of-Fat will share his bed. Fiercely anti-German, at first Ball-of-Fat is adamant in her refusal—a stance which some of the other travelers fail to comprehend. One woman remarks to another:

> "Since it is the trade of this creature to accommodate herself to all kinds, I fail to see how she has the right to refuse one more than another. . . . For my part, I find that this officer conducts himself very well. . . . And we must remember too that he is master. He has only to say, 'I wish,' and he could take us by force with his soldiers." The two women had a cold shiver. Pretty Madame Carre-Lamadon's eyes grew brilliant and she became a little pale, as if she saw herself already taken by force by the officer.[2]

As Maupassant presents it, the idea of engaging in sex with a stranger is, in fantasy, an exciting notion to these bourgeois women. Moreover, one of the women is portrayed as attracted to the officer: "The genteel Madame Carre-Lamadon seemed to think that in her [Ball-of-Fat's] place, she would refuse this one less than some others."[3]

Eventually, worn down by the self-serving cajoling of the other passengers, Ball-of-Fat agrees to the officer's demand. During the act of intercourse, the passengers joke about what is happening, and the atmosphere among them is charged with sensuality.[4] While they wait, occasionally listening for sounds from the floor above, one woman tells her husband that Carre-Lamadon is green with envy of the prostitute.[5] After it is all over, the other passengers repudiate Ball-of-Fat, treating her with utter contempt.

So beautifully does Maupassant write this story, and so naturally do the events unfold, that the travelers' behavior seems quite predictable. It may not occur to us to question the basis of their repudiation and contempt. Why do the passengers make an about-face regarding the prostitute, after she has done the very thing that they had asked her to do? From the hints dropped in the story, the best explanation seems to be that the other passengers identify with Ball-of-Fat and her act of self-abasement. Precisely because they resonate to her behavior, while also regarding it as immoral, they cannot consciously accept Ball-of-Fat; they repudiate her as a way of avoiding awareness that they, too, are capable of prostitution. Indeed, since it was they who persuaded her to sacrifice her principles, they are her accomplices in the act of harlotry.

Another portrayal of a noncriminal who, at one stage, repudiates a criminal appears in Charles Dickens's novel *Great Expectations*. In the opening pages, the small boy Pip, alone on the marshes, encounters an escaped convict, who, we subsequently learn, is named Magwitch. The convict demands that Pip obtain some food and a file for him. Terrified, Pip steals the wanted items from his sister and brother-in-law and returns to the marshes, where he nearly stumbles upon another convict before turning over the provisions to Magwitch.

During this phase of the story, Dickens repeatedly refers to Pip's guilt-ridden identification with Magwitch. For example, Pip feels like a thief, because he is stealing from his sister: "I felt fearfully sensible of the great convenience that the Hulks were handy for me. I was clearly on my way there. I had begun by asking questions, and I was going to rob Mrs. Joe."[6] Projecting his sense of guilt onto the world around him, he imagines the cows he passes calling out to him: "A boy with somebody else's pork pie! Stop him! Halloa young thief!"[7] While running back to the marshes, Pip compares the cold riveted to his feet, "as the iron was riveted to the leg of the man I was running to meet."[8]

In a later scene, when Pip and his brother-in-law participate in a search for the escaped criminals, Pip refers to Magwitch with the words "my convict."[9] Ostensibly, he employs this phrase to distinguish the man he had talked to, whose name he does not know, from the other felon. However, the expression, which is repeated as often as nine times in two pages, also conveys an affectionate and proprietary attitude toward the escaped felon. Pip's sympathy is, indeed, with the criminals, for he whispers to Joe that he hopes the party doesn't catch the men. Nevertheless, they are caught, and, in what will be the last communication between Pip and "his convict" for many years, Pip tries to signal to Magwitch that he has not betrayed him.

Thus far in the story, we have seen only empathy and identification in Pip's attitude toward the criminal. His reaction is markedly different the next time he meets Magwitch. Now a young gentleman, Pip has risen in the world thanks to an unknown benefactor whom he always assumed to be Miss Havisham, guardian of the beautiful Estella. One night, alone in his flat, Pip receives a visitor he quickly recognizes: the convict he had aided on the marshes so many years before. It becomes clear that it was Magwitch who financed Pip's advancement, and now the old man has returned to delight in the creature he has made.

At this stage, Pip describes his feelings toward Magwitch in the language of loathing; for example: "The abhorrence in which I held the man, the dread I had of him, the repugnance with which I shrank from him, could not have been exceeded if he had been some terrible beast."[10] Significantly, the criminal's affection for Pip only increases Pip's disgust: Pip "recoiled from his touch as if he had been a snake,"[11] and when Magwitch kisses Pip's hands, "the blood ran cold"[12] within Pip. So intense is Pip's revulsion that one night he experiences the impulse to leave the country to get away from him:

> Every hour so increased my abhorrence of him, that I even think I
> might have yielded to this impulse . . . but for the knowledge that

Herbert [his friend] must soon come back. Once, I actually did start out of my bed in the night, and begin to dress myself in my worst clothes, hurriedly intending to leave him there with everything else I possessed, and enlist for India as a private soldier.[13]

In this phase of the novel, the disgusted young man presents a powerful contrast to the empathic little boy he had been, as we see in the grown Pip's description of Magwitch eating: "He ate in a ravenous way that was very disagreeable, and all his actions were uncouth, noisy and greedy. Some of his teeth had failed him since I saw him eat on the marshes, and as he turned his food in his mouth, and turned his head sideways to bring his strongest fangs to bear upon it, he looked terribly like a hungry old dog."[14] As a child, Pip had also employed the metaphor of a dog to describe Magwitch's way of eating. But where, as a child, Pip's description was neutral, free of disgust, here it is pervaded by a profound repugnance.

Why does Pip, who formerly exhibited empathy and identification with the convict, now show such extreme loathing—to the point where he actually considers leaving everything and running off to India? To be sure, the discovery that the convict has been his benefactor is a disappointment; it means that his supposed patron, Miss Havisham, had not, as he had thought, been grooming him all those years to be Estella's mate. Moreover, Pip must acknowledge the painful truth that his rise in life has been contaminated because it was financed by a convict. Finally, Pip finds Magwitch's boorish ways more appalling now that he is a gentleman. However, none of these explanations seems adequate to account for the exaggerated quality of Pip's reactions.

In psychoanalysis, any extreme trend in one direction is considered an indication that the person may be defending against awareness of the opposite impulse.[15] The prototypical example of this defense mechanism, termed a "reaction-formation," is the adult's disgust at feces, which fascinate small children. In this case, it is Pip's extreme disgust that seems exaggerated, and the opposite of disgust is identification or fascination. What evidence is there that Pip is, indeed, defending against a feeling of kinship with Magwitch? Apart from the indications that Pip powerfully identified with the criminal as a child, another manifestation of Pip's now-largely repressed fascination with Magwitch appears in the following passage: "Words cannot tell what a sense I had, . . . of the dreadful mystery that he was to me. When he fell asleep of an evening, . . . I would sit and look at him, wondering what he had done, and loading him with all the crimes in the Calendar."[16]

That Pip's disgust for Magwitch represents a disgust for his own prison-imbued life can be seen in the following excerpts describing his thoughts after he has visited Newgate prison:

> I consumed the whole time in thinking how strange it was that I should be encompassed by all this taint of prison and crime; that in my childhood out on our lonely marshes on a winter evening I should have first encountered it; that, it should have reappeared on two occasions, starting out like a stain that was faded but not gone; that it should in this new way pervade my fortune and advance-ment.[17]

Pip goes on to wish that he had not chanced to enter the prison on that particular day, when he was to meet Estella's coach,

> so that, of all days in the year on this day, I might not have had Newgate in my breath and on my clothes. I beat the prison dust off my feet as I sauntered to and fro, and I shook it out of my dress, and I exhaled its air from my lungs. So contaminated did I feel, remembering who was coming, that the coach came quickly after all, and I was not yet free from the soiling consciousness.[18]

In these passages we see the typical motifs of anality: taint, stain, dust, contamination, and soil. Pip's preoccupation with these themes, though couched in the language of disgust, reflects an underlying attraction—an attraction that is inadmissible to his conscious mind. Rather than acknowledge his fascination with criminals and prisons, Pip develops a quasi-paranoid fantasy that Newgate prison has gotten inside of him, into his very breath, and has become a part of his being.[19]

The meaning of Pip's attraction to criminals becomes still clearer if we look at the images of the criminal in the life of his creator, Dickens. As all Dickens-lovers know, Charles Dickens's father was confined in the Marshalsea prison for inability to pay his debts. Unquestionably, this was a traumatic experience for Dickens, who, while he did not reside in the prison himself, often visited his family there and cried with his father over their frightening role reversal.[20] Adding to the pain and the lasting effects of this period was Dickens's own simultaneous immurement in a blacking factory—"a crazy, tumble-down old house . . . literally overrun with rats."[21] Working at his parents' behest to alleviate the family penury, Dickens spent his days monotonously pasting labels on pots of paste blacking. As an adult, he would describe "the secret agony of his soul" during this time when he felt his "early hopes of growing up to be a learned and distinguished man, crushed in [his] breast."[22] Significantly, he believed that only good fortune had prevented his becoming a criminal himself: "I know that, but for the mercy of God, I might easily have been, for any care that was taken of me, a little robber or a little vagabond."[23]

Thus, in Dickens's childhood, the theme of criminality appears in two forms: his father's punishment for indebtedness, and Dickens's fantasy about the thief that he himself might have become. In addition, Dickens's maternal grandfather was an embezzler who fled to the Isle of Man to avoid imprisonment for his crime.[24] Occurring only two years prior to Dickens's birth, this event may have cast a taint over Dickens's early years—a taint like the one that Pip describes as "pervading his fortune and advancement." These facts suggest that underlying Pip's revulsion at the very presence of Magwitch is Dickens's profound consciousness that the criminal was, indeed, *his* convict—his father, his grandfather, and himself.

I have argued that some people experience repugnance toward criminals, proclaiming their disgust and loathing, avoiding physical contact, fearing contamination by the criminal's very presence or affection; yet, on the unconscious level, this revulsion functions to defend the noncriminals against their own fascination with criminals, who are perceived as self-indulgent (Ball-of-Fat) and free to dwell in the pleasures of anal messiness and instinctual greed (Magwitch and the other convicts in *Great Expectations*).

If, in some people, admiration for criminals is transmuted into loathing and avoidance, in others, it undergoes a different transformation: being changed into loathing and persecution. Noncriminals in the latter category may attempt to punish criminals in a one-time incident or build lives centering on the role of avenger. Whereas those who shun criminals employ a reaction-formation, defending against attraction through avoidance, those who build lives around punishing criminals exhibit a compromise-formation.[25] They simultaneously gratify both their attraction to and their revulsion from criminals—the attraction through their ongoing involvement with lawbreakers, and the revulsion through the persecutory nature of their involvement. In the next section I will examine this improbable and complex vicissitude of admiration for criminals.

A COPPER NEEDS CRIME: ADMIRATION, LOATHING, AND PERSECUTION

> They say that coppers suppress crime. My own belief is that they create it: they spread a criminal atmosphere where none existed. . . . A soldier to succeed needs wars. . . . In just the same way as a copper, to get on, needs crime.
>
> —C. MacInnes, *Mr. Love and Justice*

For our first illustration of this theme, let us return to Wilkie Collins's mystery novel *The Woman in White*. As we have seen, the heroine, Marian Halcombe, initially feels a strong attraction for the psychopathic villain, Count Fosco. To her journal she confides: "In two short days he has made his way straight into my favorable estimation—and how he has worked the miracle, is more than I can tell."[26] As with Nicol Jarvie in *Rob Roy* and Marlow in *Heart of Darkness*, Marian's puzzlement suggests that her attraction to the criminal has an unconscious basis. This nonrational pull to the criminal is all the more striking in a woman who is portrayed as having excellent judgment.

As the story develops, Marian learns that the Count is capable of any vile deed, including murder, and that he has attempted to condemn her sister to a living death in a sanatorium. Horrified as she is at these revelations, Marian's most intense feeling of revulsion emerges in connection with the Count's continued admiration for her. Describing her encounter with the Count to her friend Walter Hartright, she says: "All the horrible time at Blackwater came back to me the moment I set eyes on him. All the old loathing crept and crawled through me, when he took off his hat with a flourish, and spoke to me, as if we had parted on the friendliest terms hardly a day since."[27] Marian feels so polluted by the Count's attentions that she cannot bring herself to repeat his words to Walter. Later, it becomes clear that the Count has hesitated in doing an evil act out of consideration for Marian. When she learns of this, Marian again experiences disgust:

> It's hard to acknowledge it, Walter—and yet I must! *I* was his only consideration. No words can say how degraded I feel in my own estimation when I think of it—but the one weak point in that man's iron character is the horrible admiration he feels for *me*. I have tried, for the sake of my own self-respect, to disbelieve it as long as I could.[28]

Why should it be the Count's fondness for Marian that most evokes Marian's loathing? And why should the *Count's* feelings threaten *Marian's* self-respect? So normal (in the sense of typical) is Marian's reaction that we may be disinclined to analyze it. Yet, to follow this disinclination would be to lose an important insight. For Marian's revulsion, I would submit, is not, at bottom, a revulsion for the Count, but for herself and for whatever it was in her that allowed her to be so powerfully drawn to him. Since Marian is not a patient on the couch, it is impossible to be sure that this analysis is correct. But the strength of her earlier, "half-unwilling" fascination with the Count, together with the exaggerated quality of her disgust at his attentions, make this a highly plausible interpretation.

When Marian begins to loathe Count Fosco, her impulse is not to snub the criminal or to remove herself physically from him. Rather, she seeks his destruction. Thus, after reading a note to herself from the Count, she urgently begs her friend Walter Hartright: " 'Walter! . . . if ever those two men [Sir Percival and the Count] are at your mercy, and you are obliged to spare one of them—don't let it be the Count.' "[29] And again, when Walter is discussing how to build a case against the two criminals, Marian flushes and whispers: " 'Begin with the Count! . . . For my sake, begin with the Count.' "[30]

The theme of admiration transmuted into loathing and persecution is even more richly developed in John Millington Synge's classic drama *The Playboy of the Western World*. The action revolves around a young man, Christy Mahon, who arrives in a poor, isolated Irish village claiming to have killed his father. The villagers, who have already been depicted as leading a limited and oppressed existence, welcome the ostensible patricide as a hero. So positive is the villagers' reaction that, on the first night of his arrival, Christy goes to sleep thinking: "Well it's a clean bed and soft with it, and it's great luck and company I've won me in the end of time—two fine women fighting for the likes of me—till I'm thinking this night wasn't I a foolish fellow not to kill my father in the years gone by."[31]

Early the next morning, three young women arrive to see him, worrying as they come that they may have missed their chance to meet a patricide: "Well, it'll be a hard case if he's gone off now, the way we'll never set our eyes on a man killed his father, and we after rising early and destroying ourselves running fast on the hill."[32]

Upon meeting the supposed murderer and fugitive, they welcome him and offer him gifts: duck's eggs, cakes, and chicken. Some time later, the father of the female protagonist, Pegeen Mike, agrees to Christy's engagement with his daughter, even though she is already engaged to another, a cowardly, timid man. Joining the hands of the newly betrothed couple, the father proclaims: "A daring fellow is the jewel of the world, and a man did split his father's middle with a single clout, should have the bravery of ten, so may God and Mary and St. Patrick bless you, and increase you from this mortal day."[33]

While Christy is basking in the villagers' esteem, his father appears, not dead, but very much alive, with only a wounded head from the blow his son had given him. In a flash, the peasants turn on Christy, ridiculing and condemning him for having made himself out to be a murderer. Furious in her disillusionment, Pegeen lashes out: "And it's lies you told, letting on you had him slitted, and you nothing at all."[34] Ruefully, she observes: "And to think of the coaxing glory we had given him."[35]

Overcome with all that he has lost along with the status of patricide, Christy again picks up a loy [a long, narrow spade] and bashes his father on the head. The onlookers believe old Mahon to be dead. This time, however, instead of reacting to the crime with "coaxing glory," they repudiate Christy's deed and make plans to hang him. Pegeen herself turns persecutor as she participates in the group that slips the noose over Christy's head and sadistically brands his leg with a burning stick. Explaining the change in the community's reaction, Pegeen observes: "I'll say, a strange man is a marvel, with his mighty talk; but what's a squabble in your back-yard, and the blow of a loy, have taught me that there's a great gap between a gallous story and a dirty deed."[36]

Before the villagers can complete the lynching, old Mahon revives. Father and son go off together, leaving Pegeen to undergo yet another change of heart. In the final scene of the play, realizing that she now must marry the dull, fearful Shawn, she puts her shawl over her head and laments: "Oh my grief, I've lost him surely. I've lost the only playboy of the Western World."[37]

Synge's play embodies our conflicting attitudes toward the criminal, our simultaneous admiration and condemnation for the one who dares to break society's laws. The slang word *gallous*, which Pegeen uses to describe Christy's story, epitomizes this conflict with its two opposed meanings: (1) deserving the gallows; hence, villainous; and (2) very great, fine, dashing.[38] Not only the play itself, but also the audiences' and the critics' reactions to it, highlight the simultaneous love and hatred for the criminal that pervade our culture. During the play's opening performances at the Abbey Theater in 1907, audiences rioted against it, disrupting the show. Expecting to see a play that glorified Irish culture, they violently rejected the play's portrayal of their countrymen lauding a criminal. In self-defense, Synge emphasized that he had based his play on actual events: on the Aran Islands, peasants had protected a patricide from the authorities until he could escape to America, even though a substantial reward had been offered for his capture.[39]

For our purposes, one of the fascinating aspects of this play is the villagers' involvement in creating Christy's criminal persona and fostering his criminal deed. By their selective enthusiasm for the parts of his story centering on the patricide, the peasants encourage Christy to think of himself as a dashing murderer. By their scoffing repudiation of him when his father turns up alive, the community generates his second act of violence—an act that is more culpable than the first since it is without legal provocation. We have already seen that in real life, too, noncriminals sometimes foster criminality in others to gratify vicariously their own criminal impulses. After unwittingly generating, and enjoying, the criminal behavior, the noncriminals often proceed to prosecute the criminal, who thus becomes a scapegoat—a symbol of everyone's unacknowledged guilt.

Another interesting issue raised by this play concerns the reversal that the community undergoes after the second supposed patricide. Christy Mahon himself is stunned by the disparity between the two reactions—the villagers' glorification of the criminal when he arrives, a stranger, announcing a previously committed crime, and their violent persecution of him when he commits the same crime in their presence. From a psychoanalytic perspective, the divergence in the community's responses to the two supposed crimes is not surprising. For what is important in the unconscious is not one extreme or another, but *polarities.* Surface behavior that seems highly contradictory, then, may reflect some larger unconscious preoccupation, embracing both sides of the contradiction. In the play, the villagers' initial attraction to the criminal and their subsequent repudiation and persecution of him are but two sides of their abiding fascination with crime and the criminal. Their superficial shift from the roles of follower and admirer to the role of persecutor seems to reflect a need for the criminal to be, in some sense, a *stranger*. When his crimes are committed in, as Pegeen says, their "back yard," the villagers' own complicity becomes too apparent for their superegos to tolerate. They then undergo a shift from the id's delight in an act of aggression against authority to the superego's denunciation of the same act.

On a deeper level, we can view the villagers' persecution of Christy not as a gratification of the superego following a gratification of the id, but rather as a compromise formation: behavior that simultaneously gratifies both sides of their inner conflict over criminality. For in branding and preparing to lynch Christy, the villagers themselves are behaving like criminals; they are acting outside the law. They are thus expressing their own sadistic and criminal impulses and also their defense against these impulses— their need to see themselves as opposed to crime. If imitation is the sincerest form of flattery, then their illegal behavior represents admiration for criminals.

As in literature, so also in life: people may permit a breakthrough of their own antisocial impulses in the guise of bringing criminals to justice. For instance, in California in the early 1970s, government undercover agents intentionally and illegally slaughtered seven elk, sheep, and polar bears in the process of building a case against suspected hunting violators. The federal district judge who presided over the successful prosecution commented: "The fascinating aspect of this case is that the agents go out and kill these same animals that the defendant is charged with killing. They (the government) brought a road contractor all the way from Vermont to illegally kill animals. No matter what happens here, I am going to pursue this."[40] In the conventional view, such illegal behavior by prosecutors is a lamentable accident resulting from excessive zeal. From the perspective I am advocating, however, the phenomenon of prosecutors crossing over the line into illegality can best be understood as a foreseeable breakthrough of their repressed admiration for criminals.

Even where there is not, as in the preceding examples, a breakthrough of criminal behavior on the part of the prosecutor, it may

still make sense to interpret prosecutorial behavior as a compromise formation—a symbolic expression of both instinctual and
anti-instinctual forces, of attraction to the criminal and defense
against this attraction. Victor Hugo's novel *Les Miserables* provides
an example in the character of Javert, the police officer who
obsessively, over the years, pursues the criminal Jean Valjean.
Valjean is guilty only of having violated the conditions of his
probation; however, Javert harbors an abiding contempt for this
criminal, as he does for all those who exist outside the law. The
all-consuming quality of Javert's belief in the law comes through
in Hugo's description: "Order was his dogma and was enough for
him; since he had been of the age of a man, and an official, he had
put almost all of his religion in the police."[41]

As with Pip, Marian, and the other characters discussed in this
study, Javert's aversion to criminals can be understood as a defense
against feelings that are inadmissible to his conscious mind. Hugo
tells us that Javert himself was born in prison of a mother who was
a "tramp" and a father who was a galley slave. Together with the
exaggerated quality of his behavior, Javert's origins suggest that
his prosecution of criminals fulfills an important psychological
function: to defend against awareness of his own identification
with criminals. But beyond serving a defensive function, Javert's
profession also serves to gratify the very impulses he is defending
against. For his role as a police officer allows him to be where the
criminal is, to think like the criminal and think *about* the criminal
for years on end—all the while justifying this behavior as required
by his fight against criminality.

The best evidence that Javert indeed feels an attraction to the
criminal appears toward the end of the book, when Javert's defense
mechanism fails as he becomes conscious of his admiration for
Jean Valjean. As Hugo describes this development, "Javert felt that
something horrible was penetrating his soul, admiration for a
convict. Respect for a galley-slave, can that be possible?"[42] In
succeeding passages, Javert characterizes Valjean with oxymorons
that bespeak his own confusion: "a beneficent malefactor, a com-
passionate convict . . . Javert was compelled to acknowledge that

this monster existed .... this infamous angel, this hideous hero."[43] As circumstances force him to recognize the goodness in his longtime prey, Javert loses his psychological balance. Perceiving Valjean as high-minded, he is no longer able to maintain his view of himself as pure. The rigid compromise formation had kept his self-loathing, his sense of inner pollution, repressed. Now, as these feelings surface, Javert commits suicide.

Conclusion to Part Two: This Unforeseen Partnership

> The disappearance of repulsive (and, considered in isolation, destructive) energies does by no means always result in a richer and fuller social life (as the disappearance of liabilities results in larger property) but in as different and unrealizable a phenomenon as if the group were deprived of the forces of cooperation, affection, mutual aid, and harmony of interest.
>
> —Georg Simmel, *Conflict*

In Part Two I have pursued three interrelated goals: (1) to show the pervasiveness and conflictive nature of our admiration for criminals; (2) to explore the bases of our admiration for criminals—not only the articulated, conscious explanations but also the unacceptable, darker sources of the criminal's appeal; and (3) to uncover the high regard for criminals that is hidden beneath such defense mechanisms as loathing, repudiation, and persecution.

In choosing to focus on our admiration for criminals, I have not intended to deny the negative side of our ambivalence toward criminals, nor have I sought to minimize the terrible costs that lawbreakers inflict on their victims. Fear of criminals, anxiety about their likely acts, and nondefensive contempt and hatred for their ways—all these have been assumed throughout this study. But admiration for criminals is also an important aspect of our nature—an aspect that an adequate theory of criminal justice must include.

The question arises whether the preceding analysis can shed any light on the causes of criminality. If it can, the illumination might best be found at those junctures where admiration spills over into action. We have already glimpsed a few such instances: the parents cultivating criminality in their children, the beginning psychiatrists encouraging antisocial acts in their patients, and the prosecutors violating the law while in pursuit of criminals. On a larger scale, whole communities have sometimes exhibited a remarkable insouciance about criminality going on in their midst. By deliberately ignoring such illegal activity, members of these communities have been able to enjoy the criminal behavior without incurring the guilt they would feel for doing the acts themselves.[1]

Extrapolating from these examples, we may conjecture that a society might contrive to foster criminality to guarantee that its citizens' psychological needs would be met.[2] This theory would help to explain, for example, our own nation's continued reliance on the penitentiary despite its poor record in deterring criminal acts and reforming criminals.[3] To the degree that this hypothesis is valid, it implies an unusual tactic in the "war on crime"—that of cultivating self-awareness. For if we noncriminals can truly accept the criminal impulses in ourselves, we will find it unnecessary to deal with these impulses by externalizing them. When, like Pip, we can call the convict "my convict," or when, like Porfiry Petrovich, we can admit our similarity to the criminal without being derailed, as Javert was, by the recognition of this kinship, then at least we will be able to see clearly and to act wholeheartedly as we endeavor to cope with criminal behavior.

In the meantime, we must content ourselves with a world that is nonutopian in principle, a world in which criminals and noncriminals are inseparably and profoundly bound together, in which criminals, by their very existence, perform psychological functions for noncriminals—gratifying their antisocial impulses, reassuring them of their comparative innocence, and assuaging their guilt through vicarious punishment. From this perspective, criminals are far from being an unequivocal evil; they are, in fact, necessary for us to be what we are. They are the Sancho Panza to our Don Quixote, the Fool to our King Lear, the partner we need to perform our complicated dance.

Part Three will focus on the metaphor comparing criminals to soft, wet dirt or slime. The reader may wonder how this topic relates to the basic thesis of my book; namely, that criminals and law-abiding citizens exist in a complex symbiosis. But I will seek to penetrate and expose the common-sense view of the metaphor, showing that even our strongest denunciations of criminals express and conceal our romantic idealization of them.

PART THREE

In Slime and Darkness: The Metaphor of Filth in Criminal Justice

The Tao that can be spoken is not the real Tao.

—Lao-tzu, *Tao Te Ching*

If Shakespeare had decided to let the Weird Sisters inhabit water, like the Rhine Maidens, instead of "fog and filthy air," the whole play of *Macbeth* would have been profoundly different.

—Philip Wheelwright, *Metaphor and Reality*

Prologue to Part Three

Philosophers have long proclaimed the essential role of metaphors in generating meaning. Words that say one thing and suggest another are necessary for the growth of our thought and may be an inevitable aspect of language itself.[1] Nevertheless, metaphors can hamper understanding when we lose sight of their status as tropes and take them for reality.[2]

One of the most common metaphors in our culture is that of the criminal as filth. References to criminals as "dirt," "slime," and "scum" pervade the media and everyday conversation. Yet, despite the familiarity of these figures of speech, scholars have devoted little attention to such questions as the following: What is the origin of the metaphor likening criminals to filth? Is this metaphor accidental or essential to our thinking about lawbreakers? And, to the degree that this metaphor governs our understanding of criminals, what are the consequences for our criminal justice system?[3]

These questions beckon with special urgency at a time when the United States keeps more than one million people behind bars;[4] when penologists urge other ways of combatting crime, yet many legislators resist their call;[5] when sentencing guidelines mandate severe punishments for venial offenses[6]—all highlighting the irrational sources of our attitudes toward criminals.

Theoretical no less than practical considerations imbue these questions with a special allure. For filth is a concept of exceptional richness and power, an archetypal symbol with roots lying deep in childhood, in early parental warnings and primordial experiences of the body. Contradictory and paradoxical, filth in its ultimate form of excrement unites radically opposed meanings. On the one hand, it signifies meaninglessness: the nullifying reduction of all

things to one homogeneous mass. On the other hand, as psychoanalysts inform us, excrement represents many good things: an
artistic creation, a gift, wealth.[7]

Strongly repelling and strongly attracting, filth serves as an apt
metaphor for criminals, who likewise evoke our simultaneous hate
and love, repudiation and admiration. The evidence suggests that
we may be incapable of reflecting about criminals without concepts such as slime, scum, and excrement.

If this is so, then our liberation from the metaphor may depend
not on rejecting this figure of speech, nor in finding substitutes
for it, but rather in seeing clearly the vicissitudes of the metaphor
in criminal justice. This study suggests that the metaphor leads to
a view of criminals as diseased and contagious and to a policy
requiring segregation of contaminated criminals from uncontaminated noncriminals. In addition, on a measure-for-measure theory
of punishment, the metaphor may cause authorities to imprison
criminals in places that are conceived as suitably filthy and malodorous.

Chapter 10 employs literature, history, and theology to demonstrate the pervasiveness of the metaphor equating criminals with
filth. More specifically, the chapter explores the reasons we associate evil with darkness, the relationship between crime and foul
odors, and the fantasy that criminals are made specifically of soft,
wet dirt, or slime. In chapter 11, I offer an extended illustration, a
case study in legal history; namely the Botany Bay venture, Britain's 1786 decision to found a penal colony in Australia and its
eighty-one-year-long practice of banishing criminals to that remote continent. Chapter 12 shows how the metaphor of filth
sheds light on other areas of criminal justice: vagrancy law, with its
emphasis on "cleaning up" neighborhoods and towns; eighteenth-
century prison reform, with its goal of "perfect order and perfect
silence"; and juvenile justice, with its effort to remove children
from messy cities of contagious criminality to rural homes of
supposed order and purity. In the final pages, I discuss American
cases in which judges, prosecutors, and defense attorneys reveal
their vision of criminals as filth.

Eject Him Tainted Now: The Criminal As Filth in Western Culture

COME, THICK NIGHT: CRIME, DIRT, AND DARKNESS

> Lighten our darkness, we beseech thee, O Lord; and by thy great mercy defend us from all perils and dangers of this night.
>
> — *The Book of Common Prayer*

> The day is for honest men, the night for thieves.
>
> — Euripides

Early in Dickens's novel *A Tale of Two Cities*, during the first trial of Charles Darnay, an intriguing scene occurs. The British attorney general has been attempting with circumstantial evidence to show that Darnay passed state secrets to the French. He has just asked the witness, Mr. Jarvis Lorry, when he has seen the prisoner before. As Mr. Lorry answers him, the following dialogue ensues:

> "I was returning from France a few days afterwards, and at Calais, the prisoner came on board the packet-ship in which I returned, and made the voyage with me."
> "At what hour did he come on board?"
> "A little after midnight."
> "In the dead of the night. Was he the only passenger who came on board at that untimely hour?"
> "He happened to be the only one."
> "Never mind about 'happening,' Mr. Lorry. He was the only passenger who came on board in the dead of the night?"
> "He was." [1]

In this exchange, the attorney general intimates that a mere appearance in deepest night justifies an inference of criminality—an idea that we see again in an actual legal case, *United States v. Barker,* one of the cases that emerged from the Watergate burglary.

At the end of his dissenting opinion, Judge Leventhal writes: "I come back—again and again, in my mind—to the stark fact that we are dealing with a breaking and entering *in the dead of night,* both surreptitious and forcible, and a violation of civil rights statutes."[2] As in the preceding fictional example, here too the association with profound darkness suffices to render an act more suspect than it would have been if done in the light. To be sure, the common law differentiated between illegal entries at night and during the day, but Judge Leventhal also gains rhetorical power from the timeless association between darkness and criminality.

The question arises why darkness should be so closely associated with wrongdoing. At first blush, the answer may seem obvious. Human beings rely heavily on their sense of sight; in the dark, their diminished ability to see renders them more helpless and more vulnerable to predators. Criminals, then, really do enjoy an advantage in the dark. Yet this answer, while containing an element of truth, surely cannot be the whole explanation. For one thing, nearly as many violent crimes occur in the daytime as at night.[3] More importantly, noncriminals' fear of darkness exhibits a primordial quality, deeper than rational cause and effect, as we see in this old Scottish prayer:

> From ghoulies and ghosties and long-leggety beasties
> And things that go bump in the night, Good Lord, deliver us![4]

In her mystery novel *Devices and Desires,* P. D. James captures the irrational power of darkness in this scene in which the detective remembers his childhood: "[T]he small Adam Dalgliesh was already dreading those last twenty yards of his walk home, where the rectory drive curved and the bushes grew thickest. Night was different from bright day, smelled different, sounded different; ordinary things assumed different shapes; an alien and more sinister power ruled the night."[5] As if the darkness were an active, conscious enemy, the child Adam would plan a strategy to outsmart it: "Once through the gate to the drive he would walk fast, but not too fast, since the power that ruled the night could smell out terror."[6] Here we see that darkness is associated not merely with particular acts of wrongdoing, but with an abstract force, evil itself.

If the association of darkness with evil exhibits a primitive, elemental quality, such that its origin cannot be purely rational, then we must search further for the complete explanation of this linkage. I suggest that a clue may lie in the kinship between darkness and filth. Etymology supports this proposition, for the English word *dark* derives from a root meaning *to soil*.[7] Although English speakers today may be oblivious of this origin, the etymology shows that at an earlier time in our history, human beings viewed darkness and dirt as closely linked. Moreover, it makes sense that this should be so, because, as psychiatrist Robert Coles points out, "Dirt is dark, and summons in hygienic middle-class minds all sorts of fears—germs and illness, contamination. Man's waste products are dark, and if they are not expelled he grows sick."[8] Like Coles, who makes this observation in a study of racism, Patricia Williams adduces the relationship between blackness and dirt as a partial explanation of racial prejudice: "The blackness of black people . . . has always represented the blemish, the uncleanness, the barrier separating individual and society."[9]

If the association between darkness and crime flows partly from the affinity between darkness and filth, it follows that the closer this affinity is made to seem, the more darkness will evoke thoughts of crime. Most kinds of filth have a mass to them; they occupy space in such a way that other objects cannot occupy the same space at the same time. Darkness does not exhibit these properties. Yet, creative writers frequently describe darkness as if it, like dirt, had a mass and occupied space. This is especially so when the writer wants to create a crime-ridden ambience. Consider, for example, the following scene from *Macbeth*, where Lady Macbeth, planning Duncan's murder and fearing her own weakness, cries out for the help of a dark night:

> Come, thick night,
> And pall thee in the dunnest smoke of hell,
> That my keen knife see not the wound it makes,

> Nor heaven peep through the blanket of the dark
> to cry "hold, hold!" [10]

Here Shakespeare imagines the night as "thick," a conception that we find again two acts later when Macbeth, having just arranged the murders of Banquo and Fleance, calls on darkness to hide the evidence of his heinous deeds:

> Come seeling night,
> Scarf up the tender eye of pitiful day,
> And with thy bloody and invisible hand
> Cancel and tear to pieces that great bond
> which keeps me pale. Light thickens, and the crow
> Makes wing to the rooky wood. [11]

With the phrase "light thickens," Shakespeare associates darkness with a viscous form of light, an image that resonates with the "gruel thick and slab" that the witches brew in a later scene. Darkness is portrayed not as the absence of light, or a void, but rather as a denser, more solid form of light. Compare the rendering of darkness in this sentence from the modern novel *Before and After* by Rosellen Brown. The author is describing the thoughts of a man who has just learned that his son is a murderer: "[I] lay there for many hours staring up as if the dark were dirt and I was buried under it." [12]

Besides describing darkness as thick and suffocating, creative writers often employ fog, rain, and turbulence to render darkness more viscous, more dirty, and more evocative of crime. Notice in this connection a remarkable autobiographical statement by the French mystery writer Georges Simenon: "I was born in the dark and the rain, and I got away. The crimes I write about—sometimes I think they are the crimes I would have committed if I had not got away." [13] Using a diaphor—a metaphor that compares through juxtaposition—Simenon likens being in the darkness and rain to being a criminal.

For a more elaborate illustration of this theme, let us return to *Macbeth*. We begin with the stormy opening scene and the first witch's questions:

When shall we three meet again?
In thunder, lightning, or in rain?[14]

If these images give substance to the darkness, thus implicitly bringing it closer to filth, the resemblance between moisture-laden darkness and dirt is made explicit at the end of the scene, when the witches chant together:

Fair is foul, and foul is fair,
Hover through the fog and filthy air.[15]

The way Macbeth addresses the witches, the instigators of crime, likewise serves to equate darkness and filth, for he sometimes calls them "filthy hags" and at other times "secret, black and midnight hags."[16] By using interchangeably words meaning *obscure* and words meaning *filthy*, Shakespeare prepares us to see as filthy the many scenes of stormy darkness that pervade this play.

Toward the end of *Macbeth*, the predominant image changes from darkness to slime as the witches celebrate Macbeth's vile deeds by making a particularly slimy stew, a "gruel thick and slab."[17] That the gruel epitomizes evil there can be no doubt, for, as they make it, the witches chant:

All ill come running in, all good keep out.[18]

Here, too, slime and darkness are confounded; among the macabre ingredients in this brew, none is associated with light, while two are explicitly linked to darkness:

Root of hemlock digged i'th dark,
. . . and slips of yew
slivered in the moon's eclipse[19]

Like Shakespeare, the novelist Daphne du Maurier uses fog and rain to make darkness more solid, dirty, and ominous. These images pervade her novel *Jamaica Inn*, a story about ruthless men who lure ships to their destruction and murder all survivors. Here is how the novel begins:

It was a cold grey day in late November. The weather had changed overnight, when a backing wind brought a granite sky and a miz-zling rain with it, and although it was now only a little after two o'clock in the afternoon the pallor of a winter evening seemed to have closed upon the hills, cloaking them in mist. It would be dark by four.[20]

The threat of darkness alone has power to elicit apprehension, but here the author's particular rendering of the scene magnifies the effect upon the reader's imagination. On the next page, du Maurier openly compares the misty, rainy darkness to uncleanness when one of the travellers observes "for at least the twentieth time that it was the dirtiest night she ever remembered."[21] Once again, etymology corroborates the affinity between darkness and filth; the word *mist* derives from a word meaning *urinate*, to excrete fluid waste.[22]

In a parallel example from another genre, the renowned film director Alfred Hitchcock sets a scene of driving rain and pitch blackness as *Psycho* heroine Marian Crane pulls up in front of the Bates Motel, where she will be murdered. As in *Jamaica Inn*, the resemblance to filth is made explicit, for one of the first things Norman Bates says to his victim is, "Dirty night." The final scene of the movie reemphasizes the association between murder and filth. It shows Crane's car as the authorities retrieve it from a muddy swamp; the car is laden with ooze.[23]

The associations between darkness, filth, and criminality, which are employed as chance images in *Psycho*, are elevated to a symbolic level in Dickens's novel *Bleak House*. In this book Dickens sets himself a remarkable task, to cast a *court* in the role of a villainous criminal. He embarks on this task in the opening paragraph, where he describes, in exaggerated terms, a muddy, sooty scene: "As much mud in the streets, as if the waters had but newly retired from the face of the earth, and it would not be wonderful to meet a Megalosaurus, forty feet long or so, waddling like an elephantine lizard up Holborn Hill."[24] In addition to mud, there is darkness—not just any darkness, but an especially filthy form of it: "Smoke lowering down from chimney-pots, making a soft black drizzle, with flakes of soot in it as big as full-grown snow-flakes— gone into mourning, one might imagine, for the death of the sun."[25]

In the second paragraph, Dickens introduces the motif of fog—in our terms, a viscous kind of darkness: "Fog everywhere. Fog up the river, where it flows among green aits [islets] and meadows; fog down the river, where it rolls defiled among the tiers of shipping, and the waterside pollutions of a great (and dirty) city."[26] Since he describes the fog as "defiled," Dickens hardly means us to see it as a pristine morning mist; as in the preceding paragraph, here too, the images of dirt and darkness are inextricably entwined. Having detailed this scene of filth and darkness, Dickens goes on to enhance and combine both elements as he applies them to the judicial system: "The raw afternoon is rawest and the dense fog is densest, and the muddy streets are muddiest, near the leaden-headed old obstruction . . . Temple Bar."[27] And at the very center of this filth, "at the very heart of the fog, sits the Lord High Chancellor in his High Court of Chancery."[28]

In the following paragraphs, Dickens openly characterizes the Court as the villain of the piece, describing it as the "most pestilent of hoary sinners," and referring to "all the injustice it has committed, and all the misery it has caused."[29] Nevertheless, his images have already showed us—and more effectively than any explicit condemnations—that the Court is the criminal. That Dickens, a master of symbolism, selects entwined metaphors of filth and darkness for this purpose demonstrates both the association of these symbols with each other and their archetypal power to evoke evil.

I have suggested that the mental linkage between two ideas, darkness and criminality, derives partly from their common association with a third idea, that of filth. It is now necessary to add that crime's association is not so much with filth in general as with a particular kind of filth; namely, wet, soft dirt, or slime. In the next section, we will take up this topic of wet dirt, and, in so doing, we will also shift our focus from one human faculty to two others. For as darkness is the manifestation of our metaphor that appeals mainly to the sense of sight, so slime is the manifestation that appeals predominantly to the senses of touch and smell.

The Real Black Hound Is the Moor: The Fantasy of the Criminal As Wet Dirt

Vile I am.
I'm evil because I'm a man.
And I feel within me
the primeval slime.
—Iago, in Verdi's *Otello*

In his essay *The Fantasy of Dirt*, Lawrence Kubie reports that, on the hierarchy of dirtiness, human beings almost universally regard softness and wetness as dirtier than hardness and dryness.[30] We recognize the truth in this statement, but why should it be so? According to Kubie, our attitudes toward dirt originate more in fantasy than in realistic concerns. He asserts: "Because once in a hundred times somebody else's toothbrush or spoon might carry to one a pathogenic organism, does not mean that in all the other ninety-nine times there is an objective aesthetic or bacteriological difference between one's own spittle and that of the rest of the world."[31]

If our notion of dirt is not based on realistic concerns, on what theory *is* it based? By investigating those substances that we avoid touching and even seeing, Kubie reaches this conclusion: "[Dirt is] anything which either symbolically or in reality emerges from the body, or which has been sullied by contact with a body aperture."[32] For example, we may be content with a certain amount of dust in the air, but when that dust enters someone's nostrils, mixes with water salts, and a few watered-down molecules of mucoprotein, and emerges in a sneeze, we consider the resulting substance filthy.[33]

Consistent with Kubie's formulation is an analysis presented by Erwin Strauss. In his monograph *On Obsession*, Strauss writes: "Separation from the integrity of the living organism turns the physiognomy from delight to disgust."[34] Extrapolating from this finding, he goes on: "This transition indicates a transition from life to death; it signifies decay. Disgust is directed more against decay, the process of decomposition, than against the dead."[35]

Neither Kubie nor Strauss applies his findings to the criminal justice system; nevertheless, certain conclusions about our attitudes toward criminals follow from their analyses. For example, if we intimately associate criminals with slime, then we evidently imagine them not simply as filth, but as the quintessence of filth. Furthermore, we associate criminals with human mortality, and not merely in the trivial sense that some lawbreakers are murderers; rather, we seem to equate criminals with the decomposing, reeking matter that our bodies will one day become.

Slime is sometimes conceived as the matrix from which we came as well as the fate to which we go. Consider, for example, the following versions of the creation story in *Genesis:* "And the Lord God formed man of the slime of the earth."[36] And again: "Yahweh shaped an earthling from clay of this earth."[37] Elaborating on the second version, the noted literary critic Harold Bloom observes: "[Yahweh] picks up the moistened clay and molds it in his hands rather like a solitary child making a mud pie."[38] The poet Langdon Smith provides a humorous and touching variation on this theme:

> When you were a tadpole, and I was a fish,
> In the Paleozoic time,
> And side by side in the ebbing tide
> We sprawled through the ooze and slime.[39]

If we imagine ourselves as slime, or as originating in slime, or as fated to end in slime, then the zeal with which we denounce criminals as "slime" becomes more understandable. The denunciation represents a defense against awareness of our own mortality.

Later in this book, we will explore further the defensive functions of our attitudes toward criminals, but first, let us examine some works of literature and see how profoundly and pervasively our culture identifies criminals with slime. I begin with the illustration *par excellence* of this theme, a novella in which wet dirt serves as a leitmotif of evil and, in the words of one of its characters, a "worthy setting" for crime—Arthur Conan Doyle's *The Hound of the Baskervilles.*[40]

As this nineteenth-century novella begins, a prospective client, Dr. Mortimer, is reading Holmes and Watson a letter about a deadly black hound. The letter concludes with the following warning: "I counsel you by way of caution to forbear from crossing the moor in those dark hours when the powers of evil are exalted."[41] Although the warning places special emphasis on night as a time when evil reigns, an equally important theme is the association of criminality with the moor. Indeed, it is difficult to separate the two motifs, because the narrator frequently describes the moor as black or dark.[42] For example, at one point Watson states: "the dark, void spaces on either side of the narrow road told me that we were back upon the moor."[43]

But the moor has one aspect that literal darkness lacks; it connotes not just dirt, but wet dirt. Derived from a root meaning *damp*, *moor* means a "broad tract of open land, . . . poorly drained, with patches of heath and peat bogs."[44] Bogs, in turn, are even more closely associated with moist filth, being quagmires "filled with decayed moss and other vegetable matter; wet spongy ground, where a heavy body is apt to sink."[45]

A particular bog, the great Grimpen Mire, looms throughout the story as a symbol of danger and evil. In the final scene, having learned that the murderer keeps a refuge on an island in the Mire, Holmes and Watson venture into the deadly swamp to look for him. Here the narrator describes in ominous tones the wet, decomposing earth: "Rank reeds and lush, slimy water-plants sent an odour of decay and a heavy miasmatic vapour into our faces, while a false step plunged us more than once thigh-deep into the dark, quivering mire, which shook for yards in soft undulations around our feet."[46] As Watson imagines it, this slime is not a passive evil, but an aggressive, almost human force: "Its tenacious grip plucked at our heels as we walked, and when we sank into it, it was as if some malignant hand were tugging us down into those obscene depths."[47]

If there could still be any doubt whether the story means to associate evil with slime and decay, that doubt would be resolved by the fate of the murderer: "Somewhere in the heart of the great Grimpen Mire, down in the foul slime of the huge morass which had sucked him in, this cold and cruel-hearted man is for ever buried."[48] In death as in life, the criminal and the Mire are united.

In *The Hound of the Baskervilles*, the metaphors of wet dirt are not chance images but are embedded in an entire network of related images.[49] So integral are they to the story that it is impossible to imagine the work without them. As the novelist John Fowles observes in his "Foreword" to the 1974 edition, "[T]he real black hound is the Moor itself."[50]

The motif of evil as wet dirt did not appear for the first time in the nineteenth century. Rather, in his brilliant rendering of crime, Conan Doyle was drawing on a symbol with origins deep in the Judeo-Christian tradition. Thus, the sixteenth-century allegorist John Bunyan chose a slimy bog, the "Slough of Despond," to represent evil in *The Pilgrim's Progress*.[51] Soon after the protagonist, Christian, flees his home in the City of Destruction to seek eternal life, he falls into a bog, becomes "grievously bedaubed with dirt," and begins to sink. With the assistance of a man named Help, he struggles free of the bog, and then inquires why the hazard is not remedied, so that travellers might pass safely through the region. Help explains: "This miry slough is such a place as cannot be mended. It is the descent whither the scum and filth that attends conviction for sin doth continually run, and therefore it is called the Slough of Despond."[52] Like the witches' brew in *Macbeth*, this slough serves as a receptacle of evil. More specifically, it symbolizes the state of moral turpitude into which an individual has sunk. This meaning has been captured beautifully in *Webster's New International Dictionary*, which defines *slough* as "an engulfing depth of sin."[53]

Writing a thousand years before Bunyan, the Roman philosopher Boethius also conceived of evil as slime, in a line that some have translated: "Seest thou not then in what mire wickedness wallows . . . ?"[54] By contrast, in Queen Elizabeth's translation, this line reads: "See you not in what a great slowe . . . wicked things be wrapped in."[55] Here the queen makes a play on words. To the idea of evil encased in mud, she adds an allusion to the other meaning of *slough*: the outer skin that a reptile periodically sheds.

The metaphor of the criminal as a reptile or, more exactly, a *slimy* reptile, is important in our culture. In the following passage from *Middlemarch*, George Eliot chooses this metaphor to describe Bulstrode's feelings after a horrifying encounter with his blackmailer: "It was as if he had had a loathsome dream, and could not shake off its images with their hateful kindred of sensations—as if on all the pleasant surroundings of his life a dangerous reptile had left his slimy traces."[56]

Reptiles are not, of course, actually slimy, but when used to represent criminals, they are imagined as such—a conception we see again in Dickens' novel *Oliver Twist*. In the following passage, Dickens is describing the villainous gang leader, Fagin: "As he glided stealthily along, creeping beneath the shelter of the walls and doorways, the hideous old man seemed like some loathsome reptile, engendered in the slime and darkness through which he moved: crawling forth by night, in search of some rich offal for a meal."[57] As Dickens portrays him, the criminal could hardly be more closely associated with filth. Fagin, he tells us, was secreted out of the very mud through which he crawls, seeking garbage to eat.

In his later novel *Great Expectations*, Dickens returns to this vision of the criminal as a slimy creature. In the opening scene, he describes the "raw afternoon towards evening," when Pip encounters Magwitch, who is "soaked in water, and smothered in mud."[58] After the convict has threatened Pip and enlisted his help, Pip stutters the words, "Goo-good night, sir." Magwitch replies, " 'Much of that!' . . . glancing about him over the cold wet flat. 'I wish I was a frog. Or a eel!' " [*sic*][59]

Like these nineteenth-century novels, the twentieth-century musical, *Peter Pan*, resorts to the metaphor of a wet, filthy creature to highlight the badness of its villain, Captain Hook. Bragging about his evil deeds to the other pirates, Hook sings: "Who's the slimiest rat in the pack?"[60] At the end of the song, Captain Hook and the pirates alternately sing:

> Slimy . . .
> Slimy . . .
> Cap'n Hook![61]

Since slimy dirt is sometimes in a state of decomposition, this dirt may be putrid; therefore, evil is associated not merely with filth, but specifically with filth that stinks. In the following passage from *A Portrait of the Artist as a Young Man*, James Joyce conveys the evil of hell by vividly rendering its stench:

Imagine some foul and putrid corpse that has lain rotting and decomposing in the grave, a jellylike mass of liquid corruption. Imagine such a corpse . . . giving off dense choking fumes of nauseous loathsome decomposition. And then imagine this sickening stench, multiplied a millionfold and a millionfold again from the millions upon millions of fetid carcasses massed together in the reeking darkness, a huge and rotting human fungus. Imagine all this and you will have some idea of the horror of the stench of hell.[62]

Not only evil places, but also evil deeds, are conceived as malodorous. For example, in *Hamlet*, King Claudius condemns his own fratricide with the words: "O, my offense is rank, it smells to heaven."[63] Conversely, the acts of pure, good people smell sweet. For example, Paul describes Christ's sacrifice as a "sweet-smelling savour" or, in another translation, a "fragrant offering."[64]

Because of its association with evil, smelliness in itself may be taken as an indicator of reprehensibility. In Dostoevsky's novel *The Brothers Karamozov*, when Father Zossima's corpse begins to smell the day after his death, the monks take the odor as a sign that the Father was not holy after all. In a chapter entitled "The Odor of Corruption," the smell issuing from the coffin not only diminishes the Father's reputation; it also engenders "coarsely unbridled" temptations among the monks.[65] For example, some who had envied the Father were pleased that his noisome corpse had diminished his aura of sanctity. In the same novel, the brother who killed his father is named Smerdyakov, "[son] of the stinking one."[66] Ivan refers to him as "the stinking lackey."[67] Moreover, Smerdyakov was conceived in the fetid passageway when his father had "passed through the 'backway.' "[68]

Perhaps the most extended association between bad smells and criminality appears in Dostoevsky's other masterpiece, *Crime and Punishment*, in which St. Petersburg, the site of the crime, is repeatedly described as fetid. Consider, for example, this passage from the opening scene:

> The stuffiness, the jostling crowds, the bricks and mortar, scaffolding and dust everywhere, and that peculiar summer stench so familiar to everyone who cannot get away from St. Petersburg . . . all combined to aggravate the disturbance of the young man's nerves. The intolerable reek from the public houses . . . completed the mournfully repellent picture.[69]

Throughout the novel, Dostoevsky characterizes the air as "foul smelling, contaminated," and "reeking with its familiar odours."[70] It is amid this fetid atmosphere that Raskolnikov plans his crime. By contrast, before committing the murder, Raskolnikov walks to the Petersburg island, where the air is clean and fresh. Here he dreams of his childhood and awakens horrified at what he is planning to do.[71]

Literature's portrayal of crime and criminals as smelly lends support to the idea that we imagine lawbreakers as the filthiest of filth, as decaying matter, or the paradigmatic type of filth, excrement. On first examination, this finding may seem unsurprising, because the available repertoire of powerful negative symbols is small; we had to choose one symbol from this repertoire, and that one was filth. On closer inspection, however, the metaphor appears to be a revealing choice, a choice that shows our simultaneous hatred and love, repulsion and attraction, toward filth and the criminal.

But why do I speak of love and attraction to filth, or, for that matter, the criminal? To take up first the issue of filth, psychoanalysis no less than everyday observation suggests that filth holds an unconscious allure for us all. Human infants enjoy playing with feces, while older children exhibit a special fascination with mud pies, fingerpaints, and other slimy, smeary things.[72] Currently, there is a toy on the market that consists of a green gelatinous ooze; it is called, simply, *Slime*.[73]

As children grow older, their attraction to slime is overlaid with a veneer of repugnance, and mental conflict results. This conflict has been acknowledged in an amusing way by the creators of another contemporary toy, *Icky-Poo*. On the back cover of *The Official Icky-Poo Book*, which accompanies a container of sticky slime, the editors declare, "You'll be disgusted with yourself for loving it."[74] Conscious mental conflict is painful; therefore, children develop defense mechanisms to avoid awareness of their attraction to dirt. For example, psychologist Ruth Munroe reports that her children became so intolerant of filth that they insisted on changing the dishwater several times during the washing up.[75] In their fastidiousness, Munroe's children were employing a reaction-formation—defending against the impulse to be messy by extravagantly representing the impulse to be clean.

Besides exaggerating their repugnance, children often defend against recognizing their interest in filth by attributing this interest to others—a dynamic we see in the following incident from my own experience. During the period when I was writing this book, my seven-year-old niece asked me whether I wanted to hear a "really disgusting poem." Before I could reply, she began to recite:

> Ooshy-Gooshy was a worm;
> A mighty worm was he.
> He sat upon the railroad tracks.
> Squish. It was not for me!

Thinking that the poem might come in handy some day, I asked her to repeat it, so I could write down the words. She did so, then asked forcefully, "What do you want to know for?" I explained that I was writing about criminals and the language we use to describe them. I added, "We like slime, but we also don't like it. And your poem shows that we like it." Indignantly, she replied, "No it doesn't! It shows that we don't like it!" I asked, "But if we don't like slime, why are we writing poems about it?" My niece pondered this briefly, then defended her position in a tone of utter repudiation: "That's a two-year-olds' poem!" In other words, it is not we who like slime, but the members of another, devalued, group. This defense mechanism, the attribution to others of unacceptable feelings in ourselves, is known as projection.[76]

As the preceding vignette illustrates, filth is not unequivocally despised, but is rather an object of inner conflict. When the polarities of filth and cleanliness, mess and order, are central to a person's mental life, we speak of obsessive-compulsive neurosis.[77] This neurosis derives from an unusually strong attachment to the anal zone—what Erik Erikson has called the " 'other' end of the human anatomy, that factory of waste-products and odorous gases which is totally removed from our own observation and is the opposite of the face we show to the world."[78]

We may not all be full-blown obsessive-compulsives, but we do all exhibit some compulsive traits, some attachment to the anal zone. In our dealings with criminals, I submit, we are especially apt to behave like the classic obsessive-compulsive patient, seeing dirt and contamination everywhere,[79] and using measures such as washing, neatening, and segregating to contend with this perceived threat. In the next section, I take up these measures as they appear in literary portrayals of criminality. I begin with the theme of washing.

Waters on the Hand of Blood: Washing and the Unavailing Effort to Regain Innocence

> I will sprinkle clean water upon you, and you shall be clean from all your uncleannesses.
> —*Ezekiel* 26:25

> Cleanliness is, indeed, next to godliness.
> —John Wesley

From the cultural equation of crime with filth it follows that water will play a central symbolic role in efforts to control crime. With its two properties as a cleansing agent and a giver of life, water serves as an archetypal symbol.[80] In the Judeo-Christian tradition, as in other traditions throughout the world, cleansing with water represents the abandonment of an evil existence and rebirth into a life of innocence and purity.[81]

The Pilgrim's Progress illustrates the symbolic power of water in the scene where Christian visits a large parlor that is filthy with dust. When a man tries to sweep away the filth, he only succeeds in creating more dust, causing Christian to choke. Then a damsel sprinkles the room with water, and when she has finished, it becomes possible to sweep and cleanse the room. The Interpreter explains: "This parlor is the heart of a man that was never sanctified by the sweet grace of the Gospel; the dust is his original sin and inward corruptions. . . . He that began to sweep at first is the Law; but she that brought water and did sprinkle it is the Gospel."[82]

Although this example depicts water as potentially effective in the struggle against guilt, a stronger literary tradition portrays cleansing as futile where the crime is heinous. For instance, in Sophocles' *Oedipus Tyrannus*, a messenger professes hopelessness in this way after the revelation of Oedipus's horrible deeds:

> Though stream on stream should pour
> Their swift-cleansing waters on the hand of blood,
> The old stain shall not be washed away.[83]

Likewise, Lord Byron's Cain, after slaying his brother Abel, recognizes sorrowfully:

> And I who have shed blood
> cannot shed tears.
> But the four rivers would not
> cleanse my soul.[84]

And again, in the most famous literary version of this theme, Macbeth raises the prospect of washing away his guilt, only to despair of success:

> Will all great Neptune's ocean wash this blood
> Clean from my hand? No, this my hand will rather
> The multitudinous seas incarnadine,
> Making the green one red.[85]

Later, Lady Macbeth, her mind crazed from guilt, seeks peace and blamelessness by enacting the same metaphor. Repeatedly, for as long as a quarter of an hour at a time, she rubs her hands together, as though washing them. Yet, like her husband, she harbors no illusion of recovering innocence:

All the perfumes of Arabia
will not sweeten this little hand. O, O, O![86]

Psychoanalysis confirms the idea that Lady Macbeth's efforts, however much repeated, will avail nothing. Ritualistic handwashing is a classic obsessional symptom, an *undoing*, which aims to ward off the pain of remorse through an expiatory gesture that annuls the wrongful act.[87] Typically, the undoing must be repeated over and over, and this very repetition is itself a sign that the conflict remains unresolved. As Ruth Munroe explains:

> Compulsive rituals of negative magic are especially repetitive because in one way or another they usually include a positive expression of the impulse either in the undoing itself or in the thought or act which precipitates the undoing. . . . The one meaning (doing) tends to intrude upon the other, and the patient is never sure just how many acts will undo the eternally recurrent positive impulse.[88]

Thus, the stain that imbues the criminal is an indelible stain, and the criminal, being irreclaimable, must be thrown away. So basic is this idea that *Webster's New International Dictionary* alludes to criminals illustratively in the very sentence defining *offal*. *Offal*, it says, is "[a]nything that is thrown away as worthless; carrion; refuse; rubbish; garbage; as the *offal* of jails."[89] But the image of the criminal as ineradicably stained is not the only source of banishment. Indeed, the powerful appeal of banishment (including internal banishment, or imprisonment) may stem from its ability to unite the notion of discarding worthless garbage with that of removing a diseased group from a healthy one, to prevent contamination.

A Great Gulf Fixed: Banishment of the Diseased Criminal

> They flung me down like a heap of carrion, and retreated as if they fled from the pollution of my touch.
> —Charles Maturin, *Melmoth the Wanderer*

Our earliest encounters with the notion of dirt often occur in the context of parental prohibitions related to illness; for example,

"Don't touch; it's dirty; it will make you sick." Because of this common experience, and because of the causal connection between dirt and illness, the notion of filth readily becomes assimilated to the notion of disease.[90]

Literature supports the idea that we tend to imagine criminals as not merely dirty but also contagious and diseased. A vivid illustration of this theme appears in Dickens' novel *A Tale of Two Cities* after the lawyer, Stryver, discovers that Charles Darnay is acquainted with the Marquis St. Evremonde. "I am sorry for it," Stryver comments. When Darnay insists on knowing why, Stryver answers:

> Here is a fellow who, infected by the most pestilent and blasphemous code of deviltry that ever was known, abandoned his property to the vilest scum of the earth that ever did murder by wholesale, and you ask me why I am sorry that a man who instructs youth knows him? Well, but I'll answer you. I am sorry because I believe there is contamination in such a scoundrel. That's why.[91]

So contagious is evil, in Stryver's view, that one may acquire it through mere acquaintance with a "scoundrel." Shakespeare's plays reveal that he too regards evil as an infectious disease. In *Hamlet*, a play about an unpunished act of murder, the central image is disease, in particular, as Caroline Spurgeon notes, "a hidden corruption infecting and destroying a wholesome body."[92]

If crime is a contagious disease, it makes sense that noncriminals should adopt measures to prevent criminals from contaminating them. Jaggers, the barrister in *Great Expectations*, employs cleansing for this purpose. As Pip relates:

> I embrace the opportunity of observing that he washed his clients off, as if he were a surgeon or a dentist. He had a closet in his room, fitted up for the purpose, which smelt of the scented soap like a perfumer's shop. It had an unusually large jack-towel on a roller inside the door, and he would wash his hands and wipe them and dry them all over this towel, whenever he came in from a police-court, or dismissed a client from his room.[93]

So also Wemmick, the solicitor who works with Jaggers, attempts to avoid defilement by the criminal milieu. Every evening, upon returning home, Wemmick crosses a drawbridge over a chasm and then pulls the bridge up behind him. To Pip, he observes, "After I have crossed this bridge, I hoist it up—so—and cut off the communication."[94]

Whereas Wemmick avoids criminal contamination through this nocturnal rite of self-banishment, literature's more common theme is the banishment of evildoers. Thus, King Oedipus, having discovered that he himself is the criminal who slayed his father and married his mother, demands to be punished in the traditional way, with banishment.[95] Likewise, Adam and Eve, after disobeying God in the Garden of Eden, are punished with exile. In Milton's retelling, Christ intercedes for the couple; nevertheless, God declares that Man, being sullied, may no longer abide in paradise:

> But longer in that Paradise to dwell,
> The Law I gave to nature him forbids:
> Those pure immortal Elements that know
> No gross, no unharmoneous mixture foule,
> *Eject him tainted now*, and purge him
> off . . . .[96]

As a Milton scholar explains, Adam and Eve may not remain in Paradise because "what is immortally pure and untaintable cannot assimilate what is soiled by any admixture of pollution."[97] Thus, the motive behind segregating these transgressors is not so much to avoid contracting their disease as to render the nonexpelled remnant utterly pure.

In a variation on the story of the Fall, Adam and Eve's son Cain, in a jealous rage, kills his brother Abel. Like his parents before him, Cain receives the punishment of exile for his crime. Condemned by God to be a "fugitive and a vagabond" on the face of the earth, he goes forth to the land of Nod, East of Eden, out of the Lord's presence.[98]

The theme of removing the wicked from the righteous runs through the *New Testament* as well as the *Old*. For example, in explaining the Final Judgment, Jesus describes God as separating the sheep from the goats, putting the goats on his left hand and sending them, cursed, into everlasting punishment. Significantly, this story associates darkness with wickedness; Syrian sheep, the breed that would have been familiar to the Gospel writers, were white, while the goats were black. Even in the dusk, they could be told apart.[99]

Jesus' story of the rich man and Lazarus provides another vivid example of the segregation motif. In this parable the rich man, dressed in purple, enjoys everything good while he lives. Meanwhile, a beggar, Lazarus, lies "at his gate and desire[s] to be fed with crumbs from the rich man's table."[100] After both men die, Lazarus rests in heaven in Abraham's bosom, whereas the rich man lies agonizing in hell. The rich man begs Abraham to let Lazarus put his finger in the water and cool his tongue to alleviate his torment. In denying the rich man's request, Abraham explains: "[B]etween us and you there is a great gulf fixed: so that they which would pass from hence to you cannot, neither can they pass to us, that would come from thence."[101]

Rituals of separation, defilement, and contagion—such are the themes of these stories, and they suggest that banishment has its roots in a concept we associate with primitive peoples, an ancient concept we know by its Polynesian name, *taboo*. As defined by anthropologists, *taboo* refers to rules of pollution: superstitious prohibitions on touching certain persons or objects. In his seminal work *The Golden Bough*, James Frazer describes the persons to whom the taboo applies: "[T]he common feature . . . is that they are dangerous and in danger."[102] The purpose of the taboo, then, is to "seclude these persons from the rest of the world so that the dreaded spiritual danger shall neither reach them nor spread from them."[103]

If the anthropological concept that illuminates banishment is *taboo*, the psychoanalytic counterpart is the defense mechanism of *isolation*. Though now used primarily to mean the separation of thoughts from their corresponding emotions, isolation once had a more general meaning: the spatial or temporal separation of the spheres that (it is thought) should not be in contact. As Otto Fenichel explains, "Numerous compulsive symptoms regulate the modes in which objects should be or must not be touched. The objects represent genitals or dirt. 'Clean' things must not communicate with 'dirty' ones."[104]

Its parallels with taboo and isolation suggest that banishment cannot be understood as merely a straightforward, rational response to evildoing. Rather, its origins lie deep in superstition and magical thinking. Later, in analyzing the Australian penal colony, we shall return to this topic, but first let us examine the places that evildoers inhabit beyond the "great gulf."

The Land of Gloom and Chaos: Darkness and Dirt As Essential Qualities of the Criminal's Punishment

Beyond the great gulf that separates the ungodly from the virtuous, evildoers are imagined as dwelling in conditions that mirror the characteristics of the punished—conditions known in theology as "measure-for-measure" punishments.[105] Since, as we have seen, criminals are commonly associated with slime, darkness, and foul odors, their places of punishment must likewise reflect these qualities.

The Hebrew concept of *Gehenna* provides a particularly interesting illustration of the ways in which the metaphor of filth has influenced human beings' thinking about punishment. Originally Gehenna was an actual place, a valley outside Jerusalem where garbage burned perpetually. In Jesus' preaching, Gehenna took on an eschatological meaning, becoming the site of evil-doers' eternal punishment. Over time, the concept of *Gehenna* was assimilated to an older idea of hell, *Sheol*, a place of mire and darkness. Since darkness and fire seemed incompatible, the Hebrews imagined Gehenna's fire as giving off no light. They willingly tolerated even this incompatibility to retain darkness as an affliction of the punished.[106]

Milton draws on this Hebrew tradition when, in *Paradise Lost*, he describes Hell as follows:

> A dungeon horrible on all sides round,
> As one great furnace flamed; yet
> from those flames
> No light; but rather darkness visible.[107]

Besides darkness, extreme removal from God characterizes the place where Milton's fallen angels dwell:

here their prison ordain'd
In utter darkness, and their portion set
As far remov'd from God and light of Heav'n
As from the center thrice to th' utmost Pole.[108]

The quality of being so far removed from light hints at an anal meaning to Milton's portrayal. This same association can be seen in actual practice in medieval times, when the unclaimed bodies of executed criminals were left to rot without a grave. The place where the corpses lay was then used as a dump; villagers threw garbage on the criminals' remains.[109] By this custom, society expressed its view of criminals as intimately related to stench and filth.

These anal meanings of criminality find another concrete expression in twentieth-century America. In the famous zoning case *Euclid v. Ambler*, the Supreme Court details the functions and institutions that the Euclid city officials have seen fit to put together in zone U-6: "plants for sewage disposal and for producing gas, garbage and refuse incineration, scrap iron, junk, scrap paper and rag storage, aviation fields, cemeteries, crematories, penal and correctional institutions, insane and feeble minded institutions, storage of oil and gasoline . . . and manufacturing and industrial operations."[110] As in the literary, theological, and historical examples, here too, criminals are associated with anal matters: waste, foul-smelling operations, and death, with its inevitable connotations of rot and decay.

How are we to understand the practice of punishing criminals in dark, dirty, smelly places? On one level, as the phrase "measure for measure punishment" implies, this practice may appeal to our sense of fairness; it seems only just that those who have engaged in crime and thus made themselves filthy should be forced to dwell in filth. On another level, the practice may signify an indulgence of the noncriminals' sadistic drive, thinly disguised as an appropriate punishment. No doubt both these explanations contain a partial validity. In addition, the practice of punishing criminals in filth can be understood as a mysophilic practice—a practice expressing a love of filth. Rather than being a defense, like washing and banishment, it represents a breakthrough of the original impulse: the attraction to dirt and the delight in playing with slimy, smeary things.

At the beginning of Part Three, I undertook to explore the ways that we employ the metaphor of filth to conceptualize criminals. But what began as an investigation of a metaphor has revealed to us an allegory—not a static image, but a dynamic story in which noncriminals perceive criminals first as slimy and dark, and then as dangerously diseased. Finally, fearing that they too will become contaminated with filth, the noncriminals banish the lawbreakers to a suitably dark, filthy, and remote place.

In the next chapter, I will show that this allegory found a resonance in late eighteenth- and nineteenth-century Britain and Australia. More specifically, I will suggest that British people living in these lands assimilated both their criminals and their new continent to this archetypal story, reenacting with real people and real places an epic drama of self-purification through banishment of the filthy.

Projecting an Excrementitious Mass: The Metaphor of Filth in the History of Botany Bay

Spewed from our country, forgotten, bound to the dark edge of
the earth.

—Timberlake Wertenbaker, *Our Country's Good*

BANISHED BEYOND THE SEAS: THE ORIGINS OF TRANSPORTATION TO AUSTRALIA

In 1786, having lost its American colonies, which had previously served as a repository for British criminals, and being
plagued by overcrowded prisons, from which typhus threatened to
spread into the surrounding communities, the British government
decided on a remarkable course of action: the creation of a penal
colony at Botany Bay, on the eastern coast of Australia.

Although it was not the only attempt at a solution to the penal
crisis—the penitentiary also developed during this period—the
"thief-colony" on the far side of the world would play an important role in the British criminal justice system for eighty-one
years, from 1787, when the First Fleet departed for New South
Wales with 736 convicts aboard, until 1868, when the last ship
landed its prisoners in Western Australia. Estimates of those forc-
ibly exiled to Australia vary, but all calculations indicate a large
number of transported convicts—probably from 156,000 to
162,000.[1] "Transportation," as forced exile was legally known, was
sometimes employed as a sentence in its own right; at other times,
it served as a merciful alternative to death.

Forced exile had, of course, been used as a punishment before
the Australian experiment, but never in the same way or on the

same grand scale. Exile, Blackstone tells us, was "a punishment unknown to the common law."[2] The *habeas corpus* act provided that "no subject of this realm . . . shall be sent prisoner, into Scotland, Ireland, Jersey, Guernsey, or places beyond the seas (where they cannot have benefit of common law) but that all such imprisonments shall be illegal."[3] Indeed, the British sovereign was not even permitted to send a subject out of the realm to be a foreign ambassador against his will, "[f]or this might in reality be no more than an honorable exile."[4]

Nevertheless, Parliament possessed the authority to override the common law, and did so in 1597, in an act providing that persistent idlers should be "conveyed . . . beyond the seas."[5] It was on the authority of this act that Britain transported convicts to the American colonies during the seventeenth and eighteenth centuries, thereby avoiding a crisis of numbers in its prisons. When, in 1776, the American colonies revolted, Britain no longer had a place to send its prisoners. Acting on the assumption that Britain would soon win the War, the British government adopted a stop-gap measure, "The Hulks Act," whereby old and rotting men-o'-war and troop transports would be used to hold convicts sentenced to be transported until their destination should be decided. As time went on, with the hulks' population increasing by one thousand prisoners a year, and with "gaol fever" rampant on the ships, the British government made increasingly frantic efforts to find a solution to its penal crisis.[6] In 1786, these efforts culminated in the appointment of a Governor, Lieutenant-Governor, and Chaplain for a penal colony to be established in Australia.[7] In late May 1787, six convict ships departed for the far side of the world.[8]

Historians have been hard pressed to make sense of the decision to create a penal colony in Australia. Some scholars, incredulous at what seems on its face an ill-conceived scheme, have sought out nontraditional explanations; specifically, they have proposed that Britain aimed at creating a strategic foothold in the Far East, or a flax industry on Norfolk Island, off of Australia's eastern coast.[9] In their quest for new interpretations, these historians have hoped to find "a less gratuitous beginning for Australia" than the plan for a penal colony.[10] Writing of the revisionists' motivation, David

MacKay observes: "The general sense is that Australia's colonial past is tawdry and requires tidying up. In their search for more noble and 'rational' explanations . . . writers have attempted to erase a blot from Australia's history." [11]

While some historians have found merit in the idea that commercial and strategic factors played a role in Britain's decision, others have rejected this view, and for powerful reasons. Thus, as to the commercial motive of growing flax on Norfolk Island, the equipping of the First Fleet tends to contradict this interpretation. The British government neglected to send either suitable tools or trained flax dressers to the colony. Not surprisingly, the flax industry got off to a slow start and was soon given up altogether. [12]

Many have found the argument for a strategic motive equally unconvincing. For example, Robert Hughes notes that the Australian colony lay thousands of miles from the areas of England's strategic interest; moreover, by the 1790s French ships no longer posed a significant threat in the Far East. Evidence about Prime Minister Pitt's state of mind also tends to belie the strategic motive, for his correspondence at the time contains only a few vague allusions to the strategic arguments. [13]

If the arguments for commercial and strategic motives are weak at best, we are left with the traditional explanation: that the British founded Australia as a place to dump criminals. But this theory, though widely accepted, is unsatisfying to virtually everyone, because it implies that the British government acted irrationally. Consider, for example, the assessment of David MacKay, author of *A Place of Exile:* "[T]he government found itself propelled towards . . . the worst possible alternative . . . the scarcely known shores of Botany Bay. Having arrived at this choice almost by default, it was then co.., ¬¹led to try to justify a decision which in reality had little to recommend it." [14] He continues: "The dispatch of the First Fleet to Botany Bay was a reckless act on the part of a desperate ministry. The intended site for the settlement was insufficiently known; the expedition itself was poorly organized and badly equipped. . . . Sending out the First Fleet without an adequate preliminary survey was irresponsible." [15]

In a similar vein, Hughes writes: "They chose the least imaginable spot on earth, which had been visited only once by white men."[16] Hughes goes so far as to characterize the plan of establishing a convict colony in a place so little known and far away as "bizarre."[17]

Geoffrey Blainey points out two other puzzling aspects of the decision to ship convicts to Botany Bay: first, transportation to eastern Australia was a terribly expensive solution to the British penal crisis; and second, it was a very slow way to solve what is thought to have been an urgent problem. Almost two and a half years elapsed between the sailing of the First Fleet of convict ships and the departure of the Second Fleet.[18] Thus, the plan to create a penal colony at Botany Bay seems curiously irrational if judged by the policymakers' conscious motives.

But psychoanalysis tells us that not all motives are conscious; indeed, a large part of mental functioning takes place outside awareness. And it is precisely when behavior makes little sense in terms of its acknowledged purposes that we have the most to gain in searching for unconscious motives. In the following pages, I undertake an examination of these unacknowledged purposes through an analysis of the imagery that the British used in discussing Australia and the criminal exiles. Based on this analysis, I will suggest that the policy of establishing a penal colony in Australia can be understood in terms of two unconscious aims: (1) to avoid a painful awareness of disavowed criminal qualities in the self by projectively identifying with those qualities in others; (2) to reenact an archetypal drama about dwellers in paradise who became tainted and were banished to a dark, remote land.

A Pervading Stain: The Language of Filth in Australian History

In contemplating Australian history, one cannot fail to be impressed by the pervasiveness of anal metaphors in the debate over transporting criminals to that far-off land. The very idea of "far-off" itself hints at anality, because, in the human body, the anal region is remote from that part of the body we identify most closely with our selves, namely, the face. A letter written by the English essayist Charles Lamb to his friend Barron Field conveys some sense of Australia's remoteness to the eighteenth-century European: "I do not know whereabout Africa merges into Asia; . . . nor can form the remotest conjecture of the position of New South Wales [the name then given to all of eastern Australia], or Van Diemen's Land [Tasmania, a large island off of Australia's southern coast]. Yet do I hold a correspondence with a very dear friend in the first-named of these two Terrae Incognitae."[19] To the men and women of eighteenth-century England, Australia was truly an unknown land. Prior to the transporting of the convicts, only one British ship had ever landed at Botany Bay, and that briefly, seventeen years earlier. The first convict fleet required two hundred fifty days to reach its destination.

The point, of course, is not that Australia was literally an unknown and remote place, but that these qualities enabled Australia to serve as a powerful *symbol* of the unknown, the remote, and the anal. Australia's function as a symbolic land meaning Britain's backside can be seen in the title of a three-volume work about Australia published in the early 1850s. Written by Colonel Godfrey Mundy, a long-term official visitor to Australia, the work is entitled *Our Antipodes.*[20]

Besides remoteness, more explicit anal metaphors were also used to speak of Australia. Consider, for example, the following passage in which Bishop William Ullathorne, Vicar-Apostolic for New South Wales, argued against the continued transportation of criminals to Australia: "We have taken a vast portion of God's earth and made it a cesspool; we have taken the oceans, which, with their wonders, gird the globe, and . . . made them the channels of a sink; we have poured down scum upon scum and dregs upon dregs of the offscourings of mankind."[21]

In England, as well, commentators imagined Australia rather vividly as a place that the British were using as a sewer. Thus, in 1819, the Reverend Sydney Smith, an occasional consultant to Home Secretary Peel, wrote in the Edinburgh Review: "There can be but one opinion. New South Wales is a *sink of wickedness.*"[22]

Similarly, in 1849, the *Times* defended transportation with these words:

> While . . . we recognize the wisdom and public spirit of those who deprecate the perversion of any colony into a mere *convict cesspool,* we must remind them that England has rights as well as her dependencies, and that . . . she will not submit to the shame and cost of maintaining an annual burden of three thousand convicted felons on her own soil.[23]

But perhaps the most graphic and conspicuously anal language about Australia comes from *Our Antipodes.* Explaining why some Australian settlers opposed the revival of transportation, Mundy states: "He who steps backwards will tumble in the mire—and what mire blacker and fouler than the Botany Swamp!"[24] Like Charles Dickens in *Oliver Twist* and Arthur Conan Doyle in *The Hound of the Baskervilles,* Mundy portrays the criminals' habitat as an alluvial ooze.

In the passages quoted above, writers conceive of Australia as a slimy receptacle of filth; hence, a toilet, or an anus, not in the sense of an expelling organ, but of a passively receiving one. If Australia was an anus, then the criminals sent there were feces, as we see in the following eloquent example from Jeremy Bentham. Speaking out against the "thief-colony" in 1812, he observed that England was projecting "a sort of excrementitious mass."[25] While not quite so explicit, other observers likewise portrayed the criminal exiles in anal terms, as refuse, scum, taint, and stain. For instance, in 1846, a colonial correspondent of *The Times* wrote: "As the foundation of a permanent convict system, no change ought to be accepted which does not abandon at once and for ever the selfish and heinous sin of casting off on infant countries the *scum and refuse* of our own society."[26] Likewise, Colonel Mundy thought that "the privilege of shooting so much moral *rubbish* upon other and distant premises . . . [was] cheaply bought."[27] And again, the British *Quarterly* declared convicts "the refuse of the trading towns" and so "unsuitable for colonial employment."[28]

Permanent settlers in Australia used the same metaphor, as we see in this 1851 example from the *Bathurst Free Press:* "[T]o invite the *scum* of the British Empire merely from pecuniary motives, would be to ask from the parent land her curse, instead of her blessing—would be to effect the complete destruction of the trifling claim to respectability which we now possess."[29] The word *scum* unites the concepts of wet dirt and darkness. Long used to mean a layer of impurities lying on top of a liquid, the word derives from a root meaning to *cover* or *conceal;* hence, to place in the darkness.[30]

The colonials often associated the convict-filth with the first point of contact between the criminal exiles and the continent, that is, the shore and its surrounding waters. Thus, orating from a bus roof, an English emigrant barrister proclaimed that "the stately presence of their city, the beautiful waters of their harbour, were this day again polluted with the presence of that floating hell—a convict ship."[31] In a similar vein, the London *Times* editorialized in 1852 about the "polluted shores" of Van Diemen's Land.[32]

While words like *pollution, refuse, garbage,* and *scum* were commonly used to refer to the convicts, the dominant metaphor was *stain* or its closely associated term *taint.* In a typical example, a British official reporting on Van Diemen's Land in 1847 wrote, "Vice of every description . . . is to be met with on every hand—not as isolated spots, but as a pervading stain."[33] In another instance, an article published in England in 1855 contains the following language about the convict who discovered gold in Australia: "[B]ut in this day and hour how many of the superior classes will be bold enough to aver that the wretched, contaminated, brutalised, *crime-stained,* flagellated Irish convict may not have discovered gold."[34] The metaphor of taint occupied a central role in the debate over eligibility for the jury in Australia. In 1833, when selected ex-convicts were permitted to serve as jurors in Australia, one faction objected that "untainted" persons could not be expected either to sit on a jury with convicted felons or to be tried by them.[35]

Stain and taint are discolorations that tend to spread; hence, it was a natural step from these images to the idea that criminals are diseased. Mundy explains the colonials' opposition to transportation with these words: "No one could desire the regrowth of an unsightly tumour which had once been painfully excised."[36] In addition to metastasizing within a single organism, the disease of criminality was thought of as spreading down through the generations. For instance, as late as 1889, a writer in the British journal *Nineteenth Century* laments: "New South Wales labours under the disadvantage of possessing . . . a population in whose veins there is an hereditary taint of criminality."[37]

Besides spreading both within the body of convicts and to the convicts' descendants, criminality was conceived as radiating to noncriminals who came into contact with the convicts. Thus, a key figure in the founding of the Australian penal colony, Prime Minister Pitt, cited the notion of contamination to justify transporting criminals to Botany Bay. In a parliamentary debate in 1791, he argued "that it was the worst policy of a state to keep [the most incorrigible] offenders . . . at home to corrupt others, and contaminate the less guilty, by communicating their own dangerous depravity."[38] In the same vein, in 1828, the British *Quarterly* argued that the "entire removal of the individual to a new scene of life affords at once the only security to society against his future crimes and the contagion of his habits."[39]

This same metaphor of criminality as a contagious disease that might spread to noncriminals played a role during the influential meetings of the House of Commons Select Committee inquiring into transportation in 1837 and 1838. At one point, the chair of the committee, Sir William Molesworth, articulated the committee's concern that the contaminating influence of a criminal influx would be greater at that time than it had been previously. In Australia's early days, he suggested, the free settlers might have arrived with their characters already formed, and so were "less liable to be corrupted than their unfortunate offspring."[40]

THE ORIGINS AND MEANINGS OF THE ANAL METAPHOR

The Metaphor of Filth As a "Pupil's Metaphor"

Metaphors involving filth and, by extension, contagious disease, so pervade the debate over transportation of convicts to Australia that it would be hard to imagine the same debate without them. Just as *Macbeth* and *The Hound of the Baskervilles* are as much about slime and darkness as they are about plot and character, so also the story of Botany Bay seems to be as much about filth—about scum, refuse, mire, and stain—as it is about arguments and policies. It is now time to ask what these metaphors can tell us about the relationship between criminals and noncriminals during this period. Were the metaphors of filth accidental or essential? If writers and speakers had referred to criminals as fire-eating dragons, or to Australia as an iceberg, or an oven, would this usage have implied something different about the meanings and functions of the criminal during the era of transportation to Australia?

Psychoanalysis, as well as literary criticism, maintains that the choice of metaphor is never accidental, for the vehicle of one's thought is inseparably entwined with its content.[41] That this is so, that the metaphors of filth were inextricably bound up with the noncriminals' understanding of criminality, can be seen more clearly with the aid of a distinction offered by C. S. Lewis in his essay "Bluspels and Flalansferes." Lewis suggests that metaphors can be categorized into two types depending on their role in the mind of the user. The Master's metaphor, he explains, is "freely chosen . . . one among many possible modes of expression; it does not at all hinder . . . the thought of its maker."[42] The Pupil's metaphor, by contrast, "is not chosen at all; it is the unique expression of a meaning we cannot have on any other terms; it dominates completely the thought of the recipient; his truth cannot rise above the truth of the original metaphor."[43]

These two types of metaphor lie, of course, on a continuum, and, doubtless, most noncriminals in Australian history were capable of defining criminals without using metaphors of filth. Yet so widespread is this imagery, and so rare is the use of other images for criminals, that we seem justified in characterizing the metaphor of filth as a Pupil's metaphor. For a powerful illustration of this point, consider the words of an emigrant's handbook published in London in 1851. The author endeavors to reassure prospective emigrants to Australia with this analogy: "The operation of the penal system has altered the face of the country where it has been set down . . . just as manure may have altered the character of a field."[44] Thus, even a Britisher writing positively about the criminal exiles makes her point with the language of filth.

The Metaphor of Filth As a Defense against Identification with Criminals

If the image of the criminal as filth was a Pupil's metaphor, essential to the noncriminals' thinking about Botany Bay, then it is worthwhile to proceed further with our inquiry, asking why the metaphors of filth were employed so abundantly to refer to criminality. I have already suggested a partial answer; to wit, the resonance between Australia's literal remoteness from Britain and the remoteness of the anal region of the human body. Similarly, the prisoners who were transported to Australia literally dwelled in conditions of filth and darkness on board the ships.[45] These actual qualities may have encouraged people to assimilate criminals to the concept of filth. Nevertheless, as we have seen, the origins of the filth-criminal equation go much wider and deeper than any mere literal similarity. I wish now to propose that these origins may be found in the similar emotional stance that we adopt toward criminals and filth; namely, a stance of ambivalence, or simultaneous hatred and love, repulsion and attraction, toward the same object.

Putting aside for the moment the topic of our attraction to criminals, let us consider again our complicated emotional stance toward filth. As we saw in the last chapter, filth holds an unconscious allure for us all. Transparently revealed in children's play, this attraction gradually undergoes an almost-universal repression. In adults, it appears mainly in sublimated forms—in the appeal of a mud-wrestling competition, for example—or indirectly, in exaggerated defenses against messiness, such as the compulsive person's undiscriminating insistence on neatness and order. From a psychoanalytic perspective, the exaggerated quality of this repudiation itself betrays the continuing power of the underlying attraction—a truth that has made its way into popular consciousness with Shakespeare's *bon mot*, "The lady doth protest too much."

If human beings generally are attracted to filth, and if noncriminals equated criminals with filth throughout early Australian history, it seems reasonable to infer that these noncriminals harbored an attraction to criminals. Yet, their language suggests, this attraction was so repugnant that they barred its admission to their conscious minds via the mechanism of repression.[46] And, since repression often requires reinforcement from other defense mechanisms, they also developed a reaction formation, converting the feeling of attraction into its opposite: loathing, or disgust. Relatedly, the noncriminals may have used the criminal-exiles to avoid awareness of disavowed criminal qualities in themselves through the mechanism of externalization.[47]

But what is the evidence for these speculations? By themselves, the anal images only hint at the interpretation I have offered; nevertheless, additional evidence comes to our assistance, in several forms. First, not only the language, but also the policy adopted toward criminals during this period displays a hyperbolic quality, as if the British were saying, "We want nothing to do with criminals, and to ensure that we do not, we will ship them to the moon!"

The extreme nature of the policy was noted by some observers at the time. For example, in 1786, the *Gentleman's Magazine* pronounced the Botany Bay venture "a most extravagant scheme."[48] Similarly, Sir Nathaniel Wraxall, a political commentator writing in 1787, ridiculed the Botany Bay expedition precisely for its outlandishness, characterizing the policy as "one of those extraordinary acts of State, which, as it never has . . . had any precedent; so I incline to apprehend, it will remain for ever without imitation."[49] To Wraxall, the almost unbelievable remoteness of the new penal colony rendered the plan ludicrous. In parodied terms, he described the expedition: "through stormy seas, and inclement latitudes, . . . [forming] a new colony of thieves and ruffians, in another hemisphere, under the Southern Pole!"[50] Wraxall could conceive of only one goal that Britain could be pursuing through this policy: to remove the criminals as far as possible from the home country.[51]

To highlight the strangeness of the Botany Bay expedition,

Wraxall contrasted Britain's practice with that of other countries. "The Romans," he wrote,

> knew the value of even the vilest and most flagitious of their sub-
> jects . . . and were content with sending their malefactors to Sar-
> dinia or Corsica. . . . France has her gallies; and Russia her mines.
> . . . And could England discover no mode of availing herself of the
> strength and corporal functions of so many of her inhabitants, the
> far greater part of whom are in the vigour of life?[52]

The British, Wraxall recognized, were discarding their fellow-citizens like refuse, or, more specifically, like *irreclaimable* refuse; that is, they were throwing them as far away as possible. To Wraxall's emphasis on the corporal strength of the exiles, we may add that many of the criminals had been charged with only trivial offenses;[53] consequently, they might have been especially capable of making a contribution to their country.

Not only the hyperbolic nature, but also the mode of Britain's Botany Bay project points to a defensive function. As we have seen, the British took people who had been a part of their body politic and cast them out, telling them that they could not re-turn—either for a lengthy period of years or forever. The struc-ture of this punishment is familiar to us, for its model is defeca-tion. In defecation, as in expulsion of criminals, something that was a part of one's "body" is removed from the "body" and be-comes refuse. This similarity hints at the policy's anal meaning and, with it, the probability that the noncriminals felt an attraction to, as well as an aversion for, the lawbreakers.

Besides its resemblance to defecation, the punishment of exile bears an affinity with a psychological mechanism, externalization, which is the experiencing of inner impulses and feelings as if they belonged to the outer world. In a simpler, more vivid definition of the same mechanism, a little boy who was the scapegoat of his family once explained to his therapist: "They put the bad onto me and they feel good."[54] Now this boy, Tommy, had, in reality, developed the characteristics that his parents perceived in him. Through the operation of a self-fulfilling prophecy, he had come to be "a regressed, soiling, snot-eating child"[55] with little self-control. Thus, at the time of Tommy's therapy, the parents' distortion of reality did not take the form of imagining things in their son that were not there at all. Rather, in a form of externalization known as projective identification, they saw qualities in Tommy that *were* there; however, they exaggerated them and used Tommy to avoid the painful recognition that they felt themselves to be damaged and messy.[56] It is this same defense mechanism, projective identification, that I suggest the British noncriminals were employing in their Botany Bay policy.

I have argued that Britain's Botany Bay policy was a means of defending against an unconscious attraction to and identification with criminals. But defense mechanisms are rarely totally successful. If my interpretation has merit, we should see expressions of the other side of the conflict at the time the policy was decided, in eighteenth-century England. Specifically, we should see indications that, besides spurning lawbreakers and expelling them from their land, noncriminals also identified with criminals and regarded them with pleasure and esteem. Let us now examine the evidence that this was the case.

The Other Side of the Conflict: Popular Identification with Criminals and Delight in Their Ways

> The law doth punish man or woman
> That steals the goose from off the common
> But lets the greater felon loose
> That steals the common from the goose.
> —Anonymous, 1764

It is surely no accident that this English folk song dates from the eighteenth century, for English literature of that era displays a profound ambivalence toward the criminal law. In his examination of eighteenth-century English fiction, David Punter finds three prominent themes, all reflective of this ambivalence. First, he reports that novels of this era consistently tend to discredit En-

glish legal mechanisms and institutions, presenting criminal sub-
groups as living by a set of rules more honorable than the rules
that characterize the dominant legal system. To mention but two
examples, the prisoners in *The Vicar of Wakefield* and the pirate
band in *Captain Singleton* exhibit a decency and humaneness in
their self-government that, the novelists imply, is lacking in the
government of England.[57]

As a second major theme in the literature of this period, Punter
finds that the line between officers of the law and lawbreakers is
regularly blurred. Lawyers, for example, are portrayed as little
different from criminals; like the criminals, they rob, but with
legal sanction. Besides lawyers, the thief-takers of this period, such
as the famous Jonathan Wild, are depicted as straddling the law.
On the one hand, they enforce the law by impeaching an occasional robber and returning stolen goods to the victims. On the
other, they themselves direct gangs of thieves, forcing noncriminals into lives of crime by threatening to report them falsely to
the authorities.[58]

As a third theme of eighteenth-century English fiction, Punter
notes that the protagonists' crimes are often justified by circumstances. To take but one famous example, the heroine of *Moll
Flanders* is a lifelong thief and prostitute who delights in her
resourcefulness and shows little remorse for her crimes. As Defoe
portrays her, Moll's life of crime is partly justified by the alternative she initially faces: a life of servitude.[59]

Since Punter confines his analysis to novels, he omits what may
be the most famous example of a criminal hero in eighteenth-
century English literature, the charismatic highwayman in John
Gay's musical, *The Beggar's Opera*. With his glamorous clothes, his
charm, and his success with women, Macheath portrays the life of
a highway robber as greatly to be desired. As we saw in chapter 7,
numerous writers and preachers publicly lamented Macheath's
popularity; meanwhile, *The Beggar's Opera* became the most successful theatrical production of the eighteenth-century.[60] The
eighteenth-century British fascination with fictional criminals carried over to real criminals as well. For instance, while highwaymen

languished in Newgate prison, awaiting death, members of society would pay them social calls.[61] Then, as each condemned prisoner journeyed from Newgate Prison to Tyburn Tree, crowds would throng the road, tossing flowers and fruits to the convict, who, arrayed in his best apparel, might use the occasion of his hanging to make a speech to the supportive mob.[62] Summing up what some saw as the perverted flavor of these spectacles, Foucault writes: "In these executions, which ought to show only the terrorizing power of the prince, there was a whole aspect of the carnival, in which rules were inverted, authority mocked and criminals transformed into heroes."[63]

Besides admiration, identification with lawbreakers was also strikingly evident during this period. For example, victims of crime frequently petitioned on behalf of the very criminals who had robbed them, after the criminals had been sentenced to transportation. Bothered by the disproportion between a sometimes trivial offense and the enormity of exile, and unwilling to bear the guilt for the breakup of a family, some victims declared their own forgiveness of the crime and begged for a legal remission of the culprit's sentence to Botany Bay. On one occasion, when forwarding such a petition with the recommendation that it be denied, a magistrate vented his frustration at popular sympathy for criminals with the words: "These are times when the current of public opinion seems to disarm the law of *all* its terrors!"[64]

In addition to these indications from eighteenth-century England, twentieth-century Australia provides longitudinal evidence of an intrapsychic conflict over criminals. In recent years, it has become quite fashionable to claim descendance from the First Fleet. Indeed, those Australians who can prove such descent have expressed their pride by forming a society in Sydney: the Fellowship of First Fleeters![65] Thus, both contemporaneous and historical testimony confirms the existence of a polarity, an ambivalence embracing love and hate, idealization and devaluation of criminals.

Thus far, I have offered three kinds of evidence to corroborate my interpretation of the Botany Bay experiment. First, the policy of expelling criminals and transporting them to a place so far away has an exaggerated quality, which suggests a struggle with feelings and impulses in the self. Second, the policy (like the language about the exiles and their island prison) exhibits an anal character, which implies the presence of the same ambivalence toward criminals that we all feel toward feces—not only an aversion, but also an attraction to and an identification with the dark, viscous matter that was once part of the self. Third, the literature and history of eighteenth-century England provide substantial evidence of the other side of the conflict: identification with criminals and admiration for criminal deeds.

There remains one final kind of confirmation to offer. If my interpretation is correct, then the criminal-exiles had a profound meaning for the British noncriminals, serving as a split-off and punished part of themselves. We would therefore expect that any interference with the noncriminals' ability to use the exiles and Australia in this symbolic way would meet with an extreme reaction. In this light, let us consider the story of Alexander Maconochie's tenure as Superintendent of Norfolk Island.

The Revilement of Superintendent Maconochie: An Epitome

About nine hundred miles northeast of Sydney, in the Pacific Ocean, lies Norfolk Island, where authorities sent the worst of Britain's transported convicts. In 1827, Australian Governor Darling stated his intention to make this settlement "a place of the extremest punishment, short of death."[66] In keeping with this goal, Norfolk Island came to be considered a hellish prison, where illegal tortures prevailed and where convicts were turned against each other by an elaborate system of informing. The awful nature of the place can be seen in an official report written in 1834, where the chaplain recounts that on one occasion all thirteen of the convicts sentenced to death knelt to thank God for their good fortune, whereas all those who received reprieves cried bitterly at the thought of a future in that place.[67]

In 1840, Alexander Maconochie, a retired naval captain and former prisoner of war who had written extensively on prison reform, was appointed superintendent of the island. Unlike most Britons of his time, Maconochie viewed imprisonment as a sufficient punishment in itself; he saw no need for additional tortures and degradations. True to this philosophy, during his four years as superintendent he presided over many humanitarian reforms: building churches, re-establishing schools, demolishing gallows, and permitting the convicts to cultivate gardens. In addition, Maconochie established indeterminate sentences and then allowed the convicts themselves to determine the length of their terms by earning "marks"; for every ten marks earned, they shortened their sentence by one day.

Maconochie's reforms proved remarkably successful in rehabilitating the supposedly unsalvageable offenders of Norfolk Island. Only three percent of the 1,450 prisoners discharged during Maconochie's tenure are known to have been reconvicted.[68] Perhaps the most spectacular instance of rehabilitation concerned the convict Charles Anderson. Irreversibly brain damaged, Anderson had been a violent and resentful person at the time he was convicted of burglary and placed on Goat Island, a rock in Sydney Harbor. For two years, he had been fastened, naked, to a chain on the rock, his only home a cavity carved out of the stone.[69] Unhealed welts festered on his back, the result of hundreds of punishments with the lash. Residents of Sydney amused themselves by rowing out to his rock and throwing crusts of bread or offal for him to eat.

Following an investigation, Anderson was removed from Goat Island to another prison, Port Macquarie. While there, serving a life sentence, he murdered an overseer in hopes of attaining escape through the gallows. His death sentence was commuted, and he was sent to Norfolk Island, where he continued violent and unrepentant until Maconochie assumed control of the prison. Maconochie gave Anderson a job taming bullocks away from the ridicule of other prisoners. After Anderson succeeded in this first assignment, Maconochie put him to work managing a signal station. Although his brain damage precluded a full rehabilitation, Anderson improved enormously under Maconochie's reforms. When Governor Gipps visited Norfolk Island in 1843, he wrote of his astonishment at seeing Anderson transformed from a wild beast to a man "trimly dressed in sailor's garb, going importantly about his duties."[70]

Notwithstanding Maconochie's effectiveness in rehabilitating convicts, his reforms inspired ridicule and revilement among non-criminals in Sydney and London. Significantly, it was a one-time event, a largely symbolic one, that elicited the most vociferous criticism among the noncriminals. To show his trust for the men, on Queen Victoria's birthday in 1840, Maconochie gave the convicts a holiday, allowing the men to roam freely over the Island and providing them with good food, rum, fireworks, and a theatrical performance. In Sydney, news of the birthday celebration caused "a wave of execration" to break on Maconochie's head.[71] As Governor Gipps described the situation, "every man was against him, every man derided his System."[72] At least as early as 1842, the authorities in London made the decision to recall Maconochie, although no replacement became available until 1844.[73] Maconochie's successor, Major Joseph Childs, obeyed his superiors' orders to make Norfolk Island the epitome of hell once again.

The question arises why the British noncriminals displayed such a hostile reaction to this man whose reforms were succeeding in transforming hardened convicts, and who would later be recognized as a pioneer in penology, one of the "few exceptional administrators of these colonies of brutality."[74] Several possible explanations come to mind: perhaps the noncriminals feared that, by turning Norfolk Island into a more pleasant place, Maconochie was eliminating the Island's deterrent value. Or, by treating the convicts with kindness and respect, Maconochie may have thwarted the noncriminals' need to exact sadistic vengeance on convicts. Finally, by going his own idealistic way, Maconochie may simply have annoyed too many of his superiors, leading them to believe that he could not be trusted to obey orders.

Without denying that these factors may have played a part, I suggest that the negative reaction to Maconochie's reforms primarily stems from the noncriminals' need to use this Australian prison as a symbol of hell. In chapter 10, we saw that places of punishment are typically imagined as mirroring the qualities of the punished. Since criminals are seen as intimately related to filth, their prison must be filthy as well. Like Gehenna, it must be dark and stinking with garbage; it must be, as the writer of *Job* puts it, "a land of gloom and chaos."[75] By undermining Norfolk Island's ability to function as a symbol of hell, Maconochie challenged the noncriminals' dualistic vision of the world and, with it, their dialectically-determined identity as the pure noncriminals, the untainted remnant. To appreciate the profundity of this challenge, one has only to remember Victor Hugo's character Javert, whom I discussed in an earlier chapter. When forced to recognize the noble qualities in his criminal prey, Javert despairs of life's meaning and drowns himself.

I have presented the story of Maconochie at some length to corroborate my view that the Australian criminal exiles played an important intrapsychic role for the British noncriminals, serving as externalized aspects of the noncriminals' selves—their disavowed greed, sadism, and hostility to authority. In developing this interpretation, I have employed a particular psychoanalytic paradigm, the conflict model, which views the mind as beset by inner polarities and conflicts. In the next section, I will attempt to enrich our understanding of the Botany Bay venture with the help of another, complementary paradigm: the narrative model. This model focuses on human beings as mythopoeic creatures, who invent stories to give their lives meaning.[76]

SYMBOLISM AS MOTIVE: THE BOTANY BAY VENTURE AS A REENACTMENT OF THE FALL

And the woman said unto the serpent, we may eat of the fruit of the trees of the garden:

But of the fruit of the tree which is in the midst of the garden, God hath said, ye shall not eat of it, neither shall ye touch it, lest ye die. . . .

. . . And when the woman saw that the tree was good for food, and that it was pleasant to the eyes, and a tree to be desired to make one wise, she took of the fruit thereof, and did eat, and gave also unto her husband with her; and he did eat.

And the eyes of them both were opened, and they knew that they were naked; . . .

. . . [And the Lord God said,] Hast thou eaten of the tree, whereof I commanded thee that thou shouldst not eat?

And the man said, The woman whom thou gavest to be with me, she gave me of the tree, and I did eat.

And the Lord God said unto the woman, What is this that thou hast done? And the woman said, The serpent beguiled me, and I did eat. . . .

. . . Therefore the Lord God sent him forth from the garden of Eden, to till the ground from whence he was taken.

So he drove out the man; and he placed at the east of the garden of Eden Cherubims, and a flaming sword which turned every way, to keep the way of the tree of life. —Genesis 3:2–24

In eighteenth- and nineteenth-century England, when books were far less prevalent than today, one book was well-known to nearly every educated person: the King James version of the Bible.[77] And of the many stories in the Bible, very likely one of the best-known was the myth of the Fall. For this myth—with its wonderful detail, its humor, its epiphany, and reversal of fortune—possesses all the elements of a powerful drama. Moreover, from a theological perspective, the episode of the Fall is "the starting point of the Christian drama of redemption, and hence is a subject of the utmost importance and the utmost sublimity from the point of view of the author and his audience."[78]

As the story is related in *Genesis*, human beings disobeyed a law and, consequently, became morally polluted with a taint that would pass down through the generations. Referring to this taint, the *New Testament* declares: "[I]n Adam all die."[79] Likewise, the *Articles of Religion*, another work that was known to the educated Britisher of this era, refers to the offspring of Adam as harboring an "infection of nature."[80] As a punishment for having violated God's law and become tainted, Adam and Eve were banished from their original home to an unpleasant place, a place where Eve would bring forth children "in sorrow," and live in subordination to her husband, and where Adam would eat bread "in the sweat of [his] . . . face," and finally return to dust.[81]

Earlier in this essay, I noted the strong resemblance between this story and the story that the British enacted in the late eighteenth and nineteenth centuries when they transported criminals to Australia. There too, people had violated the law, and there too, this violation was thought to have engendered a moral taint that would pass down to the criminals' descendants. Moreover, like Adam and Eve, the convicts were punished with banishment from their original home to a place that was conceived as unpleasant. The words that the *Interpreter's Bible* uses to describe the fate of the first humans could apply, with only slight modifications, to the British exiles: "So the past was to be irrevocable. The man and his wife must turn from all they had known to a future that was unknown. The gate was shut, and the angel with the flaming sword kept them from ever going back."[82] The British criminal exiles were rarely accompanied by spouses, and British law replaced the angel with the flaming sword, but with these exceptions, the two stories are remarkably the same.

The time has come to inquire more closely into the meaning of this resemblance. Does the resemblance suggest that the story of the Fall contributed to causing the Botany Bay venture, or merely that it added a layer of meaning to a decision made on independent grounds? While this question cannot be answered with certainty, an argument can be made for the stronger inference. It goes as follows: when, in the late eighteenth century, the British needed a new way to cope with their burgeoning class of criminals, they assimilated these wrongdoers to a myth that was already deeply embedded in their culture, the myth of the Fall. When the Botany Bay solution was proposed, its correspondence to the Biblical story made it seem a natural choice.

If, on one level, the myth of the Fall can be understood as a *cause* of the Botany Bay venture, on another, deeper level, both the myth and the Botany Bay venture can be understood as *responses* to a third factor; namely, human beings' need for stories that symbolically grapple with the central concerns of their lives.[83] We have already examined the themes of guilt and filthiness that pervade the story of Botany Bay. But there are also other concerns, related more to the metaphor's vicissitudes than to the metaphor itself, that are embedded in the narratives of the Fall and of Botany Bay. One is the disquieting recognition that we are all temporary sojourners on this earth—that our true home, if any, lies elsewhere, in a place from which we came, and to which we will eventually return.[84]

This states the theme from the perspective of our existential predicament. In terms of developmental psychology, both the Fall and Botany Bay reflect the central fear of childhood, the fear of parental abandonment. As psychiatrist Gregory Rochlin writes, "Childhood is full of a need for people and the fears of being left by them. There was never a child who did not need an adult nor was there a child who did not fear losing an adult he had."[85] Owing to its importance in the child's mental world, the dread of abandonment has been elaborated in many fairy tales where the parent dies, voluntarily forsakes the child, or allows the child to be taken away. The story of *Hansel and Gretel*, in particular, closely resembles the Botany Bay venture. In this fairy tale, the poor woodcutter and his wife take their children far from home and leave them, without the means to return.[86]

In *Hansel and Gretel*, as often in reality, it was poverty that led the parents to desert their children, but whatever the actual circumstances, children tend to blame themselves for their parents' desertion. As Rochlin writes, "[I]t is the child's view that there is no danger except if one is worthless because only what is no good is given up."[87] Thus, in the child's fantasy, the parallel of abandonment with the Fall and the Botany Bay venture becomes more complete.

At this point, the reader may object that the parallel I have drawn is imperfect because the Botany Bay story lacks a happy ending. In *Hansel and Gretel*, the exiled children are ultimately reunited with their loving father. Likewise, in the Biblical story of the Fall, human beings lose their innocence but finally gain something far greater, salvation. Indeed, according to the theological doctrine of the *felix culpa*, or "fortunate fall," Adam's sin was a necessary one. Had Adam not disobeyed God, we would have no need of salvation and would not experience God's grace.[88]

It is true that, in some versions, the Botany Bay story can offer no such joyous dénouement. Many convicts died on the voyage to Australia; others were raped by their fellow exiles, or treated cruelly by the masters to whom they were assigned. Still other criminals, however, did manage to make a new life in their place of exile. Like Jean Valjean in *Les Miserables*, they found in the "sewer" a place of salvation.[89] Such positive experiences reveal the truth in the facetious words of a 1786 ballad describing the Australian prison colony as "this Garden of Eden, this new promised land."[90]

In part because of such success stories, Botany Bay soon lost its power as an unequivocally negative symbol, a deterrent to crime in the mother country. According to Hughes, it was difficult to convince the British lower classes that transportation was a terrible fate.[91] By 1840, Charles Dickens was writing to the Whig home secretary stating that most British criminals viewed transportation as a chance to improve their lives. To counter such positive perspectives, he offered to write "a vivid description of the terrors of Norfolk Island and such-like places, told in a homely narrative with a great appearance of truth and reality and circulated in some very cheap and easy form."[92] Confirming the reality underlying Dickens's concern, anecdotal evidence suggests that some nineteenth-century Britons may actually have committed crimes in hopes of being transported to Australia.[93] Whatever the truth of these accounts, it is clear that the beckoning image of Botany Bay as a place of "newness and freedom"[94] offered serious competition to its official image as a hellish and isolated abode. Similar to the more traditional prisons that we examined in Part One, this "prison of infinite space"[95] became, for some, a beloved prison.

Like the myth of the Fall, the narrative of Botany Bay gave symbolic form to human beings' deepest anxieties: the sense of being dirty and bad, the dread of abandonment, the experience of exile, and the hope of redemption. Though not a written text, or a dramatic production, the story of Botany Bay may have offered its listeners what all great stories offer: a way to avoid immersion in quotidian detail and to live life with a sense of transcendent meaning.

Thus far, I have attempted to accomplish two goals: to show the depth and cultural pervasiveness of the metaphor likening the criminal to filth, and to demonstrate that the theory of anality can shed light on an important episode in criminal justice, the Botany Bay venture. But the Botany Bay experiment is now finished, and Britain no longer uses transportation to punish criminals. The question arises, then, whether the theory I have proposed has application beyond this particular historical instance—to the criminal justice system of the United States, for example, and to more recent times. In the next chapter, I will address this question, briefly identifying three areas of criminal justice that invite exploration in terms of anal themes: vagrancy law, penology, and juvenile justice. In addition, I will discuss American legal cases in which lawyers and judges describe defendants with the metaphor of filth.

CHAPTER 12

Stirring the Odorous Pile: Vicissitudes of the Metaphor in Britain and the United States

PERFECT ORDER AND PERFECT SILENCE: THE OBSESSIONAL MOTIF IN CRIMINAL JUSTICE

Vagrancy Law

Laws against vagrants criminalize a lifestyle that many people find aesthetically offensive, in part because of its association with filth. For example, a county court in New York State characterized vagrants as the "sordid individuals who infest our stations such as the dirty, disheveled, besotted characters whose state is but a step short of intoxication."[1] In a similar vein, a 1941 Supreme Court opinion describes vagrants as follows: "They avoid our cities and even our towns by crowding together, in the open country and in camps, under living conditions shocking both as to sanitation and social environment."[2]

Besides being actually grimy by the standards of the dominant culture, vagrants are associated with filth in a more profound way. In her classic study, *Purity and Danger,* anthropologist Mary Douglas defines dirt as "matter out of place." She elaborates: "Shoes are not dirty in themselves, but it is dirty to place them on the dining table; food is not dirty in itself, but it is dirty to leave cooking utensils in the bedroom, or food bespattered on clothing."[3]

Now vagabonds are, by definition, people who lead an unsettled existence. For instance, in one old English formulation, they are "all persons wandering abroad."[4] In Blackstone's more colorful description, they are "such as wake on the night, and sleep on the day, and haunt customable taverns, and ale houses, and routs about; and no man wot from wence they came, nor wither they go."[5] Modern American statutes likewise make wandering central to the offense of vagrancy, as we see in this definition of a night walker: "an idle or dissolute person who roams about at late or unusual hours and is unable to account for his presence."[6] Moreover, many modern vagrancy statutes use language such as "tramps," "gypsies," and "railers"[7]—all terms that harken back to the old British condemnation of "persons wandering abroad." Since vagabonds either have no place or are out of their place, by Douglas's definition they are dirt.

The idea that wandering bears an essential, not accidental, relationship to filth finds confirmation in the traditional figure of Satan. Called the "Prince of Darkness" and typically depicted as "black and filthy," Satan leads a wandering existence. As Daniel Defoe writes in *The History of the Devil:*

> Satan, being thus confined to a vagabond, wandering, unsettled condition, is without any certain abode; for though he has, in consequence of his angelic nature, a kind of empire in the liquid waste or air, yet this is certainly part of his punishment, that he is . . . without any fixed place, or space allowed him to rest the sole of his foot upon.[8]

As we saw in our examination of Botany Bay, so also in vagrancy—the metaphor of dirt leads naturally to the metaphor of contagious illness. Thus, in the traditional view, the vagrant is "the chrysalis of every species of criminal,"[9] and vagrancy statutes are designed to prevent the spread of "a parasitic disease."[10] As the New York Court of Appeals graphically articulated, the goal of vagrancy laws is to "prevent crime by disrupting and scattering the breeding spot."[11] This conception of vagrancy is particularly interesting in view of statistics showing little correlation between pauperism and serious criminality, between dirtiness and law-breaking.[12]

Because vagrancy is imagined as a contagious disease, the solution to this problem is conceived as segregation. More specifically, the goal of vagrancy laws, as evident today as it was in the sixteenth century, is to keep vagrants in their own place.[13] If they have drifted into other areas, they are banished from them to the districts where they "belong." Once returned to their place, presumably, they are no longer dirt.

Penology

A second episode of criminal justice that calls for analysis in terms of anal themes is the creation of the penitentiary in the late eighteenth and early nineteenth centuries. Before that era, prisons played a relatively minor role in punishment; they served mainly as holding places prior to execution, or, in the case of debtors' prisons, as places to keep people temporarily, until they paid their creditors. Prior to 1775, prisons were rarely used, as they are today, to punish for felonies.[14]

The earlier prisons differed from their successors in other ways as well, above all in the blurring of lines between dissimilar categories of people. Men and women, grownups and children, hardened criminals and more innocuous offenders, convicted felons and those awaiting trial—all were confined together. As an historian writing in the early eighteenth century described Newgate prison, it was "a confused Chaos without any distinction, a bottomless pit of violence, and a tower of Babel. . . . There is mingling the noble with the ignoble, the rich with the poor, the wise with the ignorant, and debtors with the worst of malefactors."[15] In addition, the very boundary between prisoners and nonprisoners was a much more fluid one than we are accustomed to today. As one student of the eighteenth century writes: "An easy familiarity existed between prisons and the world they so pungently distilled. Crowds of visitors sustained familial communication . . . and prisons, like Bedlam, were treated as holiday curiosities."[16]

When, in the eighteenth and nineteenth centuries, prison reformers in Europe and America pressed for a new system of punishment, revulsion against this indiscriminate mingling was a prominent theme. Thus, after an inspection tour of the Cook County Jail in 1869, the Chicago Board of Visitors observed: "The effects of herding together of old and young, innocent and guilty, convicts, suspected persons and witnesses, male and female, makes the jail a school of vice. In such an atmosphere, purity itself could not escape contamination." [17]

There are, to be sure, rational reasons for protesting such conditions, but there is also an obsessional-compulsive undercurrent to these protests. For the reformers were objecting to confusion, and confusion may lie at the heart of what we imagine as dirt. As Mary Douglas explains: "For us dirt is a kind of compendium category for all events which blur, smudge, contradict, or otherwise confuse accepted classifications." [18] In a similar vein, psychoanalyst Janine Chasseguet-Smirgel emphasizes that forbidden mixtures, mixtures that confound dissimilar things, are the essence of anality. The prototype of such chaotic mixtures is excrement, a homogeneous blend of substances that were originally distinct. In contrast to the Biblical world of division and separation stands this "universe of perversion." [19]

If one sign of the obsessional theme in prison reform is a revulsion from the indiscriminate mingling of the old-style prisons, another is the preoccupation with order and separation in the new prisons. This preoccupation can be seen in the following passage from the First Annual Report of the Boston Prison Discipline Society, written in 1826:

> At Auburn, we have a more beautiful example still, of what may be done by proper discipline, in a Prison well constructed. . . . The whole establishment, from the gate to the sewer, is *a specimen of neatness.* The unremitted industry, the entire subordination and subdued feeling of the convicts, has probably no parallel among an equal number of criminals. In their solitary cells they spend the night, with no other book than the Bible, and at sunrise they proceed, in military order, under the eye of the turnkeys, in solid columns, with the lock march, to their work-shops; then, in the same order, at the hour of breakfast, to the common hall, where they partake of their wholesome and frugal meal in silence. Not even a whisper is heard through the whole apartment. [20]

In a detail that brings to mind the French expression *la manie de précision,* the report goes on to describe how convicts were obliged to raise their right hands to obtain more food and their left hands to relinquish unwanted food. At the end of the day, the prisoners returned to their cells, where they ate supper and spent the evening and night in solitude.[21]

The system at Auburn was named "the silent system" because prisoners were allowed no verbal intercourse with each other at any time. Alexis de Tocqueville and Gustave de Beaumont, who visited Auburn in 1831, wrote this description of the prison's awful stillness: "[E]verything passes in the most profound silence, and nothing is heard in the whole prison but the steps of those who march, or sounds proceeding from the workshops." At night, the authors continued, "the silence within these vast walls . . . [was] that of death. . . . [W]e felt as if we traversed catacombs; there were a thousand living beings, and yet it was a desert solitude."[22]

Though isolated at night, prisoners under the Auburn plan were allowed to work together silently during the day. In a competing model known as the "separate" system, prisoners were kept apart both day and night. On occasions when they had to venture from their cells, the prisoners in the separate system wore dark hoods with only two holes cut for their eyes. By this means, they were prevented from recognizing and contaminating each other.[23] Here we see a fanatical striving after purity that implies, by its very fanaticism, an attraction to the opposing qualities of dirtiness and defilement.

To the nineteenth-century reformers, the silent and separate systems were sufficiently different to warrant a prolonged, often-heated debate over their respective merits: was it best to keep prisoners silent *and* separate both day and night, or only silent during the day and separate at night? An "epic struggle" over this question raged in American penological circles from 1800 to 1870.[24] Vitriolic attacks on one's opponents and flagrant misuse of statistics permeated the conflict, which even attracted the attention of distinguished European reformers and novelists.[25] To the twentieth-century interpreter, the very existence of this debate over two such similar systems may appear as yet another sign of the reformers' compulsiveness. For the controversy reflects a cognitive style that is typical of the obsessive-compulsive—a style characterized by an absorption in technical detail and a failure to notice what David Shapiro has called "the flavor or impact of things."[26]

As to impact, it is not surprising that these extraordinarily rigid systems of "perfect order and perfect silence"[27] led to a high incidence of insanity among the prisoners. For example, in the English prison of Pentonville, which followed the separate system, there were twenty times more cases of mental illness than in any other prison in the country.[28] That the reformers' preoccupation with order was not entirely rational can be seen in these results.[29]

Juvenile Justice

The assumption that criminality is fundamentally a problem of dirt and disorder, which must be corrected through various kinds of cleansing, neatening, and segregating measures, pervades nine-teenth-century juvenile justice as it does vagrancy law and adult penology. A thorough examination of juvenile justice is beyond the scope of this book; I wish only to intimate the obsessional motifs in two important "child-saving" institutions: the Houses of Refuge and the Orphan Train Movement.

Prior to the early nineteenth century, children were not pun-ished by confinement, but rather by a variety of other measures, including corporal punishment, apprenticeship, banishment from the community, and, in a few cases, capital punishment.[30] In the 1820s and the succeeding decades, many states established places of confinement for incorrigible and delinquent children; these institutions were called by such names as Houses of Refuge, Re-form Schools, and Houses of Reformation. Similar to the peniten-tiaries, the Houses of Refuge placed "discipline, routine, and cleanliness" at the core of their philosophy.[31] Also like the peni-tentiaries, these institutions exhibited an obsessional ethos in which extreme orderliness and cleanliness became ends in them-selves. For an illustration of this point, consider the following passage from August Aichhorn's 1925 classic, *Wayward Youth:*

The superintendent [of the Reform School] . . . once called my attention to wash basins that had been in use for twenty years. He was proud of the fact that they remained so long undamaged and still shone like new. In the dormitories the beds stood in a row, twenty-five on each side, like rows of soldiers, not an inch out of line. The covers were all folded at correct right angles and fell like a plumb-line. Everywhere was the same meticulous order.[32]

Besides orderliness with respect to objects, the Houses of Refuge also endeavored to inculcate orderliness with respect to time. This purpose comes through vividly in the following excerpt from a report of the New York Society of the Reformation of Juvenile Delinquents. The passage describes life in the New York House of Refuge in the early 1830s.

At sunrise, the children are warned, by the ringing of a bell, to rise from their beds. Each child makes his own bed, and steps forth, on a signal, into the Hall. They then proceed, in perfect order, to the Wash Room. Thence they are marched to parade in the yard, and undergo an examination as to their dress and cleanliness; after which, they attended morning prayer. The morning school then commences, where they are occupied in summer, until 7 o'clock. A short intermission is allowed, when the bell rings for breakfast; after which, they proceed to their respective workshops, where they labor until 12 o'clock, when they are called from work, and one hour allowed them for washing and eating their dinner. At one, they again commence work, and continue at it until five in the afternoon, when the labors of the day terminate. Half an hour is allowed for washing and eating their supper, and at half-past five, they are conducted to the school room, where they continue at their studies until 8 o'clock. Evening Prayer is performed by the superintendent; after which, the children are conducted to their dormitories, which they enter, and are locked up for the night, when perfect silence reigns throughout the establishment. The foregoing is the history of a single day, and will answer for every day in the year, except Sundays, with slight variations during stormy weather, and the short days in winter.[33]

In the last sentence of this remarkable report, we glimpse the authors' pride in their rigid time schedule, which varies so little, even during bad weather.

Attentiveness to time is, of course, a well-known obsessive-compulsive trait. Beyond observing a scrupulous punctuality, some obsessional neurotics display a great interest in all sorts of time-tables, and even organize their entire lives by detailed schedules.[34] In extreme cases, such persons become like "living machines."[35] But what exactly is the function of such orderliness in time? As Otto Fenichel explains: "The compulsion neurotic who is threatened by a rebellion of his . . . sensual and hostile demands feels protected as long as he behaves in an 'orderly' manner, especially concerning money and time."[36] Spontaneous behavior, then, represents danger—the danger that one will commit, or has committed, the sins that one fears.

For some obsessional neurotics, it is not enough that they themselves observe the prescribed system, but other persons are required to serve as "witnesses"; they too must follow the system, and thereby validate its demands.[37] The severity of the regimen in the Houses of Refuge can perhaps be understood in terms of this compulsive need for "witnesses" to a system of ordered time. If this explanation has merit, it follows that these reformatories were unconsciously designed to meet the psychological needs of the reformers as much as the needs of the confined children. Indeed, it is unlikely that delinquent children would improve under such orderly regimens when they had failed to meet far less rigorous standards in the world outside.[38]

Besides the Houses of Refuge, the nineteenth century witnessed the rise of another child-saving institution, the "placing out system," or Orphan Train Movement. One of its founders, Charles Loring Brace, criticized the Houses of Refuge as too controlling and prison-like for children;[39] yet, his movement too exhibited pronounced obsessional features. The goal of the Movement was to save children from lives of delinquency and crime by removing them from the city to the countryside—from what was conceived as a dirty, contaminated place to a place of supposed purity and order. Notice, for example, the images in the following passage from the 1857 Annual Report of the New York Children's Aid Society:

The poor vagabond boy, or the child whom misfortune has made wretched and homeless, goes to a quiet country home. . . . [T]he poor lad, remembering the dirty cellars, and the alleys piled with garbage and the filthy holes of the great city, wonders with delight at the gardens and lilacs and the green grass and the pure air of his new home.[40]

In addition to the New York Children's Aid Society, the Boston Children's Mission also transplanted city children to farm families for "moral disinfection."[41] Several thousand children per year were uprooted in this way between the mid-nineteenth century and 1929.

The Orphan Train Movement is now considered controversial and even, in some quarters, discredited.[42] Nevertheless, one of the driving assumptions behind the Movement remains embedded in our culture; to wit, the assumption that criminality is natural to the cities and alien to the suburbs and the country. That we associate criminality with cities is a commonplace, but this idea is usually thought to spring from the actual correlation between high crime rates and urban concentration. I suggest that the roots of the idea lie deeper, that criminality and cities are linked by their common association with filth. If this is so, then our nation's inability to fight crime effectively may stem partly from a belief that the affinity between crime and cities is deep-seated and inexorable.[43]

INTO THE DIRT, INTO THE SLIME: THE METAPHOR OF FILTH IN AMERICAN CASE LAW

Besides its manifestations in discreet areas and episodes of criminal justice, the anal metaphor runs through criminal trials generally. My research has turned up thirty-four American cases in which the prosecutor's characterization of the defendant as filth was an issue on appeal.[44] Ranging from 1885 to 1990, these cases show prosecutors calling defendants by such terms as "little scums," "slimy creature," "type of worm," and "skunk." Since not all cases are appealed, and since some prosecutors may suppress the impulse to use such language to avoid reversal, we can assume that these thirty-four cases represent only a fraction of the instances when the metaphor appeared in a prosecutor's mind.

Among the themes that appear in these cases, one of the most fascinating is the idea that law-enforcement personnel may, in the course of their duties, become defiled. Consider, for example, this language from the prosecutor's closing argument in *Peterson v. State:* "This is sale of heroin, sale of cocaine, and this is a case that was done in the only way it could be done by a police officer, trained, that had to go undercover, that had to go *down into the dirt, into the slime* with the pushers, deal with them at their level, and bring the case to court."[45] This case was reversed in part because of these evocative metaphors, but what is important for our purpose is the insight this passage gives into the prosecutor's mind—specifically, his conception of the police officer, Dante-like, descending into a filthy hell.

The risk of contamination from such a descent, which was only implicit in Peterson, was overtly stated in *United States v. Corona.* In this Fifth Circuit case, the prosecutor made the following observation about undercover agents of the Drug Enforcement Agency who had testified at trial: "[T]he agents are human beings and they're doing a dirty, nasty job, and they're associating daily with dirty, nasty people."[46] To justify the use of another government witness, a former co-defendant who had pleaded guilty before trial, the prosecutor remarked: "The [agents are] handling garbage, ladies and gentlemen, and there's an old saying, 'When you handle garbage your hands are going to stink.' "[47] Believing that criminals inevitably contaminate those they touch, this prosecutor would have reason to imitate Dickens's barrister Jaggers, washing his hands with scented soap after every foray into the criminal realm.

Like prosecutors, defense attorneys, too, sometimes see criminals through the lens of filth. For example, in language reminiscent of Magwitch's in *Great Expectations*, a defense attorney described the government witness against General Manuel Noriega as "the slimiest of eels."[48] In a similar vein, the Supreme Court of Delaware quoted the defense counsel as describing the state's witnesses, who had admitted to various felonies, as "scum" and "snakes."[49] In yet another example, in a New York case from the 1970s, the court censured the defense attorney for characterizing the prosecution witness, a man with a criminal record, as "the scum of the earth" and for closing his cross-examination with the words, "I think I have to throw up."[50] Of course, these attorneys may only be using the metaphor of filth as rhetorical hyperbole— to evoke strong reactions from the judge or jury. Nevertheless, in view of the risk that such imagery may lead to censure, it seems likely that the language also reflects the speakers' genuine feelings about criminals.

Let us turn now to the way judges regard the metaphor comparing criminals to filth. At times, judges acknowledge the metaphor's power, for in six of the cases in which the prosecutor compared the criminal to filth, the appellate court reversed in part on this basis.[51] Moreover, in another case, the appellate judge himself introduced the metaphor to explain why the defendant had not received a fair trial. Here, the prosecutor had exceeded the legitimate bounds of cross-examination, questioning defense witnesses about the defendant's involvement in eighteen different kinds of egregious misconduct—from coercing women into prostitution to attempting to incite arson. In reversing the conviction of conspiracy to commit arson, the judge stated: "[T]he jury must indeed have thought this defendant to be a slimy gutter rat."[52]

Significantly, in seeking to explain why the prosecutor's conduct was prejudicial, the judge could find no better language than a metaphor of filth. Like Captain Hook, he chose the image of the rat, a creature that dwells in sewers and ravenously eats garbage, a creature that is "filth incarnate."[53] Whereas in this case and in the others that were reversed, the court recognized the metaphor's evocative power, more typically, the court merely criticized the prosecutor, while holding that the metaphorical language was nonprejudicial error.

Four of the cases are especially interesting. In these, the court neither reversed on the basis of the metaphor nor treated the metaphor as nonprejudicial error; rather, it held that the metaphor

was, for one reason or another, appropriate.[54] For instance, in a
1951 Oklahoma case, the court stated, "We agree with the prosecutor that an adult who would commit the acts done by the
defendant shows that he is 'lowdown, degenerate, and filthy.' "[55]
Or again, in a 1966 case concerning the murder of a ten-year-old
girl, the Supreme Court of Illinois declared that the prosecutor's
description of the defendant as a "slimy beast" with morals "like a
snake" was "a legitimate reply to the defense argument concerning
normality."[56]

And yet again, in a 1986 case before the United States Army
Court of Military Review, the court upheld a conviction where the
prosecutor had referred to the defendant as a "slavering animal"
and "degenerate scum." According to the court, these metaphors
did not prejudice the defendant's rights, because they were "based
on evidence found in the record" and on "reasonable inferences
drawn from that evidence."[57]

What is striking about all the cases in this group is the judges'
failure to appreciate the difference between metaphors, with their
special power, and the more literal approximations of reality. It is
as if, for these judges, criminals *were* slime. Yet, as philosopher
Owen Barfield reminds us, "[T]he aptness of a metaphor to mis-
lead varies inversely with the extent to which it continues to be
felt and understood as a metaphor and is not taken in a confused
way semiliterally."[58]

Besides the cases in which judges agreed with prosecutors who
described criminals as filth, judges themselves have sometimes
employed the metaphor uncritically in their opinions. For example, in the 1920s, a judge on the Supreme Court of Ohio referred
to the "slimy . . . trail of the man who committed the crime."[59] In
a more elaborate illustration from the 1970s, a district court judge
had been asked to decide whether a prisoner was entitled to more
than two showers a week. In a footnote to his opinion, the judge
wrote: "[T]his court has too much work to do to call for additional
pleadings, or *stir the odorous pile* this and other cases of this sort
represent."[60] Ostensibly objecting to the waste of his time that
such cases entailed, the judge vented his disgust by characterizing
prisoners' concerns as smelly. In another footnote, the same judge

asked, "Is the next opinion going to require the district judge to say how many times a person should brush his teeth, go to the bathroom, wipe his nose, comb his hair, or scratch?"[61] Here the judge went out of his way to remind the reader of prisoners' bodily functions; by his choice of examples, he made one think of prisoners eliminating urine and feces, and oozing with mucous and sweat.

Judges have characterized criminals as filthy by implication as well, typically in cases focusing on the improper behavior of government agents. Thus, in *United States v. Valencia*, the government had used a lawyer's secretary as an informant to obtain evidence of the lawyer's involvement in a criminal conspiracy with his clients. Reluctantly dismissing the charges against the lawyer and three co-defendants, the district court refused to allow "the law in its majesty . . . to be equally slimy."[62] Justice Frankfurter used similar language to express a similar admonition in his dissenting opinion in *On Lee v. United States*. He wrote that criminal prosecution "should not be deemed to be a dirty game in which 'the dirty business' of criminals is outwitted by 'the dirty business' of law officers."[63] An unusual twist on the theme of contamination by criminals appears in *Oakland v. Detroit*. In this case several counties had brought suit under federal antitrust laws and RICO against the City of Detroit in its capacity as a provider of sewage services. Dismissing the complaints for lack of standing, the district court granted summary judgment for the defendants. The Court of Appeals reversed. In a footnote to its opinion, the Court of Appeals wrote as follows: "Given the nature of their crimes and the elements in which these dabblers in sludge and scum worked, Shakespeare could almost have been speaking for the convicted defendants when he wrote . . .

> And almost thence my nature is subdu'd
> to what it works in, like the dyer's
> hand."[64]

By working in actual filth, the court suggested, people become metaphorically filthy, or criminal.

Even if the metaphor of filth means only what it says, it can have damaging effects on the criminal justice system, affecting both the process and the result, the appearance of fairness and actual fairness. Beyond this, when the metaphor of filth functions to defend against a deep-seated, illicit attraction to criminals, undesirable consequences follow. First, the attorney or judge's anticriminal behavior will tend to be exaggerated and undiscriminating. Second, since repression is never complete, there will be occasional expressions of the other side of the conflict—admiration and attraction to the criminal—the so-called "breakthrough of the repressed." We cannot predict exactly what outward form the inner conflict will take, but we can say this: when an attorney uses criminals to maintain his own intrapsychic equilibrium, his behavior toward criminals will often be inappropriate, because he is responding to internal as well as external forces.

With these points I come to the end of the argument I have developed through literary works, legal history, and American case law, and it is time now to reflect on where this journey has brought us.

Conclusion to Part Three: Metaphor Understood

In these pages I have endeavored to explore the metaphor likening the criminal to filth—to penetrate its origins and unravel its vicissitudes in criminal justice policy. In the course of this exploration, I have sometimes treated the metaphor of filth as a cause, at other times as a symptom of a deeper dynamic. Viewing it as a cause, I have argued that the metaphor of filth has functioned as a powerful determinant of criminal justice policies. In particular, it has led to a view of criminals as contaminated and contagious. This perspective, in turn, has promoted an emphasis on various pollution-avoidance measures, such as segregation and banishment of the criminal. In addition, when combined with the measure-for-measure theory of punishment, the metaphor has fostered a tendency to immerse criminals in dark, dirty, fetid places.

On a deeper level, I have examined the metaphor of filth as a symptom of noncriminals' unconscious ambivalence, or simultaneous love and hate, toward criminals. Viewed in this way, the metaphor serves to explain the hyperbolic quality of some criminal justice practices; for instance, the masks that prisoners were required to wear in the separate system, the ousting of Alexander Maconochie, when he rehabilitated the most hardened offenders, and the transportation of convicts to a little-known place on the far side of the globe. Such practices, which some historians have looked upon as "bizarre" or "reckless," become readily comprehensible in light of the metaphor of filth and the theory of intrapsychic conflict. For the exaggerated nature of these practices reflects the noncriminals' struggle with powerful feelings in themselves—feelings of attraction to, and identification with, criminals. As we have seen, these feelings have sometimes emerged transparently, as in the crowds that cheered the condemned criminals who rode to Tyburn tree in eighteenth-century England. More often, these feelings are barred from consciousness, finding expression only in excessive condemnation and shunning of criminals, to prevent succumbing to their allure. It would seem then, that in the course of our efforts to understand the metaphor likening the *criminal* to filth, we have arrived at a new metaphor— one that likens the criminal justice *system* to the expression of noncriminals' inner conflict over criminals.

This perspective, I have said, can enhance our understanding of past and present criminal justice policies, but can it do more? Can this model go beyond explanation to evaluation and prescription? It is at this juncture—where a theory is obliged to address practical and future-oriented concerns—that efforts to apply psychoanalysis to law encounter their greatest difficulty. For whereas law is a system designed to transform gray into black and white,[1] psychoanalysis is a system designed to transform black and white into gray. And a discipline that yields black-and-white results is better suited to offer unequivocal proposals for action than a discipline that focuses on complex idiosyncratic meanings.

To make this point more compelling, let us consider what options might be available to us, were we to try to squeeze blood from the stone—to make our psychoanalytic model yield normative judgments and practical solutions. If we were to take such an approach to our subject, our reasoning might go something like this: the metaphor of filth, like all metaphors, abstracts from reality and, in so doing, obfuscates some aspects of its subject, while highlighting others. For example, the equation of the criminal and filth tends to hide the criminal's humanity while encouraging us to see the criminal as an object. Moreover, the metaphor invites a particular emotional response to the criminal, the same one we consciously feel toward slime: disgust.

Having judged the metaphor to be a problem, we might proceed to consider appropriate solutions. For instance, we might try to abolish the metaphor of filth and supplant it with another, such as the criminal as "an unfortunate one,"[2] or "one who made a mistake."[3] But this solution seems utopian, for several reasons. First, unlike other figures of speech such as "standing," "ripeness," and "fruit of the poisonous tree," the metaphor equating the criminal with filth has never been incorporated into legal doctrine. Since it has not been adopted by law, the metaphor of filth cannot be supplanted by law. In addition, the metaphor is extraordinarily pervasive and deepseated. As we have seen, it goes back millennia, traversing cultures and continents in a way that suggests an archetypal symbol. Besides, the metaphor of filth seems uniquely suited to reflect our emotional stance toward the criminal—our mingled loathing and admiration, our repudiation and attraction.

If it is not possible to supplant this metaphor with another, might we dispense with metaphors altogether when talking about criminals? Upon reflection, this solution too must be rejected, for virtually all our words are metaphors, or originate in metaphors. We are left, as C. S. Lewis notes, with only one option: "Either literalness, or else metaphor understood: one or other of these we must have; the third alternative is nonsense. But literalness we cannot have."[4] To many lawyers, "metaphor understood" will seem a poor solution, or no solution at all, but I believe, as Socrates did, that there is no voluntary evil, only ignorance.[5] It follows that understanding automatically leads to change; more exactly, understanding, in itself, *is* change.

Conclusion: The Romanticization of Criminals and the Defense against Despair

> The mass of men lead lives of quiet desperation.
> —Henry David Thoreau

> We tell ourselves stories in order to live.
> —Joan Didion

In the essays that form the core of this book, I have explored three central paradoxes of criminal justice: beloved prisons, romantic outlaws, and a metaphor that renders criminals as attractive filth. In this final chapter, I will discuss themes present in all three essays, themes that we—like travelers looking back over the country we have crossed—are only now in a position to survey.

A pervasive theme, perhaps the most general one, is that of complexity: the highly differentiated and paradoxical nature of our feelings about crime and punishment. More specifically, I have tried to show that the criminal justice system, far from being a simple, straightforward expression of our antipathy for crime and criminals, is in fact deeply psychologically rooted and based upon conflicting feelings of attraction and repulsion, love and hatred. In the American criminal justice system at the present time, one side of this ambivalence is on the rise. The increased use of capital punishment, the rage of prison construction, and such policies as "Three Strikes and You're Out"—all express a conscious fear and hatred of criminals and a desire to restrain lawbreakers and wreak vengeance upon them. But this book has attempted to highlight the dialectical underside of our ambivalence: the romantic allure of both criminals and their prison homes.

What is the origin of this strange attraction to the very people and places we would expect to abhor? On one level, the intricate, many-faceted character of our feelings toward criminals stems from our inability to apprehend reality directly. As Juliet Mitchell has written, we "acquire" reality, and do so in a process heavily mediated by our early-life experiences and unconscious mental processes.[1] That our feelings toward criminals must be complex is inevitable on this account, though not on this account alone.

For besides the mediating process through which "events" become "experience," there is an additional reason why the law, crime, and punishment tend to evoke complicated responses. As we have seen, the law, which enjoys authority over the citizen, represents the parent, who enjoys authority over the child. Thus, the law inherits powerful feelings of love and hatred that were directed toward the parent in early life. More particularly, the law stands for both father and mother. Insofar as it manifests itself as an infallible judge or an agent of punishment, the law resonates with the archetypal father. When it finds expression as a prison, on the other hand, the law evokes the archetypal mother, the great container who nurtures and holds.

If the law is the parent, then the criminal is the child. More exactly, the criminal is the *perpetual* child that we all, at times, yearn to be. It seems strange at first that criminals, who are thought of as guilty, should be equated with children, who are imagined as the most innocent of beings. Yet we have seen numerous examples of imprisoned lawbreakers who conceive of themselves as dependent children enveloped in a protective womb. Moreover, they experience this womb as timeless, evoking the child's happy obliviousness to the passage of the years.

From the perspective of the noncriminal, as well, the criminals' allure flows partly from their childlike qualities—their "charming" unscrupulousness, their refusal to accept responsibility, and their embodiment of freedom. Criminals are, of course, free in their refusal to abide by the laws that other people obey, whereas children symbolize freedom in their incarnation of limitless potential. As Friedrich Schiller has written, it is this quality of the child that fascinates adults:

We are moved in the presence of childhood, but it is not because from the height of our strength and of our perfection we drop a look of pity on it; it is, on the contrary, because from the depths of our impotence . . . we raise our eyes to the child's determinableness and pure innocence. . . . In the child all is disposition and destination; in us all is in the state of a completed, finished thing, and the completion always remains infinitely below the destination. . . . This is the reason why . . . the child will always be a sacred thing."[2]

As this passage suggests, we romanticize children, endowing them with a greatness we no longer possess, and viewing them as exotic creatures who "cometh from afar."

Similar to the children with whom they are linked, criminals likewise are viewed as glamorous and romantic figures. Not only are they associated with the exotic (as we saw, for instance, in *The Great Gatsby* and *Kidnapped*), but also they are connected with a view of life as intense and exalted, with a romantic "denial of the present" and a "rejection of the world-as-it-is."[3] This theme pervades the prison memoirs we examined in "Cradled on the Sea." Thus, Nerzhin, the inmate in *The First Circle*, expressed his fear of wallowing in daily living with the Russian proverb: "It's not the sea that drowns you; it's the puddle." Penal confinement, Nerzhin reflected, was the sea, the place where he had avoided immersion in the mundane and trivial, where he had been able to learn "about people and events about which he could learn nowhere else on earth." In another romantic appraisal of penal confinement, Eugenia Ginsburg declared: "There are no more fervent friendships than those made in prison."

Just as these prisoners invest their prisons with a romantic aura, so also society endows criminals with a passion and intensity that enhance life's meaning. One thinks, for instance, of Martin Dysart, the psychiatrist in *Equus* who poignantly expressed his envy of Alan Strang, the boy who had stabbed horses, putting out their eyes. While recognizing that the boy had been dangerous, and might be again, Dysart could not help but contrast his own "shrunken," "pallid," and "provincial" life with the passionate existence that Alan's crime reflected. In another example, Marlow, in

Heart of Darkness, admired the criminal Kurtz, notwithstanding that the man had committed "abominable terrors," for Kurtz at least had a vision, in contrast to the ordinary citizens of Brussels with their "insignificant and silly dreams."

If criminals, who defy the law, are "romance-empurpled,"[4] larger-than-life figures, it follows that lawyers, who serve the law, are romance*less* figures, prosaic and dull. In this vein, the English essayist Charles Lamb observed dubiously: "Lawyers, I suppose, were children once."[5] Distant from childhood, lawyers are portrayed as uncomfortable with lifelong yearnings. For example, in *Great Expectations*, when Pip tries to tell his guardian how he had always longed for an education, Jaggers cuts him off with the words: "Never mind what you have always longed for, Mr. Pip, . . . keep to the record. If you long for it now, that's enough."[6]

Although in theory the law is pedantic and dull, this dullness is partly a defense; in practice, the law is often driven by the very romanticism it claims to despise. For example, in Part Three of this book we saw how a fascination with criminals motivated seemingly straightforward policies of criminal justice—policies emphasizing order, routine, and segregation of the "contaminated" criminal from the "uncontaminated" law-abiding citizen. Nor did the romantic roots of these policies remain submerged; rather they surfaced in the legal institution of banishment, which featured the criminal as the protagonist of an exotic drama, the Fall.

What is the function of romanticizing criminals and their place of punishment? Romanticism serves to ward off the various narcissistic wounds to which our flesh is heir—the fear of leading prosaic, meaningless lives and the pain of recognizing our ultimate solitude and our mortal condition. A scene from a work we have examined in another context beautifully illustrates the defensive function of romancing the criminal. I refer to the scene in *The Playboy of the Western World* where Pegeen Mike and the other villagers have just learned that Christy has not, after all, killed his father. Pegeen speaks scornfully to Christy: "And it's lies you told, letting on you had him slitted, and you nothing at all."

In ceasing to be a patricide, Christy has become, not an ordinary, decent citizen, but "nothing at all." Pegeen's language reflects the narcissistic premise that without greatness, one is nothing. In the dreams of our youth, we aspire to greatness; we demand that life give us everything. But as time goes on, we must relinquish such expectations; in the end, in death, we face the relinquishment of everything.[7] With Wordsworth, we must ask: "Where is it now, the glory and the dream?"[8] As I discussed in "A Strange Liking," we never completely accept these losses. Rather, we defend against awareness of our limited, mortal state by imagining ourselves as "extraordinary" and "great," or by identifying with those we conceive of as having these qualities. In the construction of such defenses, criminals, we have seen, play a special role. Because they ignore the limits and moral compunctions that bind ordinary people, they are easily assimilated to the category of greatness.

And so Christy, as a glamorous patricide, invested the villagers' drab lives with excitement and meaning. When it turns out that he has not, in fact, killed his father, the villagers feel diminished by his loss of criminal stature. Reflecting the collective disappointment, Pegeen Mike says ruefully: "And to think of the coaxing glory we had given him."

For my final example, I turn to the classic children's book *A Little Princess*, by Frances Hodgson Burnett. Like *The Playboy of the Western World*, this story shows the defensive use of the criminal to participate in glory and assuage feelings of powerlessness. In addition, it depicts a variation on our theme: the noncriminal who, on the verge of hopelessness, gratefully embraces the status of prisoner. Near the beginning of the book, Sara Crewe, a pupil at Miss Minchin's London School, is banished to the garret and forced to work as a servant after her father dies penniless. In the following scene, Sara's friend Ermengarde visits Sara in her cold and cheerless abode:

> Ermengarde looked around the attic with a rather fearsome curiosity.
> "Sara," she said, "do you think you can bear living here?" Sara looked round also.

"If I pretend it's quite different, I can," she answered. "Or if I pretend it is a place in a story."

She spoke slowly. Her imagination was beginning to work for her. It had not worked for her at all since her troubles had come upon her. She had felt as if it had been stunned.

"Other people have lived in worse places. Think of the Count of Monte Cristo in the dungeons of the Chateau d'If. And think of the people in the Bastille!"

"The Bastille," half whispered Ermengarde, watching her and beginning to be fascinated. . . .

A well-known glow came into Sara's eyes.

"Yes," she said, hugging her knees. "That will be a good place to pretend about. I am a prisoner in the Bastille. I have been here for years and years; and everybody has forgotten about me. Miss Minchin is the jailer—and Becky"—a sudden light adding itself to the glow in her eyes—"Becky is the prisoner in the next cell." She turned to Ermengarde, looking quite like the old Sara.

"I shall pretend that," she said, "and it will be a great comfort."[9]

Like Sara, like the villagers, we too use criminals and prisons to exalt our lives, to comfort ourselves in the face of our finitude, to defend against despair. This paradox, of course, is not the whole story; it is only one strand of a mingled yarn, the silver lining of a sable cloud.

Appendix

AMERICAN CASES WHERE PROSECUTOR DESCRIBED
DEFENDANT, DEFENDANT'S WITNESS, OR
DEFENDANT'S ACTS OR MILIEU WITH A METAPHOR
OF FILTH

1. Filthy, Filth

U.S. v. Lowenberg, 853 F.2d 295, 302 (5th Cir. 1988) ("filthy")
State v. Comer, 799 P.2d 333, 346 (Ariz. 1990) ("filth")
People v. McMahon, 254 P.2d 903, 906 (Cal. App. 1953) ("filthy")
People v. Stiff, 542 N.E.2d 392, 395 (Ill. App. 1 Dist. 1989) ("dirty,
   filthy . . . needs")
State v. Connors, 76 S. 611, 612 (La. 1917) ("filthy hides")
Williams v. State, 226 P.2d 989, 997 (Okla. Crim. App. 1951) ("filthy")

2. Slime, Slimy

U.S. v. Moran, 194 F.2d 623, 625 (2d Cir. 1952) ("slimy underworld")
Volkmor v. United States, 13 F.2d 594, 595 (6th Cir. 1926) ("skunk,"
   "slimy crow")
Rogers v. State, 157 So.2d 13, 17 (Ala. 1963) ("slimy crow")
Biondo v. State, 533 So.2d 910, 911 (Fla. App. 1988) ("slime")
People v. Myers, 220 N.E.2d 297, 311 (Ill. 1966) ("slimy beast," "like a
   snake")
Commonwealth v. Cicere, 128 A. 446, 447 (Pa. 1925) ("slimy creature")

3. Scum, Scumbag

Lindsey v. Smith, 820 F.2d 1137, 1155 (11th Cir. 1987) ("scum," "de-
   generate scum")
People v. Apalatequi, 147 Cal. Rptr. 473, 474 (Cal. App. 1978) ("scum")
People v. Nightengale, 523 N.E.2d 136, 141 (Ill. App. 1 Dist. 1988)
   ("scum")
Ferguson v. Commonwealth, 512 S.W.2d 501, 504 (Ky 1974) ("two little
   scums")
State v. Burge, 515 S.2d 494, 505 (Ct. App. La. 1987) ("scum")

People v. Guenther, 469 N.W.2d 59, 65 (Mich. App. 1991) ("scum")

Monk v. State, 532 So.2d 592, 601 (Miss. 1988) ("scum")

Ohio v. Watkins, No. 46144, slip. op. at 11 (Ohio Ct. App. Nov. 23, 1983) ("scum and filth")

State v. Earich, No. 80–C-54, slip. op. at 14 (Ohio Ct. App. Nov. 19, 1981) ("scum")

Duque v. State, 498 So.2d 1334, 1337 (Fla. App. 2 Dist. 1986) ("scumbag")

4. Dirty, Dirt

U.S. v. Tisdale, 817 F.2d 1552, 1555 (11th Cir. 1987) ("dirty")

U.S. v. Fowler, 608 F.2d 2, 9 (D.C. Cir. 1979) (prosecutor characterized offenses charged against defendants as "dirty")

U.S. v. Crane, 445 F.2d 509, 520 (5th Cir. 1971) ("dirty work")

Peterson v. State, 376 So.2d 1230, 1231 (Fla. App. 1979) ("into the dirt, into the slime")

People v. Buckner, 293 N.E.2d 622, 623 (Ill. App. 1 Dist. 1973) ("snake," "dirty, rotten")

Anderson v. State, 4 N.E. 63, 67 (Ind. 1885) ("dirty")

State v. Young, 12 S.W. 879, 883 (Mo. 1890) ("dirty")

Hathcox v. State, 230 P.2d 927, 937 (Okla. Crim. App. 1951) ("dirty rats," "three rats")

Brito v. State, 459 S.W.2d 834, 836 (Tex. Crim. App. 1970) ("dirty")

5. Worm

U.S. v. Walker, 190 F.2d 481, 484 (2d Cir. 1951) ("type of worm")

State v. Green, 432 N.W.2d 547, 550 (Neb. 1988) (defendant and her sister, a defendant in another trial, described as "two worms")

6. Viruses

U.S. v. Wolfson, 322 F. Supp. 798, 825 (D. Del. 1971) ("viruses," "germs")

Notes

NOTES TO THE INTRODUCTION

1. Morton Sobell, *On Doing Time* (New York: Charles Scribner's Sons, 1974), 502.

2. Erica Wallach, *Light at Midnight* (Garden City, N.Y.: Doubleday, 1967), 285.

3. Northrop Frye, *The Great Code: The Bible and Literature* (New York: Harcourt Brace Jovanovich, 1982), xviii.

4. Walter Scott, *Rob Roy* (Boston: Houghton Mifflin, 1923), 104.

NOTES TO CHAPTER I

1. Aleksandr Solzhenitsyn, *The Cancer Ward*, trans. Rebecca Frank (New York: Dial Press, 1968), 576–77 (emphasis added).

2. Ibid., 562.

3. James Blake, *The Joint* (Garden City, N.Y.: Doubleday, 1971), 326 (emphasis added).

4. Ibid., 72–73.

5. See, e.g., Eugenia Ginzburg, *Journey into the Whirlwind*, trans. Paul Stevenson and Max Hayward (New York: Harcourt, Brace and World, 1967); Malcolm Braly, *False Starts: A Memoir of San Quentin and Other Prisons* (Boston: Little, Brown, 1976), 251. Eldridge Cleaver also perceived the similarity between prisons and monasteries, but denied the allure of either. See Eldridge Cleaver, *Soul on Ice* (New York: Dell, 1968), 32.

6. Blake, *The Joint*, 330 (emphasis added).

7. Ibid., 147. For the rock as a symbol of the eternal, see M. L. von Franz, "The Process of Individuation," in *Man and His Symbols*, ed. Carl Jung (Garden City, N.Y.: Doubleday, 1964), 209 ("man's innermost center is in a strange and special way akin to it. . . . In this sense the stone symbolizes what is perhaps the simplest and deepest experience—the experience of something eternal").

8. William Shakespeare, *The Tragedy of King Lear: The Folio Text*, 5.3.8–19 (emphasis added).

9. Aleksandr Solzhenitsyn, *The First Circle*, trans. Thomas P. Whitney (New York: Bantam Books, 1969), 340 (emphasis added).

10. Ibid., 339–40.

11. Ibid., 181 (emphasis in original).

12. Stendhal, *The Charterhouse of Parma*, trans. C. K. Scott Moncrieff (New York: Boni and Liveright), 2:86.

13. Ibid., 2:87.

14. Ibid., 2:88.

15. Ibid. For a discussion of the happy prison theme in Stendhal and other nineteenth-century French writers, see Victor Brombert, *The Romantic Prison: The French Tradition* (Princeton, N.J.: Princeton University Press, 1978), 62–87. In this fascinating book, Brombert explores a number of themes, focusing on the relationship between physical confinement and artistic freedom. In the concluding pages, however, he suggests that the Holocaust and the Soviet penal camps have changed the way we imagine prison, relegating the nineteenth-century motif to the "status of a reactionary anachronism." He observes that the Romantics' "dream of a happy prison has become hard to entertain in a world of penal colonies and extermination camps, in a world which makes us fear that somehow even our suffering can no longer be our refuge."

Like Brombert, linguist Joseph Shipley assumes that the paradoxical image of prison as a refuge and a place of freedom has become difficult to maintain in the context of contemporary prison conditions. In discussing *kagh*, the Indo-European root of the word *jail*, Shipley quotes Richard Lovelace's famous poem "To Althea, from prison" (1642), which reads as follows:

> Stone walls do not a prison make,
> Nor iron bars a cage;
> Minds innocent and quiet take
> That for an hermitage,
> If I have freedom in my love
> And in my soul am free,
> Angels alone, that soar above,
> Enjoy such liberty.

Shipley comments: "There is little room for such feelings in the overcrowded prisons of today." Joseph Shipley, *The Origins of English Words: A Discursive Dictionary of Indo-European Roots* (Baltimore: Johns Hopkins University Press, 1984), 153. By contrast, the present study demonstrates that the psychological sources of the attraction to prison are deeper than either Brombert or Shipley perceived, and that, in consequence, the theme of the happy prison has withstood the realities of the twentieth century's particularly nightmarish forms of incarceration.

16. Aleksandr Solzhenitsyn, *One Day in the Life of Ivan Denisovich*, trans. Ronald Hingley and Max Hayward (New York: Bantam Books, 1963), 198 (emphasis added).

17. Ibid., 199.

18. Graham Greene, *The Power and the Glory* (New York: Viking Press, 1970), 206 (emphasis added).

19. Solzhenitsyn, *The First Circle*, 38.

20. Ibid.

21. Leo Tolstoy, *War and Peace*, trans. Louise and Alymer Maude (New York: W. W. Norton, 1966), 1176.

22. Samuel Melville, *Letters from Attica* (New York: Morrow, 1972), 101.

23. Malcolm X and Alex Haley, *The Autobiography of Malcolm X* (New York: Ballantine Books, 1965), 180. Compare the remarks of an anonymous prisoner quoted in Jaakov Kohn, "Time: Two Interviews," in *Getting Busted: Personal Experiences of Arrest, Trial, and Prison*, ed. Ross Firestone (N.p.: Douglas Book Corp., 1970), 249–50.

> The situation I got myself into [in prison] was just perfect for me. For a
> long time prior to getting busted, I lived a very hectic life. Running
> around like crazy trying to make a lot of money and do a lot of things. . . .
> What I needed and what I always was aware of needing was some literary
> enrichment.
>   . . . After coming to Auburn, I started right from the beginning and
> went through the Myths, the Greek Classics and everything else from Cervantes to Dostoevsky, Tolstoi, and Balzac.

For other illustrations of the theme of prison as an academy, see Brendan Behan, *Borstal Boy* (Boston: David Godine, 1959); Thomas Gaddis, *Birdman of Alcatraz: The Story of Robert Stroud* (New York: Random House, 1955); Wallach, *Light at Midnight*, 196–97, 396; Michael Kroll, "Counsel Behind Bars," *California Lawyer* (June 1987): 34.

24. Solzhenitsyn, *The First Circle*, 340.

25. Ginzburg, *Journey into the Whirlwind*, 99.

26. Vera Figner, *Memoirs of a Revolutionist* (New York: Greenwood Press, 1968), 302.

27. Ibid., 303.

28. Solzhenitsyn, *The First Circle*, 340.

29. Ibid., 372 (emphasis added).

30. See Julian Beck, "Thoughts on the Theater from Jail: Three Letters to a Friend," in *Getting Busted*, 319.

31. Blake, *The Joint*, 209.

32. Eugenia Ginzburg, *Within the Whirlwind*, trans. Ian Boland (New York: Harcourt Brace Jovanovich, 1981), 156–57 (emphasis in original).

33. Cf. Semyon Gluzman, "Fear of Freedom: Psychological Decompensation or Existentialist Phenomenon," *American Journal of Psychiatry* 139 (1982): 57 (Soviet psychiatrist arguing that political prisoners who fear freedom are healthy in that they are experiencing specific, realistic fears).

34. Robert Lane, *Political Ideology: Why the American Common Man Believes What He Does* (New York: Free Press, 1962), 27 (emphasis added).

35. Ibid. (quoting Freud, "Beyond the Pleasure Principle," in *The Standard Edition of the Complete Psychological Works of Sigmund Freud* [London: The Hogarth Press and the Institute of Psycho-analysis], 18: 53).

36. Fyodor Dostoevsky, *Notes from a Dead House*, trans. L. Navrozov and Y. Guralsky (Moscow: Foreign Languages Publishing House, 1950), 63.

37. Immediately following the passage I have quoted, Dostoevsky writes: "It may be that his life before was miserable, that he never ate his fill and was compelled to work for his master from morn till night, while the work in the convict prison is easier, there's enough bread, and better bread than he ever hoped to eat, let alone meat on holidays." Ibid.

38. Wallach, *Light at Midnight*, 207. In our own society, the Depression-era movie *Modern Times* depicts Charlie Chaplin preferring life in jail to the difficulties of keeping a job outside. One inter-title describes Chaplin as "[h]appy in his comfortable cell." When the sheriff tells him, "Well, you're a free man," Chaplin objects, "Can't I stay a little longer? I'm so happy here." After his release, Chaplin is characterized as "[d]etermined to go back to jail." In an effort to get arrested he buys more food than he can pay for. The police do arrest him; however, Chaplin's new acquaintance, Paulette, pushes him out of the van and back to the hardships of life outside prison. *Modern Times*, prod. Charles Chaplin, United Artists, 1936.

39. See Nadezhda Mandelstam, *Hope against Hope: A Memoir*, trans. Max Hayward (New York: Atheneum, 1975), 88, 334, and passim.

40. Ruo-Wang Bao and Rudolph Chelminski, *Prisoner of Mao* (New York: Coward McCann and Geoghegan, 1973), 12 (emphasis added). Cf. Gluzman, "Fear of Freedom: Psychological Decompensation or Existentialist Phenomenon," *American Journal of Psychiatry* 139 (1982): 61 ("A paradoxical conclusion can be reached: the transition from life in the prison to 'free' life in the U.S.S.R. is characterized by a substantial reduction of the degree of internal freedom and of the possibilities of defending one's dignity from encroachment by social institutions").

41. Robert Brain, *Friends and Lovers* (New York: Basic Books, 1976), 256–60.

42. Ibid., 257.

43. See Edith Jacobson, "Observations on the Psychological Effect of Imprisonment on Female Political Prisoners," *Searchlights on Delinquency*, ed. Kurt Eissler (New York: International Universities Press, 1949), 341. Dr. Jacobson made all of her observations between 1935 and 1938 during her confinement in a Nazi State Penitentiary. By contrast with the concentration camps, the City and State Prisons at that time were not under the control of the Gestapo. Ibid., 342.

44. Ibid., 359, 363.

45. Ibid., 359.

46. Ibid., 359–60.

47. See ibid.

48. Ibid., 365.

49. Robert J. Lifton, *Thought Reform and the Psychology of Totalism* (New York: W. W. Norton, 1969), 238.

50. Ibid., 238–39.

51. See Otto Kernberg, *Borderline Conditions and Pathological Narcissism* (New York: Aronson, 1975), 12.

52. Otto Fenichel, *The Psychoanalytic Theory of Neurosis* (New York: W. W. Norton, 1945), 368.

53. See ibid., 369.

54. Blake, *The Joint*, 60 (emphasis added).

55. Ibid., 137 (emphasis added).

56. Ibid., 132.

57. Ibid., 135.

58. Consider, for example, the following description of a love affair he has in prison: "But the beauty part is the shared laughter, I've never known that in a relationship before, it's novel and precious to me." Ibid., 195. See also ibid., 197.

59. Brian Moore, review of *Brendan*, by Ulick O'Connor, *New York Times Book Review*, 25 April 1971, 35.

60. Ibid.

61. Françoise D'Eaubonne, "Jean Genet, Or, The Inclement Thief," in *Genet: A Collection of Critical Essays*, ed. Peter Brooks and Joseph Halpern (Englewood Cliffs, N.J.: Prentice Hall, 1979), 65–66.

62. Roberto Suro, "A Model and a Murder: Italy's High Life on Trial," *New York Times*, 16 June 1986, sec. A, p. 6.

63. Carol Kirschenbaum, "Women: The New White-Collar Criminals," *Glamour* 306 (March 1987): 359.

NOTES TO CHAPTER 2

1. Blake, *The Joint*, 148.

2. Ibid., 51.

3. Diana Christina and Pat Carlen, "Christina: In Her Own Time," in *Criminal Women*, ed. Pat Carlen (Cambridge, England: Polity Press, 1985), 88.

4. Ibid., 100 (emphasis added).

5. Ibid., 89.

6. Ibid., 92.

7. Malcolm Braly, *False Starts: A Memoir of San Quentin and Other Prisons* (Boston: Little, Brown, 1976), 10.

8. Ibid., 7.

9. Ibid., 9.

10. Ibid., 16.

11. Ibid., 372 (emphasis added).

12. Ibid., 369.

13. Ibid., 346.

14. Malcolm Braly, *It's Cold Out There* (New York: Pocket Books, 1966), 35, 64. On the theme of prison as a place where one feels cared for, consider the words of an old Russian prisoners' ballad:

> Here are we, the Emperor's guests,
> As befits our station.

Ginzburg, *Journey into the Whirlwind*, 325.

15. Tamsin Fitzgerald, *Tamsin* (New York: Dial Press, 1973), 112 (emphasis added). Margaret Drabble expresses the same idea in her fictional work, *The Ice Age* (New York: Knopf, 1977). The protagonist, Anthony Keating, searches for a place where he will be protected from choice, eventually finding it in prison. See, e.g., ibid., 225 ("Yet again, he was going to have to decide what to do with his life. It was too exhausting. It was too much of an effort. . . . He wished profoundly that he was where Len Wincobank was [in prison], out of harm's way").

16. Dylan Thomas, "Fern Hill," in *Selected Writings* (New York: New Directions, 1946), 79.

17. Blake, *The Joint*, 149.

18. Braly, *False Starts*, 217 (emphasis added).

19. Mary Renault, *The King Must Die* (London: Sceptre, 1958), 169 (emphasis added).

20. Algernon Charles Swinburne, *The Triumph of Time*, in *The Complete Works of Algernon Charles Swinburne* (New York: Russel and Russel, 1925), st. 33.

21. Charles Dickens, *Little Dorrit*, edition de luxe (New York: Nottingham Society, n.d.), 2:837.

22. Blake, *The Joint*, 378–79.

23. For the seminal discussion of the concept of the total institution, see Erving Goffman, *Asylums* (Garden City, N.Y.: Anchor Books, 1961). Goffman defines a total institution as "a place of residence and work where a large number of like-situated individuals, cut off from the wider society for an appreciable period of time, together lead an enclosed, formally administered round of life." Ibid., xiii.

24. Blake, *The Joint*, 379.

25. See Franz Alexander and William Healy, *Roots of Crime: Psychoanalytic Studies* (1935; reprint, Montclair, N.J.: Patterson Smith, 1969), 284.

26. See ibid.

27. See Norman O. Brown, *Life against Death: The Psychoanalytical Meaning of History* (Middletown, Conn.: Wesleyan University Press, 1959), 284. Cf. Erich Fromm, *Escape from Freedom* (New York: H. Holt, 1941), passim. Fromm maintains that over the course of history people have been liberated from prejudices and limitations. Such liberations, however, have exacted a high price: loneliness and anxiety owing to the loss of a sense of belonging. These feelings, in turn, may give rise to the longing for a *Fuehrer* and sado-masochistic submission.

NOTES TO CHAPTER 3

1. Aleksandr Solzhenitsyn, *The Gulag Archipelago*, trans. Harry Willetts (New York: Harper and Row, 1978), 98 (emphasis added).

2. Literally, "chthonic" means "in or under the earth," "dwelling or reigning in the underworld," or "relating to infernal deities or spirits." *Webster's Third New International Dictionary* (1981) (unabridged), s.v. "chthonic."

3. See Philip Wheelwright, *The Burning Fountain: A Study in the Language of Symbolism*, rev. ed. (Bloomington: Indiana University Press, 1968), 176.

4. Bill Sands, *My Shadow Ran Fast* (New York: New American Library, 1964), 48–49 (emphasis added).

5. John Cheever, *Falconer* (New York: Ballantine Books, 1977), 203–4.

6. Ibid., 211.

7. Malcolm X and Haley, *The Autobiography of Malcolm X*, 170.

8. Charles Colson, *Born Again* (Old Tappan, N.J.: Chosen Books, 1976), 283.

9. Christina and Carlen, "Christina: In Her Own Time," in *Criminal Women.*

10. Manuel Puig, *Kiss of the Spider Woman*, trans. Thomas Colchie (New York: Vintage Books, 1978), 261 passim.

11. Greene, *The Power and the Glory*, 153.

12. Ibid., 162.

13. Ibid., 199.

14. Figner, *Memoirs of a Revolutionist*, 209.

15. Jawaharlal Nehru, *Toward Freedom: The Autobiography of Jawaharlal Nehru* (Boston: Beacon Press, 1963), 181.

16. Telephone interview with Professor James Jacobs, author of *Stateville* and Director, Center for Research in Crime and Justice, NYU Law School (23 June 1987).

17. John Edgar Wideman, *Brothers and Keepers* (New York: Holt, Rinehart and Winston, 1984).

18. Ibid., 201–2 (emphasis added).

19. See *John* 15:1–8.

20. Eleanor Blau, "Poet Rebuilds Life in U.S. after Soviet Prison Term," *New York Times*, 24 March 1987, sec. C, p. 13. Compare Chekhov's exulting words after his 1890 sojourn on the island of Sakhalin, which the Russian government had selected as the place of exile for its most dangerous criminals: "I am so filled with joy and satisfaction that it would not bother me in the least if I succumbed to paralysis or departed this world by way of dysentery. I can say: *I have lived! I have had everything I want!* I have been in Hell, which is Sakhalin, and in Paradise, which is the island of Ceylon!" Letter to Leontiev-Shcheglov, quoted in Robert Payne, introduction to *The Island: A Journey to Sakhalin*, by Anton Chekhov (New York: Washington Square Press, 1967), xxxiv. Before undertaking this journey, Chekhov had been suffering from a severe depression over the death of his brother Nikolay. Ibid., xii-xiii.

21. For a discussion of the two kinds of hero myth, see Joseph L. Henderson, "Ancient Myths and Modern Man," in *Man and His Symbols*, ed. Carl Jung (Garden City, N.Y.: Doubleday, 1964), 120.

22. Cf. ibid., 132, picture caption (describing the "archetypal great mother" as "the container of all life"); Joseph Campbell, *The Hero with a Thousand Faces*, 2d ed. (Princeton, N.J.: Princeton University Press, 1968), 91 (explaining that in the belly of the whale motif, the hero "goes inward, to be born again").

23. See, e.g., *Romans* 5:3–5 ("tribulation worketh patience; and patience, experience; and experience, hope: And hope maketh not ashamed; because the love of God is shed abroad in our hearts by the Holy Ghost which is given unto us").

24. See Fenichel, *Psychoanalytic Theory of Neurosis*, 105, 293.

25. Ginzburg, *Within the Whirlwind*, 153.

NOTES TO CHAPTER 4

1. Edgar Smith, "Life in the Death House," in *Getting Busted*, 346.

2. For the distinction between positive and negative liberty see Sir Isaiah Berlin's seminal essay, "Two Concepts of Liberty," in *Political Philosophy*, ed. Anthony Quinton (New York: Oxford University Press, 1967), 141. For a discussion of Rousseau's concept of freedom, see Sheldon Wolin, *Politics and Vision* (Boston: Little, Brown, 1960), 371. For a summary of T. H. Green's "idealist revision of liberalism," see George Sabine, *A History of Political Theory*, 3d ed. (New York: Holt, Rinehart and Winston, 1961), 725–40.

3. Thomas Flynn, *Tales for My Brothers' Keepers* (New York: W. W. Norton, 1976), 46.

4. Albie Sachs, *The Jail Diary of Albie Sachs* (New York: McGraw-Hill, 1966), 134.

5. Colson, *Born Again*, 307.

6. Kohn, "Time: Two Interviews," in *Getting Busted*, 253–54.

7. Beck, "Thoughts on the Theater from Jail: Three Letters to a Friend," in *Getting Busted*, 321.

8. Figner, *Memoirs of a Revolutionist*, 297 (emphasis added).

9. Tolstoy, *War and Peace*, 1130.

10. Fitzgerald, *Tamsin*, 112.

11. Robert Bolt, *A Man for All Seasons* (New York: Vintage Books, 1960), 138.

12. For one of the classical discussions of denial, see Anna Freud, *The Ego and the Mechanisms of Defense* (New York: International Universities Press, 1966), 69–92.

13. Berlin, "Two Concepts of Liberty," 141.

14. Dostoevsky, *Notes from a Dead House*, 289.

15. Wallach, *Light at Midnight*, 256.

16. See ibid.

NOTES TO CHAPTER 5

1. Cf. Dickens, *Little Dorrit*, 22 ("'But I bear those monotonous walls no ill-will now,' said Mr. Meagles. 'One always begins to forgive a place as soon as it's left behind; I dare say a prisoner begins to relent towards his prison, after he is let

out' "). See also Tolstoy, *War and Peace*, 1123 ("All Pierre's daydreams now turned on the time when he would be free. Yet subsequently, and for the rest of his life, he thought and spoke with enthusiasm of that month of captivity").

2. Braly, *False Starts*, 211.

3. Ibid., 213, 364.

4. See, e.g., Krishna Hutheesing, *Shadows on the Wall* (New York: J. Day, 1948), 74–75 (describing a thief-arsonist who committed crimes in order to return to prison); Chris Tchaikovsky, "Looking for Trouble," in *Criminal Women*, 53 (describing her relief upon being caught and her surprising ineptness at preventing her capture).

5. Flynn, *Tales for My Brothers' Keepers*, 20.

6. Josie O'Dwyer and Pat Carlen, "Josie: Surviving Holloway . . . And Other Women's Prisons," in *Criminal Women*, 142.

7. It may be objected that political prisoners and common criminals are very different, the former breaking the law out of idealistic conviction, the latter out of necessity, passion, or antisocial personality disorder. I have ignored this distinction in this study for a simple reason; namely, that I did not find a difference between the political prisoners and the common criminals with respect to their affirmative images of prison. Indeed, one of the surprising findings of this study is precisely the similarity of themes in the two groups. For each of the positive carceral images delineated in Part One, we find examples from both types of prisoner.

8. Kenneth Lamott, review of *False Starts*, by Malcolm Braly, *New York Times Book Review*, 29 February 1976, 7. Consider also the observation of Joan Shapiro, M.D., a forensic psychiatrist who treated prisoners at Canon City Prison, Colorado. She was astonished to find that the prisoners felt cared for in prison. (Personal communication, 10 May 1987).

9. See Alexander and Healy, *Roots of Crime*, 54 ("Analyst: 'It is rather interesting that deep down the jail has some attraction for you, although consciously you don't like it at all, but this infantile longing for the mother is somehow satisfied in the prison, inasmuch as you don't have to care for yourself' "). See also ibid., 52, 67–68.

10. The findings of the late British psychoanalyst D. W. Winnicott are consistent with this thesis. Based on his clinical work with delinquents, Winnicott maintains that the antisocial tendency, with stealing at its core, reflects a hopeful search for "that amount of environmental stability that will stand the strain resulting from impulsive behavior." D. Winnicott, *Deprivation and Delinquency* (London: Tavistock Publications, 1984), 125. For an example of a murderer with some degree of attraction to imprisonment, see Ann Oberkirch, "Psychotherapy of a Murderer: Excerpts," *American Journal of Psychotherapy* 39 (1985): 505.

NOTES TO CHAPTER 6

1. Some scholars would include restraint, or incapacitation, among the traditional rationales of punishment. This theory states that we are justified in punishing offenders by isolating them from society to prevent their committing further crimes *while they are being punished*. I omit discussion of restraint theory from the text because the argument of this study has little application to it. The positive meanings of incarceration cannot alter the fact that someone physically constrained will be unable to commit new crimes against society while he is confined.

2. For basic works on the theories of punishment, see Norval Morris, *Madness and Criminal Law* (Chicago: University of Chicago Press, 1982); Nigel Walker, *Punishment, Danger and Stigma* (Oxford: Basil Blackwell, 1980); Ernest Van Den Haag, *Punishing Criminals: Concerning a Very Old and Painful Question* (New York: Basic Books, 1975); Johannes Andenaes, *Punishment and Deterrence* (Ann Arbor: University of Michigan Press, 1974); Norval Morris, *The Future of Imprisonment* (Chicago: University of Chicago Press, 1974); Hans von Hentig, *Punishment: Its Origin, Purpose and Psychology* (1937; reprint, Montclair, N.J.: Patterson Smith, 1973); Franklin Zimring and Gordon Hawkins, *Deterrence: The Legal Threat in Crime Control* (Chicago: University of Chicago Press, 1973); Stanley Grupp, *Theories of Punishment* (Bloomington: Indiana University Press, 1971); Joel Feinberg, *Doing and Deserving* (Princeton, N.J.: Princeton University Press, 1970); Raymond Saleilles, *The Individualization of Punishment* (1911; reprint, Montclair, N.J.: Patterson Smith, 1968); Leon Radzinowicz, *Ideology and Crime* (New York: Columbia University Press, 1966).

3. See Sanford Kadish and Monrad Paulsen, *Criminal Law and Its Processes*, 3d ed. (Boston: Little, Brown, 1975), 26.

4. For a poetic description of institutionalization, see George Gordon, Lord Byron, "The Prisoner of Chillon," in *The Complete Poetical Works of Lord Byron* (New York: Macmillan, 1927):

> These heavy walls to me had grown
> A hermitage—and all my own!
> and half I felt as they were come
> To tear me from a second home: . . .
> My very chains and I grew friends,
> So much a long communion tends
> To make us what we are;—even I
> Regain'd my freedom with a sigh.

5. See Braly, *False Starts*, 32.

6. See Fenichel, *The Psychoanalytic Theory of Neurosis*, 371; and Alexander and Healy, *Roots of Crime*, 109.

7. See Alexander and Healy, *Roots of Crime*, 102, 113, 67, 117.

8. My research has turned up only one legal article on this subject. See Bruce Perry, "Escape from Freedom, Criminal Style: The Hidden Advantages of Being in Jail," *Journal of Psychiatry and Law* 12 (1984): 215–30 (examining the writings of Jack Abbott and Malcolm X and concluding that these two men preferred life in prison). Another article mentions in passing that punishment may induce criminal behavior; however, it does not discuss the appeal of incarceration in particular. See C. G. Schoenfeld, "Law and Unconscious Motivation," *Howard Law Journal* 8 (1962): 15 ("What is startling, however, is the realization that by punishing criminals beset by strong unconscious guilt feelings, the law may actually encourage—rather than discourage—the commission of crimes").

By contrast, many lawyers have written of the sometime attraction of capital punishment. For a partial summary of this research, see Daniel Glaser, "Capital Punishment—Deterrent or Stimulus to Murder? Our Unexamined Deaths and Penalties," *University of Toledo Law Review* 10 (1979): 325–27.

Without focusing on any particular form of punishment, a few psychoanalytic works broach the subject of punishment as an incentive to criminality. See, e.g., Sigmund Freud, "Some Character Types Met With in Psycho-Analytic Work," in *The Standard Edition of the Complete Psychological Works of Sigmund Freud* (London: The Hogarth Press and the Institute of Psycho-analysis), 14:332–33 (discussing "criminals from a sense of guilt"), and Freud, "Dostoevsky and Parricide," in ibid., 21:186–87 ("It is a fact that large groups of criminals want to be punished. Their superego demands it and so saves itself the necessity for inflicting the punishment itself").

9. See, e.g., Gary Becker, "Crime and Punishment: An Economic Approach," *Journal of Political Economy* 76 (1968): 169–217; Richard Sullivan, "The Economics of Crime: An Introduction to the Orthodox Literature," in *Problems in Political Economy*, 2d ed., ed. David Gordon (Lexington, Mass.: D. C. Heath, 1977), 376–78.

10. See Harold Berman, *Law and Revolution* (Cambridge, Mass.: Harvard University Press, 1983), 183.

11. See Andrew Von Hirsch, *Doing Justice* (New York: Hill and Wang, 1976), 46.

12. H. L. A. Hart, *Punishment and Responsibility* (New York: Oxford University Press, 1968), 8–9.

13. See Oppenheimer, *The Rationale of Punishment*, 247 ("If we wish to remain on solid ground we shall have to avow that punishment means the infliction of evil upon the offender, and that it ceases to be punishment when it ceases to be an evil").

14. San Quentin inmate Fernando Jackson, quoted in Kroll, "Counsel behind Bars," 99.

15. See Durkheim, *The Division of Labor in Society*, 108–9.

16. Ibid.

17. See, e.g., Francis A. Allen, "The Decline of the Rehabilitative Ideal in American Criminal Justice," *Cleveland State Law Review* 27 (1978): 148 ("When I speak of the rehabilitative ideal I refer to the notion that the sanctions of the criminal law should or must be employed to achieve fundamental changes in the character, personalities, and attitudes of connected offenders, not only in the interest of the social defense, but also in the interest of the well-being of the offender himself").

18. J. Brewster, "The Use of Solitude in Prisons," in *A Companion for the Prisoner*, 5th ed. (1828), 15. Quoted in Adam Hirsch, "From Pillory to Penitentiary: The Rise of Criminal Incarceration in Early Massachusetts," *Michigan Law Review* 80 (1982): 1209.

19. Solzhenitsyn, *One Day in the Life of Ivan Denisovitch*, 198.

20. *Journal of the Senate, 1830–31*, 465. Quoted in Harry Barnes, *Evolution of Penology in Pennsylvania* (1927; reprint, Montclair, N.J.: Patterson Smith, 1968), 160.

21. Quoted in Harry E. Barnes and Negley K. Teeters, *New Horizons in Criminology*, rev. ed. (New York: Prentice Hall, 1945), 512–13.

22. See Hirsch, "From Pillory to Penitentiary," 1207–10.

23. *Journal of the Senate for 1834–35*, 467. Quoted in Barnes, *Evolution of Penology*, 162–63 (emphasis added).

24. Ibid.

25. Douglas Martin, "At a Violent Jail, Warden Strives to Ease Tension," *New York Times*, 4 May 1987, sec. B, p. 21.

26. Warden James Garvey, Jr., telephone conversation with author, 20 July 1987.

27. See, e.g., Hirsch, "From Pillory to Penitentiary," 1256.

28. See, e.g., Oppenheimer, *Rationale of Punishment*, 242 ("The curative view of punishment according to which its infliction serves to dry up the spring of evil in the soul of the offender, either for the ultimate good of society or for the benefit of the criminal alone") (emphasis added).

NOTE TO THE EPILOGUE TO PART ONE

1. Fitzgerald, *Tamsin*, 22.

NOTES TO THE PROLOGUE TO PART TWO

1. For psychoanalytic works that treat fictional characters as clinical examples, see Freud, "Some Character-Types Met With in Psycho-Analytic Work," in *The Standard Edition of the Complete Psychological Works of Sigmund Freud*, 14:309–33 (discussing Lady Macbeth and Ibsen's Rebecca West as examples of "those wrecked by success"); Arnold Rothstein, *The Narcissistic Pursuit of Perfection* (New York: International Universities Press, 1984) (examining characters in novels of Tolstoy and John Fowles to illustrate types of narcissism); Leonard Shengold, *Soul Murder* (New Haven: Yale University Press, 1989) (employing novels by Orwell, Dickens, and others to illustrate psychodynamics of child abuse and neglect).

For legal works that draw on literature to illuminate life, see Richard Posner, *Law and Literature* (Cambridge, Mass.: Harvard University Press, 1988), 25–70; Richard Weisberg, *The Failure of the Word* (New Haven: Yale University Press, 1984); Norval Morris, "The Watching Brief," *University of Chicago Law Review* 54 (1987): 1215 (one of a series of stories that Morris has written to dramatize and examine issues in criminal law); Robin West, "Authority, Autonomy, and Choice: The Role of Consent in the Moral and Political Visions of Franz Kafka and Richard Posner," *Harvard Law Review* 99 (1985): 384.

2. See Eric Hobsbawm, *Primitive Rebels: Studies in Archaic Forms of Social Movement in the Nineteenth and Twentieth Centuries* (New York: W. W. Norton, 1959), 5.

3. Eric Hobsbawm, *Bandits* (New York: Delacorte Press, 1969), 13. Based on the lives or legends of such outlaws as Robin Hood (England), Diego Corrientes (Spain), Janosik (Poland and Slovakia), Mandrin (France), and Stenka Razin (Russia), Hobsbawm delineated nine characteristic features of the social bandit:

> First, the noble robber begins his career of outlawry not by crime, but as the victim of injustice, or through being persecuted by the authorities for some act which they, but not the custom of his people, consider criminal.
>
> Second, he "rights wrongs."
>
> Third, he "takes from the rich to give to the poor."
>
> Fourth, he "never kills but in self-defense or just revenge."
>
> Fifth, if he survives, he returns to his people as an honourable citizen and member of the community. Indeed, he never actually leaves the community.
>
> Sixth, he is admired, helped and supported by his people.
>
> Seventh, he dies invariably and only through treason, since no decent member of the community would help the authorities against him.
>
> Eighth, he is—at least in theory—invisible and invulnerable.

Ninth, he is not the enemy of the king or emperor, who is the fountain of justice, but only of the local gentry, clergy or other oppressors.

Ibid., 35–36.

4. Hobsbawm, *Primitive Rebels*, 5.

5. See Paul Angiolillo, *A Criminal as Hero: Angelo Duca* (Lawrence: Regents Press of Kansas, 1979), 4–5.

6. Stephen Tatum, *Inventing Billy the Kid: Visions of the Outlaw in America 1881–1981* (Albuquerque: University of New Mexico Press, 1982).

7. Ibid., 196. For scholarly attempts to explain the love of the criminal in the United States in particular, see Robert K. Merton, "Social Structure and Anomie," in *Social Theory and Social Structure* (New York: Free Press, 1968), 195–96 (suggesting that Americans' admiration for white-collar criminals flows from a "cultural structure in which the sacrosanct goal virtually consecrates the means"); Alexander and Healy, *Roots of Crime*, 282–83 (implying that the "heroic exhibitionistic evaluation of criminal deeds in America" has its roots in the American individualistic ethos, coupled with the absence of opportunities to express one's individuality); Richard White, "Outlaw Gangs of the Middle Border: American Social Bandits," *The Western Historical Quarterly* 12 (1981): 387, 397, 402–406 (arguing that in postwar Missouri and Oklahoma in the 1890s bandits were admired because they embodied masculine virtues in a context where belief in public law enforcement had been eroded).

For an imprisoned criminal's attempt to account for what he calls the "cult of the rogue" among the American public, see Emmett Dalton, *When the Daltons Rode* (Garden City, N.Y.: Doubleday, Doran, 1931), 276–77 (suggesting that the criminal represents the common person's fight against authority, wealth, and pretension).

8. Hobsbawm, *Bandits*, 34.

9. See, e.g., Meredith Anne Skura, *The Literary Uses of the Psychoanalytic Process* (New Haven: Yale University Press, 1981), 200–201.

NOTES TO CHAPTER 7

1. Wilkie Collins, *The Woman in White* (London: Oxford University Press, 1975), 195 (emphasis added).

2. Ibid., 201 (emphasis added).

3. Joseph Conrad, *Heart of Darkness* (New York: W. W. Norton, 1971), 69 (emphasis added).

4. "Arthur Penn as Director," in *The Bonnie and Clyde Book*, ed. Sandra Wake and Nicola Hayden (London: Lorrimer, 1972), 184–85 (emphasis added).

5. See Joseph Morgenstern, "Bonnie and Clyde: Two Reviews by Joseph Morgenstern," in *The Bonnie and Clyde Book*, 218–19.

6. See Ruth Eissler, "Scapegoats of Society," in *Searchlights on Delinquency*, ed. Kurt Eissler (New York: International Universities Press, 1949), 289–90.

7. See Adelaide Johnson, "Sanctions for Superego Lacunae of Adolescents," in *Searchlights on Delinquency*, 227–28.

8. My interpretation here is consistent with the analysis of vicarious punishment in J. C. Flugel's psychoanalytic work, *Man, Morals and Society* (New York: International Universities Press, 1985), 164–74. As Johnson points out, the parents' denunciation of their children may also be an expression of hostile impulses toward the children. See Johnson, "Sanctions for Superego Lacunae," 228.

9. See Sigmund Freud, "Negation," in *The Standard Edition*, 19:235–39.

10. Brown, *Life against Death*, 160.

11. *Gangsters: A Golden Age* (WVEU television broadcast 28 September 1989).

12. Frederick Schiller, Preface to the First Edition of "The Robbers," in *The Works of Frederick Schiller* [hereinafter, *Works*], vol. 2 (n.d.) (1781), 133, 135.

13. Ibid., 135–36.

14. *Proverbs* 24:1–2.

15. Christopher Hibbert, *Highwaymen* (London: Weidenfeld and Nicholson, 1967), 103.

16. Charles Dickens, "Preface to the Third Edition (1867)," in *Oliver Twist* (1867; reprint, New York: New American Library, 1980), xv.

17. Ibid., xv-xvi.

18. See W. Hogarth, *A Harlot's Progress*, plate 3 (1732).

19. Trevor Allen, "Crooks Are So 'Romantic,' " *Contemporary Review* 210 (1967): 213–15.

20. Roger A. MacKinnon and Robert Michels, *The Psychiatric Interview in Clinical Practice* (Philadelphia: Saunders, 1971), 300.

21. Ibid., 336.

NOTES TO CHAPTER 8

1. See Howard Pyle, *The Merry Adventures of Robin Hood* (New York: New American Library, 1985).

2. See Bruno Bettelheim, *The Uses of Enchantment: The Meaning and Importance of Fairy Tales* (New York: Vintage Books, 1989), 69 ("So the typical fairy-tale splitting of the mother into a good [usually dead] mother and an evil stepmother serves the child well. It is not only a means of preserving an internal all-good

mother when the real mother is not all-good, but it also permits anger at this bad 'stepmother' without endangering the goodwill of the true mother, who is viewed as a different person").

3. Robert Louis Stevenson, *Kidnapped* (New York: New American Library, 1987), 129.

4. Ibid., 132.

5. Ibid.

6. *United States v. Nusunginya*, no. F88–063 CR (unpublished opinion, Alaska, 24 February 1989), 67.

7. Ibid., 75.

8. Ibid., 67.

9. Ibid., 75.

10. John Steinbeck, *The Grapes of Wrath* (1939; reprint, New York: Viking Press, 1958), 65.

11. Ibid., 116. The film version, even more than the book, highlights the noncriminals' delight in supposing that Tom has illegally escaped from prison. See *The Grapes of Wrath*, prod. Darryl F. Zanuck, Twentieth Century-Fox Film Corp., 1940.

12. Steinbeck, *The Grapes of Wrath*, 107.

13. Ibid., 114–15 (emphasis added).

14. Ibid., 115.

15. Ibid., 134.

16. Ibid., 181–82.

17. Ibid., 190–91.

18. Ibid., 191.

19. Ibid., 482.

20. Sophocles, *Antigone*, in *World Drama*, ed. Barrett Clark (New York: Dover Publications, 1933), 13:31–32.

21. See Edith Hamilton, *The Greek Way to Western Civilization* (New York: New American Library, 1942), 26

22. See Josue de Castro, *Dᵉath in the Northeast* (New York: Vintage Books, 1966), 7–8.

23. See Maurice Hugh Keen, *The Outlaws of Medieval Legend* (London: Routledge and Kegan Paul, 1961), 10.

24. *Webster's New International Dictionary of the English Language*, 2d ed., s.v. "bandit."

25. See Keen, *Outlaws of Medieval Legend*, 10.

26. Robert Louis Stevenson, *The Black Arrow* (New York: Airmont Books, 1963), 51–52.

27. Anton Blok, "The Peasant and the Brigand: Social Banditry Reconsidered," *Comparative Studies in Society and History* 14 (September 1972): 500.

28. Ibid., 500–501.

29. See Bill Richards, "As Legend Has It, He Used Pepper to Elude the Law," *Wall Street Journal*, 17 July 1989, sec. 1, p. 1.

30. Ibid.

31. See *People v. Goetz*, 68 N.Y.2d 96, 497 N.E.2d 41 (1986).

32. See, e.g., Joseph Berger, "Goetz Case: Commentary on Nature of Urban Life," *New York Times*, 18 June 1987, sec. B, p. 6 (quoting Professors Alan Dershowitz and Burt Neuborne to the effect that what Goetz did was illegal); Toni M. Massaro, "Peremptories or Peers?—Rethinking Sixth Amendment Doctrine, Images, and Procedures," *North Carolina Law Review* 64 (1986): 512n.77.

33. See George Fletcher, *A Crime of Self-Defense: Bernard Goetz and the Law on Trial* (New York: Free Press, 1988), 28 (referring to Goetz as a "folk hero"); Ronald Goldfarb, "Violence, Vigilantism and Justice," *Criminal Justice Ethics* 6 (1987): 2 (suggesting that Goetz became a "national hero" to many people); "Vigilante Justice," *National Law Journal* 7, 14 January 1985, p. 12 (referring to Goetz's "lawlessness" as "so easily admired by the public"); cf. Allen Lichtenstein, "Polls, Public Opinion, Pre-Trial Publicity and the Prosecution of Bernhard H. Goetz," *Social Action and Law* 10 (1985): 95–97 (describing news reports that the police hotline was inundated with calls expressing support for the still unidentified gunman, and presenting the results of polls showing that the majority of the public approved of the gunman's shooting the young men).

34. Quoted in Fletcher, *A Crime of Self-Defense*, 201 (emphasis added).

35. Ibid. (emphasis added).

36. See Fenichel, *The Psychoanalytic Theory of Neurosis*, 73. See generally Freud, "Three Essays on the Theory of Sexuality," in *The Standard Edition*, 7:123, 157–60.

37. Psychoanalysts employ the term *resistance* to describe patients' opposition to becoming aware of their unconscious mental processes. I have refrained from employing this word here, because its use is typically confined to the analytic situation. For a general psychoanalytic discussion of the difficulties of knowing oneself, see Philip Rieff, *Freud: The Mind of the Moralist* (Garden City, N.Y.: Doubleday, 1961), 71–112.

Psychoanalysis is not, of course, alone in emphasizing how painful it is for human beings to confront the truth about themselves. Consider, for example, the New Testament expression of this idea in *Luke* 6:41: "And why beholdest thou the mote that is in thy brother's eye, but perceivest not the beam that is in thine own eye?"

38. For example, it was Carmen's freedom from moral and legal scruples that attracted soprano Jessye Norman to her. Asked why she had departed from her usual repertoire to sing *Carmen*, Ms. Norman replied, "I enjoy having this character *who will do whatever is necessary to get what she wants.*" *Jessye Norman Sings "Carmen"* (WPBA television broadcast, 20 November 1989).

39. Prosper Merimee, *Carmen*, in *Colomba and Carmen* (New York: D. Appleton, 1901), 72.

40. For an explanation of the connection between the anal zone and the struggle over autonomy, see Erik Erikson, *Childhood and Society* (New York: W. W. Norton, 1963), 81–82. See also Ruth Munroe, *Schools of Psychoanalytic Thought: An Exposition, Critique and Attempt at Integration* (New York: Holt, Rinehart and Winston, 1955), 197 (discussing children whose "inner determination tends to develop *in opposition to the outside world*").

41. See Walter Slote, "Case Analysis of a Revolutionary," in *A Strategy for Research on Social Policy*, ed. Frank Bonilla and Jose Silva-Michelena (Cambridge, Mass.: MIT Press, 1967), 308 (proposing a distinction between the rebel, who fights against, and the revolutionary, who fights for).

42. Schiller, *The Robbers*, in *Works*, act 1, sc. 2.

43. Georges Bizet, *Carmen*, libretto by L. Halevy and H. Meilac (New York: Dover Publications, 1970), act 2, sc. 4 (emphasis added).

44. Merimee, *Colomba and Carmen*, 53 (emphasis added).

45. Alfred Noyes, *The Highwayman*, in *Collected Poems* (London: J. Murray, 1963), 11–14.

46. Quoted in Hibbert, *Highwaymen*, 115.

47. Quoted in Alexander Grinstein, "Vacations: A Psycho-Analytic Study," *International Journal of Psychoanalysis* 36 (1955): 183–84.

48. Ibid., 184.

49. Quoted in Hibbert, *Highwaymen*, 120.

50. Frank Aydelotte, *Elizabethan Rogues and Vagabonds* (Oxford: Clarendon Press, 1913), 137. A similar observation appears in Shakespeare's *Two Gentlemen of Verona*. Valentine, having been ambushed by outlaws and invited to join their band, receives words of encouragement from his servant Speed: "Master, be one of them. It's an honourable kind of thievery." *William Shakespeare, The Complete Works*, ed. Stanley Wells and Gary Taylor (Oxford: Clarendon Press, 1986), 4.1.35.

51. Hibbert, *Highwaymen*, 116, 117.

52. The example from the *Daily Chronicle* and the one from *Vogue* are both taken from the *Oxford English Dictionary*, vol. 7, 233.

53. For a discussion of the discrepancy between the myth and the reality of the highwaymen, see Hibbert, *Highwaymen*, 35–38, 49–51. For similar discussions about other kinds of noble bandits, see Kent Steckmesser, "Robin Hood and the American Outlaw," *Journal of American Folklore* 79 (1966): 349–54; Linda Lewin, "Oligarchical Limitations of Social Banditry in Brazil: The Case of the 'Good' Thief Antonio Silvino," in *Bandidos: The Varieties of Latin American Banditry*, ed. Richard Slatta (New York: Greenwood Press, 1987), 69; Barrington Moore, *Social Origins of Dictatorship and Democracy* (Boston: Beacon Press, 1966), 214.

54. See David Newman and Robert Benton, "Lightning in a Bottle," in *The Bonnie and Clyde Book*, 17–18.

55. Robert Louis Stevenson, *Treasure Island* (New York: Charles Scribner's Sons, 1911), 60.

56. Ibid., 76, 77.

57. Ibid., 90.

58. Ibid., 109.

59. Ibid., 260.

60. *Treasure Island*, prod. Hunt Stromberg, Metro-Goldwyn-Mayer, 1934.

61. *Treasure Island*, prod. Perce Pearce, Walt Disney, 1950.

62. Robert Louis Stevenson, *Treasure Island* (New York: Bantam Books, 1981).

63. Robert Louis Stevenson, *Treasure Island* (New York: Charles Scribner's Sons, 1911), 264–65.

64. See Susan Richmond, *Treasure Island: A Play in Six Scenes* (London: H. W. Deane, 1946); David William Moore, *The End of Long John Silver* (New York: Thomas Y. Cromwell, 1946).

65. William Shakespeare, *I Henry IV*, in *The Complete Works*, 5.4.101–4.

66. Robert Hapgood, "Falstaff's Vocation," *Shakespeare Quarterly* 16 (1965): 94.

67. Shakespeare, *I Henry IV* 2.2.86–88 (emphasis added).

68. Ibid., 3.3.64–67.

69. Ibid.

70. R. C. Bald, Introduction to *The First Part of Henry the Fourth*, by William Shakespeare, ed. R. C. Bald (New York: Appleton-Century-Crofts, 1946).

71. See Daniel Defoe, *Moll Flanders*, Norton Critical Edition (New York: W. W. Norton, 1973) (1st ed. 1722 under title *The Fortunes and Misfortunes of the Famous Moll Flanders*).

72. Arnold Kettle, "In Defense of Moll Flanders," in ibid., 391.

73. Ibid.

74. Virginia Woolf, "Defoe," in *Moll Flanders*, by Daniel Defoe, 342.

75. Ibid., 339.

76. Kettle, "In Defense of Moll Flanders," 392.

77. Ibid., 391–92.

78. See Julian Symons, *Mortal Consequences* (New York: Harper and Row, 1972), 183–84.

79. Ibid., 184.

80. Ibid. For essays offering thoughtful explanations for the widespread appeal of the detective story, see W. H. Auden, "The Guilty Vicarage: Notes on the Detective Story, by an Addict," *Harper's Magazine* 196 (1948): 406–12; Charles Rycroft, "A Detective Story: Psychoanalytic Observations," *Psychoanalytic Quarterly* 26 (1957): 229–45 (suggesting that the criminal represents the reader). For a summary of this literature and a history of crime fiction, see Symons, *Mortal Consequences*, 5–13.

81. Robert Penn Warren, *All the King's Men* (New York: Modern Library, 1953), 452.

82. Ibid.

83. Ibid.

84. Ibid., 463.

85. Peter Shaffer, *Equus* (New York: Avon Books, 1974), 94.

86. Ibid., 95.

87. Conrad, *Heart of Darkness*, 48.

88. Ibid., 72.

89. Ibid.

90. Ibid.

91. In British slang, *nark* means stool pigeon.

92. Colin MacInnes, *Mr. Love and Justice* (London: MacGibbon and Kee, 1960), 59–60.

93. E. L. Doctorow, *Billy Bathgate* (New York: Random House, 1987), 11, 23.

94. Schiller, *The Robbers*, in *Works*, act 1, sc. 2.

95. Ibid.

96. Ibid.

97. Arthur Conan Doyle, "The Adventure of the Final Problem," in *The*

Illustrated Sherlock Holmes Treasury [hereinafter, *Treasury*] (New York: Avenel Books, 1976), 317.

98. Ibid.

99. Ibid.

100. Ibid., 326.

101. Arthur Conan Doyle, "The Adventure of the Norwood Builder," in *Treasury*, 354.

102. Ibid.

103. Arthur Conan Doyle, "The Adventure of the Missing Three Quarter," in *Treasury*, 483, 491.

104. Fyodor Dostoevsky, *Crime and Punishment*, Norton Critical Edition (New York: W. W. Norton, 1975), 380 (emphasis added).

105. See ibid., 382.

106. For an analysis of Porfiry's relationship with Raskolnikov that highlights Porfiry's fascination with the criminal and willingness to acknowledge his similarity to him, see Richard Weisberg, "Comparative Law in Comparative Literature: The Figure of the 'Examining Magistrate' in Dostoevski and Camus," *Rutgers Law Review* 29 (1976): 244–48.

107. Margaret Mahler, Fred Pine, and Anni Bergman, *The Psychological Birth of the Human Infant: Symbiosis and Individuation* (New York: Basic Books, 1975), 71.

108. See ibid., 78.

109. See ibid.

110. See Arnold Rothstein, *The Narcissistic Pursuit of Perfection* (New York: International Universities Press, 1984), 22.

111. Heinz Kohut, *The Analysis of the Self* (New York: International Universities Press, 1971), 27.

112. Rothstein, *Narcissistic Pursuit of Perfection*, 45.

113. Georg Simmel, "The Stranger," in *The Sociology of Georg Simmel*, ed. Kurt H. Wolff (New York: Free Press, 1950), 402.

114. Merimee, *Colomba and Carmen*, 7 (emphasis added).

115. Stevenson, *Kidnapped*, 66.

116. F. Scott Fitzgerald, *The Great Gatsby* (New York: Charles Scribner's Sons, 1925), 44.

117. Similarly, in the Hitchcock film *To Catch a Thief*, Francine Simpson plainly wants to believe that John Robie has reverted to his former profession of jewelry thief. In her eyes, she implies, he would cut a more glamorous figure as an

active criminal than as a reformed one. *To Catch a Thief,* prod. Alfred Hitchcock, Paramount Pictures Corporation, 1954.

118. Fitzgerald, *The Great Gatsby,* 60, 49.

119. Thomas Mott Osborne, *Within Prison Walls* (1914; reprint, Montclair, N.J.: Patterson Smith, 1969).

120. Ibid., 15 (emphasis added).

121. Ibid., 18.

122. See, e.g., ibid., 11, 197; cf. 187–88.

123. Ibid., 43, 51, 63, 74.

124. Ibid., 76.

125. See Frank Tannenbaum, *Osborne of Sing Sing* (Chapel Hill: The University of North Carolina Press, 1933), 66, 71–87.

126. See ibid., 279.

127. Lev Tolstoi, *Resurrection* (Moscow: Foreign Language Publishing House, 1899). For another example of the criminal-as-stranger theme, consider Albert Camus's novel *The Stranger* (New York: Vintage Books, 1954), in which the protagonist, Meursault, unlawfully kills an Arab. Following the crime, Meursault is tried and convicted on legal irrelevancies—aspects of his character that make Meursault seem a stranger or foreigner in his society (for instance, that he did not cry at his mother's funeral and that he does not believe in God). For an analysis of Meursault's estrangement that focuses on his inability to use words, see Richard Weisberg, *The Failure of the Word* (New Haven, Conn.: Yale University Press, 1984), 115–23.

No character in the novel seems to embody an overt admiration for Meursault; however, his creator, Camus, exhibits a sympathy and regard for him. Camus chooses to write the novel in the first person, thereby allowing the reader to enter the criminal's mind. Moreover, as I have already indicated, he portrays Meursault as a victim of injustice. Richard Posner interprets Camus' portrait of Meursault as an admiring one, for he protests that *The Stranger* has "little . . . to do with law" and "much . . . to do with a form of neoromanticism in which criminals are made heroes." Richard Posner, *Law and Literature* (Cambridge, Mass.: Harvard University Press, 1988), 90.

NOTES TO CHAPTER 9

1. See Guy de Maupassant, *Ball-of-Fat,* in *The Great Short Stories of Guy de Maupassant* (New York: Pocket Books, 1955). In nineteenth-century France, the legality of prostitution was "left conveniently vague." See Jill Harsin, *Policing Prostitution in Nineteenth-Century Paris* (Princeton, N.J.: Princeton University

Press, 1985), xvi. In practice, women were allowed to work as prostitutes provided they registered with the police and abided by the regulations affecting them. Ibid. If arrested for a violation of the rules, they could be imprisoned without trial on the curious theory that by registering with the police they had put themselves "outside the law." Ibid., 6–7.

2. Maupassant, *Ball-of-Fat*, 237.

3. Ibid., 238.

4. Ibid., 244–45.

5. Ibid., 246.

6. Charles Dickens, *Great Expectations* (New York: Heritage Press, 1939), 21.

7. Ibid., 23.

8. Ibid., 24.

9. Ibid., 42–43.

10. Ibid., 307.

11. Ibid.

12. Ibid., 308.

13. Ibid., 322.

14. Ibid., 315.

15. See Munroe, *Schools of Psychoanalytic Thought*, 261 ("The power of the repressed impulses is seen in the exaggeration of the opposite tendencies. Excessive tendencies in one direction—the 'virtues to a fault' of common parlance—typically (i.e., not always but very often) represent a buttressing of the repression of unacceptable, impulses of contrary nature"). For general discussions of reaction-formation, see ibid., 251–54, and Fenichel, *Psychoanalytic Theory of Neurosis*, 151–53.

16. Dickens, *Great Expectations*, 322.

17. Ibid., 253.

18. Ibid., 254. A. O. J. Cockshut has called attention to the autobiographical significance of this passage: "In these words of Pip, Dickens expressed one of the great enigmas of his own life." See A. O. J. Cockshut, *The Imagination of Charles Dickens* (New York: New York University Press, 1962), 47. A detailed discussion of Newgate Prison as it appears in Dickens's writings can be found in Philip Collins, *Dickens and Crime* (London: Macmillan, 1962), 27–51.

19. For an interesting analysis of Pip's criminal guilt that is different from, yet compatible with, my interpretation, see Julian Moynahan, "The Hero's Guilt: The Case of Great Expectations," *Essays in Criticism* 10 (January 1960): 60–79 (arguing that Pip is associated with violent aggressiveness through his surrogates, the sadistic Orlick and Drummle).

20. Fred Kaplan, *Dickens: A Biography* (New York: William Morrow, 1988), 41.

21. Ibid., 38.

22. Ibid., 39.

23. John Forster, *The Life of Charles Dickens* (London: Dent, 1966), 1:25. Quoted in Leonard Shengold, *Soul Murder: The Effects of Childhood Abuse and Deprivation* (New Haven: Yale University Press, 1989), 191 (Shengold's emphasis deleted; mine added). For a general discussion of Dickens's experience in the blacking factory and its importance in his life, see Edmund Wilson, "Dickens: The Two Scrooges," in *The Wound and the Bow: Seven Studies in Literature* (Cambridge, Mass.: Houghton Mifflin, 1941), 4–8.

24. See Kaplan, *Dickens*, 21.

25. See, generally, Charles Brenner, *An Elementary Textbook of Psychoanalysis* (New York: International Universities Press, 1973), 201–9 (defining and providing illustrations of compromise formation); Munroe, *Schools of Psychoanalytic Thought*, 259–61 (explaining the technique of compromise).

26. Collins, *The Woman in White*, 195.

27. Ibid., 506.

28. Ibid., 507.

29. Ibid., 413.

30. Ibid., 414.

31. John Millington Synge, *The Playboy of the Western World* (London: Benn, 1975), act 1, lines 555–59.

32. Ibid., act 2, lines 30–33.

33. Ibid., act 3, lines 414–18.

34. Ibid., act 3, lines 424–25.

35. Ibid., act 3, line 434.

36. Ibid., act 3, lines 544–46.

37. Ibid., act 3, lines 624–25.

38. *Webster's New International Dictionary of the English Language*, 2d ed., unabridged, s.v. "gallows." The first meaning is now obsolete; the second is slang.

39. See Edward Hirsh, "The Gallous Story and the Dirty Deed: The Two Playboys," *Modern Drama* 26 (March 1983): 85–91; Zack Bowen, "Synge: The Playboy of the Western World," in *A. J. M. Synge Literary Companion*, ed. Edward Kopper, Jr. (New York: Greenwood Press, 1988), 69–70.

40. See Sanford Kadish and Stephen J. Schulhofer, *Criminal Law and Its Processes*, 3d ed. (Boston: Little, Brown, 1975), 686 (quoting *San Francisco Chronicle*, 7 September 1974, p. 2).

41. Victor Hugo, *Les Miserables*, trans. Charles E. Wilbour (New York: Modern Library, 1938).

42. Ibid., 1107.

43. Ibid., 1107–8.

NOTES TO THE CONCLUSION TO PART TWO

1. See Eissler, "Scapegoats of Society," in *Searchlights on Delinquency*, 299–304.

2. Ruth Eissler suggests that society, needing criminals as scapegoats, ensures the criminals' existence in two ways: (1) by seducing individuals into lives of crime, and (2) by interfering with measures to prevent delinquency. See ibid., 295.

From the discipline of sociology rather than psychoanalysis, Kai Erikson has also raised the question whether society is organized in such a way as to encourage deviant behavior, including criminality. See Kai Erikson, "On the Sociology of Deviance," in *Crime, Law, and Society*, ed. Abraham Goldstein and Joseph Goldstein (New York: Free Press, 1971), 94. Erikson's work builds on that of the great French sociologist Emile Durkheim, who observed, as early as 1895, that crime was really "an integral part of all healthy societies." Emile Durkheim, *The Rules of Sociological Method* (1895; reprint, Glencoe, Ill.: Free Press, 1958). Quoted in Kai Erikson, "On the Sociology of Deviance," 87. In his classic work *The Division of Labor in Society*, Durkheim had already proposed that crime performs an important function by uniting people in a common stance of righteous indignation, thereby strengthening the group's bond of solidarity. See Emile Durkheim, *The Division of Labor in Society* (1893; reprint, New York: Free Press, 1933), 108–9.

3. Cf. Erikson, "On the Sociology of Deviance," 94 ("[T]he agencies built by society for preventing deviance are often so poorly equipped for the task that we might well ask why this is regarded as their 'real' function in the first place"). For the suggestion that prisons actually generate crime, see Johannes Andenaes, *Punishment and Deterrence* (Ann Arbor: University of Michigan Press, 1974), 179; Peter Low, John Jeffries and Richard Bonnie, *Criminal Law*, 2d ed. (Mineola, N.Y.: Foundation Press, 1986), 27 ("[M]uch of the recent criminological literature" includes claims that "prisons breed crime"); Robert Blecker, "Haven or Hell? Inside Lorton Central Prison: Experiences of Punishment Justified," *Stanford Law Review* 42 (1990): 1194–95 (quoting prisoners who assert that doing time makes a person more dangerous upon release).

NOTES TO THE PROLOGUE TO PART THREE

1. See, e.g., Aristotle, *The Rhetoric of Aristotle*, trans. Richard C. Jebb, ed. John E. Sandys (Cambridge, England: Cambridge University Press, 1909), 149

(referring to the "supreme importance of metaphor both in poetry and prose"); Owen Barfield, "Poetic Diction and Legal Fiction," in *The Rediscovery of Meaning and Other Essays* (Middletown, Conn.: Wesleyan University Press, 1977), 45 ("But figurative expression is found everywhere; its roots descend very deep . . . into the nature . . . of language itself"); C. S. Lewis, "Bluspels and Flalansferes: A Semantic Nightmare," in *Rehabilitations* (Freeport, N.Y.: Books for Libraries Press, 1972), 135–58 passim (arguing that metaphors are necessary for meaning, which is the precondition of truth or falsehood); John M. Murry, "Metaphor," in *Countries of the Mind* (London: Oxford University Press, 1931), 1 ("Metaphor is as ultimate as speech itself, and speech as ultimate as thought").

2. See, e.g., Barfield, "Poetic Diction and Legal Fiction," 63. More specifically, Judge Cardozo warned, "Metaphors in law are to be narrowly watched, for starting as devices to liberate thought, they end often by enslaving it." *Berkey v. Third Ave. Ry. Co.*, 155 N.E. 58, 61 (N.Y. 1926).

3. I have uncovered only one legal article that touches on the metaphor of filth in criminal justice. See Peter Linebaugh, "(Marxist) Social History and (Conservative) Legal History: A Reply to Professor Langbein," *New York University Law Review* 60 (1985): 212. In a section of his article entitled "Garbage," Linebaugh addresses Professor John Langbein's claim that in eighteenth-century England, "the criminal justice system occupies a place not much more central than the garbage collection system." Ibid., 238. Linebaugh responds that the comparison between garbage collection and criminal justice is indeed apt, for prisons and courts were located near the ditch that carried sewage through London to the Thames River. Moreover, crime prevention, like garbage collection, was a basic function of government. In contrast to Langbein's belittling intent, Linebaugh argues that the metaphor actually highlights the importance of criminal justice in eighteenth-century England. At that time and place, when sewage was nearly omnipresent, the disposal of filth was hardly a trivial concern. Ibid., 238–42.

Numerous legal scholars have examined metaphors in noncriminal contexts. See, e.g., Milner S. Ball, *Lying Down Together: Law, Metaphor, and Theology* (Madison: University of Wisconsin Press, 1985); James B. White, *When Words Lose Their Meaning* (Chicago: University of Chicago Press, 1984); Michael Boudin, "Antitrust Doctrine and the Sway of Metaphor," *Georgetown Law Journal* 75 (1986): 395; Burr Henly, "'Penumbra': The Roots of a Legal Metaphor," *Hastings Constitutional Law Quarterly* 15 (1987): 81; Steven L. Winter, "The Metaphor of Standing and the Problem of Self-Governance," *Stanford Law Review* 40 (1988): 1371.

The particular metaphor comparing filth to evil has been addressed in some works of literary criticism. See, e.g., Victor Brombert, *Victor Hugo and the Visionary Novel* (Cambridge, Mass.: Harvard University Press, 1984), 112–35 passim (discussing the excremental motif in *Les Miserables*); Caroline F. E. Spurgeon, *Shake-speare's Imagery and What It Tells Us* (1935; reprint, New York: Cambridge University Press, 1968), 159–61 (showing that Shakespeare conceived of evil as dirty, black, and diseased); Gary S. Morson, "Verbal Pollution in *The Brothers Karamazov*," in *Critical Essays on Dostoevsky*, ed. Robin Miller (Boston: G. K. Hall, 1986), 234–42 passim (analyzing the theme of filth in *The Brothers Karamazov*).

4. According to the latest figures from the United States Department of Justice, 1.2 million persons were held in local jails or in state or federal prisons in 1991. See U.S. Department of Justice, *Correctional Populations in the United States, 1991* (Washington, D.C.: U.S. Department of Justice, 1993), 1.11.

5. See, e.g., Norval Morris and Michael Tonry, *Between Prison and Probation* (New York: Oxford University Press, 1990), 6–9 ("[T]here is general agreement about the need to expand 'intermediate punishments,'" such as "intensive probation, the fine, the community service order"); Fox Butterfield, "Are American Jails Becoming Shelters from the Storm?" *New York Times*, 19 July 1992, sec. E, p. 4 (citing Norval Morris, who believes that "increased imprisonment has made no difference in the crime rate," and citing exorbitant expenditures on new prisons); Don Terry, "More Familiar, Life in Cell Seems Less Terrible," *New York Times*, 13 September 1992, sec. A, p. 1 (quoting New Haven police chief Nicholas Pastore on the "mean-spirited system of justice" that warehouses criminals but lacks genuine concern for them); Joseph B. Treaster, "Two U.S. Judges, Protesting Policies, Are Declining to Take Drug Cases," *New York Times*, 17 April 1993, sec. A, p. 7 (discussing two prominent judges who refuse to preside over drug cases to protest our society's emphasis on arrests and imprisonment).

6. Thus, Judge Richard Posner cites our "exceptionally severe criminal punishments (many for intrinsically minor, esoteric, or archaic offenses)" as one of the factors making the United States "one of the most penal of the civilized nations . . . a disturbing state of affairs." Review of *Hitler's Justice: The Courts of the Third Reich*, by Ingo Muller, *The New Republic* 204 (1991): 42. On a more specific level, Judge Harold Greene recently declared the *Federal Sentencing Guidelines* unconstitutional as applied to a defendant in a drug case. The defendant had been convicted of possessing about one-fourth of an ounce of heroin and cocaine—an offense requiring thirty-years' imprisonment, according to the *Guidelines*. Sentencing the defendant to ten years in prison, Judge Greene observed that the mandated sentence was "grossly out of proportion to the seriousness" of the crime. He added, "We cannot allow justice and rationality to become casualties of a war on drugs being waged with Draconian, politically expedient sentences." Michael York, "Judge Rejects Federal Sentencing Guidelines; Mandatory 30–Year Imprisonment for Repeat Drug Offender Called Unconstitutional," *Washington Post*, 30 April 1993, sec. D, p. 5.

7. For the idea of feces as an artistic creation, consider the following incident:

"[A] three-year-old boy . . . came into the parental bedroom carrying a chamber pot containing three turds: one large, one middle-sized, and one small . . . ; the boy exclaimed with great joy, 'Look, I've made a daddy, a mommy, and a me!' " Leonard Shengold, *Halo in the Sky: Observations on Anality and Defense* (New York: Guilford Press, 1988), 46. See also ibid., 47 (quoting a letter in which Gustave Flaubert jubilantly looks forward to his future creative writing with the words, "[T]hen the shitting: and the shit had better be good!").

For the notion of excrement as a gift, see Freud, "On Transformations of Instincts Exemplified in Anal Erotism," in *The Standard Edition*, 17 (1955): 130 (describing feces as "the infant's first gift, a part of his body which he will give up only on persuasion by someone he loves").

As this quotation implies, excrement can also signify wealth. To a child, feces are "a very precious substance." Fenichel, *The Psychoanalytic Theory of Neurosis*, 281. Indeed, feces may be considered the prototypical possession, being "actually outside [the body] but symbolically inside." Ibid. Cf. N. Brown, *Life against Death*, 293 ("Possessions are worthless to the body unless animated by the fantasy that they are excrement").

NOTES TO CHAPTER 10

1. Charles Dickens, *A Tale of Two Cities* (New York: New American Library, 1936), 77.

2. *United States v. Barker*, 546 F.2d 940, 973 (D.C. Cir. 1976) (emphasis added).

3. See *Criminal Victimization in the United States*, 1990 (Washington, D.C.: U.S. Department of Justice, 1992), 73 (stating that 47.2% of all violent crimes occur in the daytime).

4. Bartlett, *Familiar Quotations*, 1098.

5. P. D. James, *Devices and Desires* (New York: Knopf, 1990), 66–67.

6. Ibid.

7. *Webster's New International Dictionary of the English Language*, 2d ed., s.v. "dark." Cf. Joseph T. Shipley, *The Origins of English Words: A Discursive Dictionary of Indo-European Roots* (Baltimore: Johns Hopkins University Press, 1984), 68 (deriving *dark* from a root meaning *muddied*).

8. Robert Coles, *Children of Crisis* (Boston: Little, Brown, 1967), 357.

9. Patricia Williams, *The Alchemy of Race and Rights* (Cambridge, Mass.: Harvard University Press, 1991), 198.

10. William Shakespeare, *The Tragedy of Macbeth*, in *The Complete Works*, act 1, sc. 5.

11. Ibid., act 3, sc. 2.

12. Rosellen Brown, *Before and After* (New York: Farrar, Straus, Giroux, 1992), 57.

13. Lucille F. Becker, *Georges Simenon* (Boston: Twayne Publishers, 1977), 31.

14. Shakespeare, *The Tragedy of Macbeth*, in *The Complete Works*, act 1, sc. 1.

15. Ibid.

16. Ibid., act 4, sc. 1.

17. Ibid., act 3, sc. 5.

18. Ibid., act 4, sc. 1.

19. Ibid.

20. Daphne du Maurier, *Jamaica Inn* (New York: Sun Dial Press, 1937), 1.

21. Ibid., 2.

22. See Shipley, *Origins of English Words*, 240.

23. *Psycho*, prod. Alfred Hitchcock, Paramount Pictures Corp., 1960. Films, which must do with pictures what books can do with words, afford many examples of our theme. See, e.g., *Murder by Decree*, prod. Bob Clark and Rene Dupont, Highlight Theatrical Production, 1979 (using thick fog to evoke an ominous feeling in this movie about Jack the Ripper); *The Princess Comes Across*, prod. Arthur Hornblow, Jr., Paramount Pictures Corp., 1936 (setting the stage for attempted murder with heavy fog and darkness).

24. Dickens, *Bleak House* (Boston: Houghton Mifflin, 1956), 1.

25. Ibid.

26. Ibid.

27. Ibid.

28. Ibid.

29. Ibid., 5.

30. Lawrence Kubie, "The Fantasy of Dirt," *Psychoanalytic Quarterly* 6 (1937): 395.

31. Ibid., 393. Likewise, the distinguished anthropologist Mary Douglas believes that realistic concerns cannot explain our attitudes toward dirt. She writes: "Nor do our ideas about disease account for the range of our behaviour in cleaning or avoiding dirt. In chasing dirt, ... we are positively reordering our environment, making it conform to an idea." Mary Douglas, *Purity and Danger* (London: Frederick A. Praeger, 1966), 2.

32. Kubie, "The Fantasy of Dirt," 391. But see Walter O. Weyrauch and Maureen A. Bell, "Autonomous Lawmaking: The Case of the Gypsies," *Yale Law*

Journal 103 (1993): 323 (discussing gypsies' view that bodily products emanating from the top half of the body are clean; only products emerging from the lower half of the body are considered polluting).

33. Kubie, "The Fantasy of Dirt," 391–92.

34. Erwin Strauss, *On Obsession: A Clinical and Methodological Study*, Nervous and Mental Disease Monographs, no. 73 (1948; reprint, New York: Johnson Reprint Corp., 1968), 13.

35. Ibid.

36. *Genesis* 2:7 (New American Catholic ed. 1952).

37. *The Book of J*, trans. David Rosenberg and ed. Harold Bloom (New York: Vintage Books, 1991), 61.

38. Ibid., 175.

39. Langdon Smith, "Evolution," in *Evolution: A Fantasy* (Boston: J. W. Luce, 1909), unpaginated.

40. Arthur Conan Doyle, *The Hound of the Baskervilles*, in *Sherlock Holmes Treasury*, 544.

41. Ibid., 535.

42. See, e.g., ibid., 575, 585.

43. Ibid., 617.

44. *The American Heritage Dictionary of the English Language*, 2d ed., s.v. "moor."

45. *Webster's New International Dictionary of the English Language*, 2d ed., s.v. "bog."

46. Doyle, *The Hound of the Baskervilles*, 625.

47. Ibid.

48. Ibid.

49. For the distinction between a chance image and a network of images, see Yevgeny Zamyatin, "Backstage," in *A Soviet Heretic: Essays by Yevgeny Zamyatin* (Chicago: University of Chicago Press, 1970), 198.

50. John Fowles, foreword to *The Hound of the Baskervilles*, by Arthur Conan Doyle (London: John Murray and Jonathan Cape, 1974), 11.

51. John Bunyan, *The Pilgrim's Progress* (Nashville: Cokesbury Press, n.d.). (Part I was first published in 1678; Part II in 1684).

52. Ibid., 8.

53. *Webster's New International Dictionary of the English Language*, 2d ed., s.v. "slough."

54. Boethius, *The Consolation of Philosophy*, trans. I.T., revised by H. F. Stewart, in *The Theological Tractates and The Consolation of Philosophy* (Cambridge, Mass.: Harvard University Press, 1918), 315.

55. Boethius, *The Consolation of Philosophy* (Queen Elizabeth trans., 1593), quoted in *Oxford English Dictionary* 15:740 (1989).

56. George Eliot, *Middlemarch* (New York: W. W. Norton, 1977), 475.

57. Dickens, *Oliver Twist* (Oxford: Oxford University Press, 1987), 135.

58. Dickens, *Great Expectations* (New York: Heritage Press, 1939), 11–12.

59. Ibid., 14.

60. *Peter Pan* (National Broadcasting Co., Inc., 8 December 1960).

61. Ibid.

62. James Joyce, *A Portrait of the Artist as a Young Man*, in *The Portable James Joyce*, ed. Harry Levin (New York: Viking Press, 1947), 374.

63. William Shakespeare, *The Tragedy of Hamlet*, in *The Complete Works*, act 3, sc. 3.

64. *Ephesians* 5:2 (King James); *Ephesians* 5:2 (Revised Standard Version).

65. Fyodor Dostoevsky, *The Brothers Karamazov*, trans. Richard Pevear and Larissa Volokhonsky (San Francisco: North Point Press, 1990), 327, 330.

66. Ibid., 783 n. 2.

67. Ibid., 225.

68. Ibid., 98. For an analysis of the theme of filth in *The Brothers Karamazov*, see Gary S. Morson, "Verbal Pollution in *The Brothers Karamazov*," in *Critical Essays*, passim.

69. Feodor Dostoevsky, *Crime and Punishment*, Norton Critical Edition, 2d ed. (New York: W. W. Norton, 1975), 2.

70. Ibid., 132, 407.

71. See George Gibian, "Traditional Symbolism in *Crime and Punishment*," in ibid., 525.

72. For a discussion of children's attraction to anal things, see Ruth Munroe, *Schools of Psychoanalytic Thought*, 194–96.

73. *Slime* (Nickelodeon trademark, MTV Networks 1992).

74. *The Official Icky-Poo Book* (Palo Alto: Klutz Press, 1990).

75. Munroe, *Schools of Psychoanalytic Thought*, 252.

76. See Brenner, *An Elementary Textbook of Psychoanalysis*, 91–93.

77. For discussions of cleanliness and orderliness as components of the obsessive character, see Karl Abraham, "Contributions to the Theory of the Anal

Character," in *Selected Papers of Karl Abraham* (London: Hogarth Press, 1948), 371, 388–89; Sigmund Freud, *Character and Anal Erotism*, in *The Standard Edition*, 9:167–75; MacKinnon and Michels, *The Psychiatric Interview*, 90–91.

78. Erik Erikson, *Young Man Luther* (New York: W. W. Norton, 1962), 246.

79. Cf. V. E. von Gebsattel, "The World of the Compulsive," in *Existence*, ed. Rollo May et al. (New York: Basic Books, 1958), 187 ("Now the image of dirt or of death afflicts him with constant contamination").

80. See Philip Wheelwright, *Metaphor and Reality* (Bloomington: Indiana University Press, 1962), 130.

81. See Han J. W. Drijvers, "Ablutions," in *Encyclopedia of Religion* (Mircea Eliade ed. 1987), 1:9–13 passim; Michel Meslin, "Baptism," in *Encyclopedia of Religion*, 2:59–63 passim.

82. Bunyan, *Pilgrim's Progress*, 22.

83. Sophocles, *Oedipus Tyrannus*, quoted in Philip Wheelwright, *The Burning Fountain: A Study in the Language of Symbolism*, rev. ed. (Bloomington: Indiana University Press, 1968), 181.

84. George Gordon Byron, *Cain: A Mystery*, act 3, lines 520–23, in *Lord Byron's Cain*, by Thomas Guy Steffan (Austin: University of Texas Press, 1968), 256.

85. Shakespeare, *The Tragedy of Macbeth*, act 2, sc. 2.

86. Ibid., act 5, sc. 1.

87. *Encyclopedia of Psychoanalysis*, s.v. "undoing." See also Fenichel, *Psychoanalytic Theory of Neurosis*, 289.

88. Munroe, *Schools of Psychoanalytic Thought*, 257.

89. *Webster's New International Dictionary of the English Language*, 2d ed., s.v. "offal."

90. See Kubie, "The Fantasy of Dirt," 416 ("That which is dirty will make one sick, and sickness and dirt become synonymous").

91. Dickens, *A Tale of Two Cities*, 237.

92. Caroline F. E. Spurgeon, *Shakespeare's Imagery and What It Tells Us* (New York: Cambridge University Press, 1968), 213.

93. Dickens, *Great Expectations*, 204.

94. Ibid., 200.

95. Sophocles, *Oedipus Tyrannus* (New York: W. W. Norton, 1970), 1st performance c. 429 b.c. For discussions of murder and pollution in ancient Greece, see Douglas M. MacDowell, *Athenian Homicide* (New York: Barnes and Noble, 1963); Richard A. Posner, "Retribution and Related Concepts of Punishment," *Journal of Legal Studies* 9 (1980): 71, 83–90.

96. John Milton, *Paradise Lost*, in *Great Books of the Western World*, 2d ed., ed. Mortimer J. Adler (Chicago: Encyclopaedia Britannica, 1990) 29:11.48–52.

97. Harry Blamires, *Milton's Creation: A Guide through "Paradise Lost"* (London: Methuen, 1971), 273.

98. See *Genesis* 4:16.

99. See *Matthew* 25:32–33; *The Interpreter's Bible* 7:563.

100. *Luke* 16:20–21.

101. *Luke* 16:26.

102. James Frazer, *The Golden Bough* (New York: Macmillan, 1950), 260.

103. Ibid. In primitive societies, persons to whom taboos apply are sometimes considered polluted, at other times, sacred. Ibid.; Mary Douglas, "Taboo," *New Society* 3 (1964): 24. So also criminals are considered unclean, and they, too, are sometimes viewed as holy. Thus, in Greek mythology, Prometheus stole fire from the gods and became, by the same act, the savior of mankind. Likewise, according to Christian theology, Christ was convicted of crimes under Roman law; in the act of being punished, he redeemed the sins of humanity. Even the ordinary criminal was, in Dostoevsky's view, "almost a Redeemer, who . . . had taken on himself the guilt which must else have been borne by others." Sigmund Freud, "Dostoevsky and Parricide," in *The Standard Edition*, 21:190. See also Philip Rieff, *Freud: The Mind of the Moralist* (Garden City, N.Y.: Doubleday, 1961), 303–5 (discussing the "ethical criminal").

104. Fenichel, *Psychoanalytic Theory of Neurosis*, 288.

105. See Martha Himmelfarb, *Tours of Hell* (Philadelphia: University of Pennsylvania Press, 1983), 106–7.

106. See I. H. Gorski, "Gehenna," in *New Catholic Encyclopedia*, vol. 6, ed. The Catholic University of America (New York: McGraw-Hill, 1967), 312–13; Leonard Bushinski and J. T. Nelis, "Gehenna," in *Encyclopedic Dictionary of the Bible*, ed. Louis F. Hartman (New York: McGraw-Hill, 1963), 847–48; A. Viard, "Gehenna," in *Encyclopedic Dictionary of Religion*, vol. F-N, ed. Paul Meagher, Thomas O'Brien, and Sister Consuelo Maria Aherne (Washington, D.C.: 1979), 1457.

107. Milton, *Paradise Lost*, book 1, lines 61–63.

108. Ibid., book 1, lines 71–74.

109. See Philippe Aries, *The Hour of Our Death* (New York: Alfred Knopf, 1981), 43–44.

110. *Euclid v. Ambler*, 272 U.S. 365, 381 (1926).

NOTES TO CHAPTER 11

1. See Robert Hughes, *The Fatal Shore* (New York: Alfred A. Knopf, 1987), 611 n. 2. I am indebted to *The Fatal Shore* for awakening my interest in Australian history. This beautifully crafted book, while not explicitly psychoanalytic, provides the kind of material that the psychoanalytically oriented interpreter requires.

2. William Blackstone, *Commentaries on the Laws of England*, 3d ed. (Oxford: Clarendon Press, 1768), 137–38.

3. Ibid.

4. Ibid.

5. See Hughes, *Fatal Shore*, 40.

6. See ibid., 40–42.

7. See C. M. H. Clark, *A History of Australia* (Parkville, Victoria: Melbourne University Press, 1962), 73–75.

8. See ibid., 76, 81–82.

9. See, e.g., Geoffrey Blainey, *The Tyranny of Distance* (South Melbourne: Macmillan, 1982), passim; D. J. Mulvaney and J. Peter White, eds., *Australians: A Historical Library* (Cambridge, England: Cambridge University Press, 1987), 394.

10. Alan Frost, *Convicts and Empire* (Melbourne and New York: Oxford University Press, 1980), 182. In significant language, Frost also observes, "The rag and bone shop of Australia's beginning was perhaps not so foul as we have for so long supposed." Ibid., 135.

11. David MacKay, *A Place of Exile* (Melbourne and New York: Oxford University Press, 1985), 3.

12. See ibid., 61; Hughes, *Fatal Shore*, 65.

13. See Hughes, *Fatal Shore*, 64–66; see also MacKay, *A Place of Exile*, 59–61 (providing detailed evidence that New South Wales had no credibility as a strategic base).

14. MacKay, *A Place of Exile*, 56.

15. Ibid., 57.

16. Hughes, *Fatal Shore*, 42.

17. Ibid., 57.

18. See Blainey, *Tyranny of Distance*, 19.

19. Coral Lansbury, *Arcady in Australia* (Carlton, Victoria: Melbourne University Press, 1970), 13 (quoting Charles Lamb).

20. Godfrey C. Mundy, *Our Antipodes*, 3 vols. (London: Richard Bentley, 1852).

21. William Ullathorne, D.D., *The Catholic Mission in Australasia* (Liverpool: Rockliff and Duckworth, 1837), iv.

22. Rev. Sydney Smith, *Edinburgh Review*, quoted in Hughes, *Fatal Shore*, 355 (emphasis added).

23. *The Times*, 29 March 1849, quoted in William Parker Morrell, *British Colonial Policy in the Age of Peel and Russell*, 404 (emphasis added).

24. Mundy, *Our Antipodes*, 3:112.

25. Jeremy Bentham, "Panopticon Versus New South Wales," in *The Works of Jeremy Bentham*, ed. John Bowring (Edinburgh: William Tate, 1843), 4:176. Nor is this an accidental choice of images, for Bentham goes on to describe the banished convicts as "this fruitlessly expelled mass of corruption." Ibid., 191.

26. *The Times*, 18 December 1846, quoted in Morrell, *British Colonial Policy*, 396 (emphasis added).

27. Mundy, *Our Antipodes*, quoted in A. G. L. Shaw, *Convicts and the Colonies* (1966; reprint, Melbourne: Melbourne University Press, 1978), 349 (emphasis added).

28. *Quarterly Review*, 1828, quoted in Shaw, *Convicts and the Colonies*, 143.

29. *Bathurst Free Press*, 11 January 1851, quoted in Michael Sturma, *Vice in a Vicious Society* (St. Lucia, Queensland: University of Queensland Press, 1983), 51 (emphasis added).

30. See *Webster's New International Dictionary*, 2d ed., 2252.

31. Hughes, *Fatal Shore*, 556.

32. *The Times*, 17 August 1852, reprinted in Lloyd Evans and Paul Nichols, eds., *Convicts and Colonial Society: 1788–1853* (Stanmore, N.S.W.: Cassell Australia, 1976), 236.

33. Morrell, *British Colonial Policy*, 393 (quoting Latrobe's report to Grey, 31 May 1847).

34. Lansbury, *Arcady in Australia*, 164 (emphasis added).

35. See Mundy, *Our Antipodes*, 1:105; Sturma, *Vice in a Vicious Society*, 20.

36. Mundy, *Our Antipodes*, 3:112.

37. *Nineteenth Century*, January 1889, quoted in Sidney Rosenberg, "Black Sheep and Golden Fleece: A Study of Nineteenth-Century English Attitudes toward Australian Colonials" (Ph.D. diss., Columbia University, 1954), 202–3.

38. Parliamentary History, xxviii, cols. 1223–25 (1791), reprinted in *Convicts and Colonial Society: 1788–1853*, 35.

39. *Quarterly Review* 27 (1828), quoted in Shaw, *Convicts and the Colonies*, 143.

40. *The Molesworth Report*, reprinted in *Convicts and Colonial Society: 1788–1853*, 76, 79.

41. This follows from the principle of psychic determinism: "In the mind, as in physical nature about us, nothing happens by chance." Brenner, *An Elementary Textbook of Psychoanalysis*, 2. Much of traditional literary criticism presupposes that the author's choice of metaphors provides insight into the author's mind. For a rare explicit acknowledgment of this assumption, see Spurgeon, *Shakespeare's Imagery*, 4: "In the case of a poet, I suggest it is chiefly through his images that he, to some extent unconsciously, 'gives himself away.' "

42. Lewis, "Bluspels and Flalansferes," 141.

43. Ibid.

44. Hughes, *Fatal Shore*, 285.

45. Chaplain Johnson, who witnessed the disembarkation of the Second Fleet, wrote that the prisoners were "covered, almost, with their own nastiness." Shaw, *Convicts and the Colonies*, 108. After the exceedingly high death rate on the Second Fleet, authorities attempted to improve conditions; nevertheless, missionaries on later ships described the "loathsomeness," "perfect darkness," and "dreary dark-ness" of the convicts' habitation. Ibid., 111.

46. For a detailed discussion of repression, see Munroe, *Schools of Psychoanalytic Thought*, 245–49.

47. See Jack Novick and Kerry Kelly, "Projection and Externalization," in *The Psychoanalytic Study of the Child* 25 (1970): 81 (defining *externalization* as "those processes which lead to the *subjective allocation of inner phenomena to the outer world*").

48. *The Gentleman's Magazine*, October 1786, quoted in Shaw, *Convicts and the Colonies*, 50.

49. Nathaniel Wraxall, *A Short Review of the Political State of Great Britain at the Commencement of the Year One Thousand Seven Hundred and Eighty-Seven*, 77–83, reprinted in *Convicts and Colonial Society: 1788–1853*, 33.

50. Ibid. This language recalls the prison to which the fallen angels were banished in *Paradise Lost*:

> As far remov'd from God and light of Heav'n
> As from the center thrice to th' utmost Pole.
> —Milton, *Paradise Lost*, book 1, lines 73–74

51. Wraxall, *A Short Review*, reprinted in *Convicts and Colonial Society: 1788–1853*, 33. Compare Jeremy Bentham's view of transportation: " 'I sentence you,' says the judge, 'but to what I know not—perhaps to shipwreck—perhaps to famine—perhaps to be devoured by wild beasts.... I rid myself of the sight of you.' " Quoted in F. L. W. Wood, "Jeremy Bentham versus New South Wales," *Royal Australian Historical Society: Journal and Proceedings* 19 (1933): 343.

52. Wraxall, *A Short Review*, reprinted in *Convicts and Colonial Society: 1788–1853*, 33.

53. See Hughes, *Fatal Shore*, 160 ("[M]any early convicts, up to the end of the Napoleonic Wars, went on board the 'Bay Ships' for small, often ridiculously slight, offenses"). Whether the people transported to Australia were serious criminals or only trivial offenders has been the subject of much debate. On the one hand, many Australians maintain that the convicts were basically innocent victims of harsh laws—poachers who needed food for starving children, for example, or oppressed political prisoners. On the other hand, historians have increasingly come to reject this view, especially as regards the later period. See, e.g., ibid., 158–60, 163; Shaw, *Convicts and the Colonies*, 146–65.

54. See Novick and Kelly, "Projection and Externalization," 69, 89.

55. Ibid.

56. Ibid., 88–89.

57. See David Punter, "Fictional Representation of the Law in the Eighteenth Century," *Eighteenth Century Studies* 16 (Fall 1982): 47, 70–72.

58. See ibid., 47, 69.

59. See ibid., 47, 68–69.

60. See Hibbert, *Highwaymen*, 65, 103.

61. See ibid., 23.

62. See Hughes, *Fatal Shore*, 31–33.

63. Foucault, *Discipline and Punish: The Birth of the Prison*, trans. Alan Sheridan (New York: Vintage Books, 1979), 61; see also Hughes, *Fatal Shore*, 33–35.

64. Hughes, *Fatal Shore*, 137 (emphasis in original).

65. See John Everingham, "Children of the First Fleet," *National Geographic* 173 (February 1988): 236, 243, 245; John Rickard, "Psychohistory: An Australian Perspective," *History Today* 31 (1981): 10.

66. John Vincent Barry, *Alexander Maconochie of Norfolk Island: A Study of a Pioneer in Penal Reform* (Melbourne: Oxford University Press, 1958), 90.

67. See ibid., 91.

68. See Christopher Hibbert, *The Roots of Evil* (1963; reprint, Westport, Conn.: Greenwood Press, 1978), 149.

69. This punishment replicates that of Prometheus, who stole fire from the gods and gave it to man. For this crime, Zeus had Prometheus seized and chained "with iron bonds" to a "friendless rock" at the outer regions of the earth. Aeschylus, *Prometheus Bound*, in *World Drama*, ed. Barrett H. Clark (New York: Dover Publications, 1933), 1:1–19.

70. Barry, *Alexander Maconochie*, 124.

71. Hughes, *Fatal Shore*, 505. See also Hibbert, *Roots of Evil*, 149.

72. See Hughes, *Fatal Shore*, 508.

73. See Barry, *Alexander Maconochie*, 146.

74. Sheldon Glueck, foreword to *Alexander Maconochie*, by Barry, vii.

75. *Job* 10:22 (Revised Standard Version).

76. For the distinction between the conflict model and the narrative model in psychoanalysis, I am indebted to Robert Michels, Address at the Atlanta Psychoanalytic Society Meeting (23 September 1992). The writings of Charles Brenner have done most to establish the dominance of the conflict paradigm. See, e.g., Charles Brenner, *The Mind in Conflict* (New York: International Universities Press, 1982). Roy Schafer has advanced the "model of narration" to explain what happens in psychoanalysis. See, e.g., Roy Schafer, *Narrative Actions in Psychoanalysis* (Worcester, Mass.: Clark University Press, 1981); Roy Schafer, "Narration in the Psychoanalytic Dialogue," *Critical Inquiry* 7 (1980): 29–53. See also Donald P. Spence, *Narrative Truth and Historical Truth* (New York: W. W. Norton, 1982); Kenneth Burke, *Permanence and Change*, rev. ed. (Indianapolis: Bobbs-Merrill, 1965), 275.

77. See Donald Greene, *The Age of Exuberance: Backgrounds to Eighteenth-Century English Literature* (New York: Random House, 1970), 93. (Eighteenth-century English writers were "writing for an audience thoroughly indoctrinated from childhood onward, with the King James Bible, the Book of Common Prayer, the Articles, the Creeds, and Catechism").

78. Eric Auerbach, *Mimesis: The Representation of Reality in Western Literature* (New York: Doubleday, 1953), 151 (writing about the *Mystere D'Adam*, a twelfth-century Christmas play based on the story in *Genesis*).

79. *1st Corinthians* 15:22. Cf. Romans 5:12 ("[S]in came into the world through one man, and death through sin").

80. "Articles of Religion," in *The Book of Common Prayer* (New York: Church Hymnal Corp., 1979), 869.

81. *Genesis* 3:16–19.

82. *The Interpreter's Bible* (New York: Abingdon Press, 1952), 1:515 n.24.

83. For works discussing human beings' need for stories to give meaning to their lives, see Bruno Bettelheim, *The Uses of Enchantment: The Meaning and Importance of Fairy Tales* (New York: Vintage Books, 1989), 3, 65–66 (explaining how fairy tales externalize a child's inner conflicts, rendering those conflicts understandable and controllable); John Hellman, *American Myth and the Legacy of Vietnam* (New York: Columbia University Press, 1986), ix ("A people cannot coherently function without myth"); J. R. R. Tolkien, "On Fairy-Stories," in *Tree and Leaf* (London: Unwin Hyman, 1988), 55–63 (arguing that fairy tales promote recovery and afford escape and consolation); cf. Carl G. Jung, "Approaching the

Unconscious," in *Man and His Symbols*, ed. Carl Jung (Garden City, N.Y.: Doubleday, 1964), 89 (discussing the need for symbols to give meaning to life).

84. For a beautiful discussion of exile as human beings' essential condition, see Hans Jonas, *The Gnostic Religion: The Message of the Alien God and the Beginnings of Christianity*, 2d ed. (Boston: Beacon Press, 1963), 62–67. See also Edward Said, "The Mind of Winter: Reflections on Life in Exile," *Harper's Magazine* 269 (September 1984): 49–55; *Hebrews* 13:14 ("For here we have no continuing city but we seek one to come").

85. Gregory Rochlin, "The Dread of Abandonment," *The Psychoanalytic Study of the Child* 16 (1961): 460. See also Bettelheim, *Uses of Enchantment*, 145 ("There is no greater fear in life than that we will be deserted").

86. See "Hansel and Gretel," in *The Complete Grimm's Fairy Tales* (New York: Pantheon Books, 1944), 86–94; see also *The Pied Piper of Hamelin*, in Robert Browning, *The Poems* (New Haven: Yale University Press, 1981), 1:383–91. For a general discussion of abandonment in fairy tales, see David Bakan, *Slaughter of the Innocents* (Boston: Beacon Press, 1971), 65–68.

87. Rochlin, *Dread of Abandonment*, 453.

88. J. Martin Evans, "Topics: Book X," in *Paradise Lost: Books IX-X*, by John Milton (Cambridge, U.K.: Cambridge University Press, 1973), 188.

89. For a fascinating discussion of "salvation from below" in *Les Misérables*, see Victor Brombert, *Victor Hugo and the Visionary Novel* (Cambridge, Mass.: Harvard University Press, 1984), 112–35.

90. "Botany Bay," reprinted in C. M. H. Clark, ed., *Sources of Australian History* (London: Oxford University Press, 1957), 76.

91. Hughes, *Fatal Shore*, 583.

92. Ibid., 584–85.

93. Everingham, "Children of the First Fleet," 240.

94. Judith Wright, *Preoccupations in Australian Poetry* (Melbourne: Oxford University Press, 1965), xi.

95. Robert Hughes refers to Australia as a "jail of infinite space." *Fatal Shore*, 596.

NOTES TO CHAPTER 12

1. *People v. Bell*, 204 Misc. 71, 74, 125 N.Y.S.2d 117, 119 (Nassau County Ct.), aff'd., 306 N.Y. 110, 115 N.E.2d 821 (1953).

2. *Edwards v. Calif.* 314 U.S. 160, 167 (1941).

3. Douglas, *Purity and Danger* (London: Frederick A. Praeger, 1966), 35–36.

4. *An Act to Amend and Make More Effectual the Laws Relating to Rogues, Vagabonds, and Other Idle and Disorderly Persons, and to Houses of Correction,* 17 Geo. 2, ch. 5 (1744) (Eng.). For a fascinating account of vagrancy laws and vagrants in the earlier, Elizabethan period, see Frank Aydelotte, *Elizabethan Rogues and Vagabonds* (Oxford: Clarendon Press, 1913).

5. Blackstone, *Commentaries,* 4:169, quoted in Gary V. Dubin and Richard H. Robinson, "The Vagrancy Concept Reconsidered: Problems and Abuses of Status Criminality," *New York University Law Review* 37 (1962): 104.

6. This definition represents two scholars' attempt to summarize a number of statutes. See Dubin and Robinson, "Vagrancy Concept Reconsidered," 109.

7. See Arthur H. Sherry, "Vagrants, Rogues, and Vagabonds—Old Concepts in Need of Revision," *California Law Review* 48 (1960): 560. Increasingly, courts have struck down vagrancy laws, usually on a void-for-vagueness rationale. For articles discussing the recent history and status of vagrancy laws, see Harry Simon, "Town without Pity: A Constitutional and Historical Analysis of Official Efforts to Drive Homeless Persons from American Cities," *Tulane Law Review* 66 (1992): 631–76; Jordan Berns, "Is There Something Suspicious about the Constitutionality of Loitering Laws?" *Ohio State Law Journal* 50 (1989): 717–36.

8. Daniel DeFoe, *The History of The Devil* (East Ardsley, U.K.: E. P. Pub., 1972), 94.

9. Christopher Tiedeman, *Limitations of Police Power* (St. Louis: F. H. Thomas Law Book Co., 1886), 117.

10. *State v. Harlow,* 174 Wash. 227, 233, 24 P.2d 601, 603 (1933).

11. *People v. Pieri,* 269 N.Y. 315, 323, 199 N.E. 495, 498 (1936). I am indebted to an article by Caleb Foote for calling my attention to this quotation and the two preceding ones. See Caleb Foote, "Vagrancy-Type Law and Its Administration," *University of Pennsylvania Law Review* 104 (1956): 625–26.

12. See Foote, "Vagrancy-Type Law," 627–28.

13. See ibid., passim. Foote quotes magistrates who repeatedly admonish vagrants to "[S]tay where you belong," and "go back where you belong." Ibid., 606.

14. See Michael Ignatieff, *A Just Measure of Pain: The Penitentiary in the Industrial Revolution 1750–1850* (New York: Pantheon Books, 1978), 15.

15. Alexander Smith, *A Complete History of the Lives and Robberies of the Most Notorious Highwaymen,* ed. Arthur L. Hayward (London: G. Routledge, 1933), quoted in John Bender, *Imagining the Penitentiary: Fiction and the Architecture of Mind in Eighteenth-Century England* (Chicago: University of Chicago Press, 1987), 26.

16. Bender, *Imagining the Penitentiary,* 14.

17. *First Biennial Report of the Board of State Commissioners of Public Charities of the State of Illinois* 175–84 (1871), quoted in Frederic L. Faust and Paul J. Brantingham, *Juvenile Justice Philosophy* (St. Paul, Minn.: West Publishing Co., 1979), 31.

18. Mary Douglas, "Pollution," in *International Encyclopedia of Social Sciences* 12 (1968): 336, 338.

19. Janine Chassequet-Smirgel, *Creativity and Perversion* (New York: W. W. Norton, 1984), 12.

20. *First Annual Report,* Boston Prison Discipline Society 36–37 (1826), reprinted in Harry E. Barnes and Negley K. Teeters, *New Horizons in Criminology,* rev. ed. (New York: Prentice Hall, 1945), 523 (emphasis added).

21. Ibid.

22. Gustave de Beaumont and Alexis de Tocqueville, *On the Penitentiary System in The United States and Its Application in France,* trans. Francis Lieber (New York: A. M. Kelley, 1970), 32.

23. For descriptions of the "silent" and "separate" systems, see Barnes and Teeters, *New Horizons in Criminology,* 505–45; David J. Rothman, *The Discovery of the Asylum* (Boston: Little, Brown, 1971), 82–83. For a discussion of the hood that prisoners wore, see Negley K. Teeters and John D. Shearer, *The Prison at Philadelphia* (New York: Published for Temple University Publications by Columbia University Press, 1957), 75, 78.

24. Barnes and Teeters, *New Horizons in Criminology,* 533.

25. See ibid., 533–34; Rothman, *Discovery of the Asylum,* 81.

26. David Shapiro, *Neurotic Styles* (New York: Basic Books, 1965), 49–50; cf. Fenichel, *Psychoanalytic Theory of Neurosis,* 288 (describing the obsessional neurotic's "inhibition in the experiencing of *gestalten*").

27. Hibbert, *Roots of Evil,* 160.

28. Ibid.

29. A modern recreation of the separate system exists at Pelican Bay State Prison in California, which is based on "extreme, around-the-clock isolation of prisoners from virtually all human contact." Jennifer Warren, "A Modern-Day Dungeon," *Los Angeles Times,* 7 September 1993, sec. A, p. 3.

During a visit to this prison in 1993, *60 Minutes* correspondent Mike Wallace expressed his amazement in language that evokes Tocqueville and Beaumont's description of Auburn a century and a half earlier:

> WALLACE: Do they mix with each, the—all the guys in this pod?
>
> LT. DEINES: No they do not. Any communication they have is through the door. If they come out of their pods, they will come in contact with no other inmate. They can talk, but they have no physical contact.

WALLACE: Good God. And—and this can go on for years in here?

LT. DEINES: Depending on the circumstances of the case, it could go on for years.

WALLACE: There's an eerie quality here, Al.

LT. DEINES: It's different from—you get when you walk into most prisons, in the—in the old prisons. You don't have the yelling and screaming.

WALLACE: Right.

LT. DEINES: It's very quiet.

WALLACE: What goes on inside those cells? What goes on inside the minds of those people in there? I mean, in this silent, otherworldly atmosphere?

60 Minutes (CBS television broadcast, 12 September 1993).

30. See Francis B. McCarthy and James G. Carr, *Juvenile Law and Its Processes* (Charlottesville, Va.: Michie, 1989), 11–12.

31. Ruth Eissler, "Scapegoats of Society," in *Searchlights on Delinquency*, 288, 297. For a detailed discussion of the Houses of Refuge, see Rothman, *Discovery of the Asylum*, 207–36.

32. August Aichhorn, *Wayward Youth* (1925; reprint, Evanston, Ill.: Northwestern University Press, 1983), 147.

33. New York Society of the Reformation of Juvenile Delinquents, *10th Annual Report* (1835), 6–7, quoted in McCarthy and Carr, *Juvenile Law and Its Processes*, 28. According to Rothman, historians agree about the central features of the prisons, reformatories, and other asylums that arose in the nineteenth century. As he summarizes, "[A]ll the institutional routines were segmented into carefully defined blocks of time, scrupulously maintained and punctuated by bells. There was nothing casual or random about daily activities." Rothman, *Discovery of the Asylum*, xxv.

34. See Fenichel, *Psychoanalytic Theory of Neurosis*, 284.

35. Wilhelm Reich, *Character Analysis*, 3d ed. (New York: Simon and Schuster, 1972), 215.

36. Fenichel, *Psychoanalytic Theory of Neurosis*, 284.

37. Ibid., 285.

38. See Eissler, "Scapegoats of Society," 297; Aichhorn, *Wayward Youth*, 147.

39. See Rothman, *Discovery of the Asylum*, 258–59.

40. Steven L. Schlossman, *Love and the American Delinquent* (Chicago: University of Chicago Press, 1977), 45. This passage recalls Dickens's *Oliver Twist*, in which Oliver oscillates between a filthy city environment where he is a captive of Fagin's thieving gang, and an idyllic country home where he is, temporarily at least, safe from the corrupting influence of criminals. See Dickens, *Oliver Twist*, 55–57, 237–39.

41. See Mason P. Thomas, "Child Abuse and Neglect, Part I: Historical Overview, Legal Matrix, and Social Perspectives," *North Carolina Law Review* 50 (1972): 307.

42. For a highly critical discussion of the Orphan Train Movement, see Richard Wexler, *Wounded Innocents* (Buffalo, N.Y.: Prometheus Books, 1990), 33–36 (citing religious bigotry and child stealing in the placing-out system). Even the more balanced account of Marilyn I. Holt concludes on this profoundly negative note: "The image of human 'cargoes'. . . or 'human freight' . . . is more reminiscent of America's history of slavery than of humanitarian efforts." See Marilyn I. Holt, *The Orphan Trains: Placing Out in America* (Lincoln: University of Nebraska Press, 1992).

43. Cf. Lewis H. Lapham, "Notebook: City Lights," *Harper's Magazine* 285 (1992): 4–6 (decrying Americans' long-standing prejudice against cities, and defending urban disorder and danger as the inevitable price of freedom).

44. For a list of these cases, see the Appendix.

45. *Peterson v. State*, 376 So.2d 1230, 1231 (Fla.App. 1979) (emphasis added).

46. *U.S. v. Corona*, 551 F.2d 1386, 1388 (5th Cir. 1977).

47. Ibid., 1388.

48. Douglas Frantz and Robert L. Jackson, "The Spooks, the Kooks, and the Dictator: If Noriega Goes Down, He's Threatening to Take the CIA, the DEA, and the White House with Him," *Los Angeles Times*, 21 July 1991, magazine sec., p. 8.

49. *State v. Bennefield*, 567 A.2d 863, 864 (Del. 1989).

50. *In re Castellano*, 361 N.Y.S.2d 23, 24 (App. Div. 1974).

51. See *Volkmor v. U.S.*, 13 F.2d 594, 595 (6th Cir. 1926); *Rogers v. State*, 157 So.2d 13, 17–18 (Ala. 1963); *Duque v. State*, 498 So.2d 1334, 1337, 1339 (Fla.App. 2 Dist. 1986); *Peterson v. State*, 376 So.2d 1230, 1232, 1235 (Fla.App. 1979); *People v. Nightengale*, 523 N.E.2d 136, 141–42 (Ill.App. 1 Dist. 1988); *State v. Young*, 12 S.W. 879, 879, 884 (Mo. 1890).

52. *People v. Tucker*, 331 P.2d 160, 163 (Cal.App. 1958).

53. Christopher Herbert, "Rat Worship and Taboo in Mayhew's London," *Representations* 23 (1988): 14. A discussion of the rat as the "demonized Other," which both fascinates and horrifies, appears in Peter Stallybrass and Allon White, *The Politics and Poetics of Transgression* (Ithaca, N.Y.: Cornell University Press, 1986), 143–47.

54. See *U.S. v. McPhaul*, 22 M.J. 808, 814 (ACMR 1986); *State v. Conners*, 76 So. 611, 612 (La. 1917); *People v. Myers*, 220 N.E.2d 297, 311 (Ill. 1966); *Williams v. State*, 226 P.2d 989, 997 (Okla. Crim. App. 1951).

55. *Williams v. State* 226 P.2d 989, 997 (Okla. Crim. App. 1951).

56. *People v. Myers,* 220 N.E.2d 297, 311 (Ill. 1966).

57. *U.S. v. McPhaul,* 22 M.J. 808, 814 (ACMR 1986).

58. Barfield, "Poetic Diction and Legal Fiction," 63.

59. *Barnett v. Ohio,* 135 N.E. 647, 649 (Ohio 1922).

60. *Taylor v. Strickland,* 411 F. Supp. 1390, 1395–96 n.15 (S.C. 1976) (emphasis added).

61. Ibid., 1395 n.13.

62. *U.S. v. Valencia,* 541 F.2d 618, 621 (6th Cir. 1976) (quoting District Judge), *cited approvingly, U.S. v. Omni Intern.* Corp. 634 F. Supp. 1414, 1440 (Md. 1986).

63. *On Lee v. U.S.,* 343 U.S. 747, 758 (1952) *cited approvingly, U.S. v. Ross,* 541 F.2d 690, 703–4 (8th Cir. 1976).

64. *Oakland v. Detroit,* 866 F.2d 839, 843 n.3 (6th Cir. 1989).

NOTES TO THE CONCLUSION TO PART THREE

1. For this way of characterizing law, I am indebted to my late colleague, Donald Fyr. But see *Estin v. Estin,* 334 U.S. 541 (1948) ("But there are few areas of the law in black and white. The greys are dominant and even among them the shades are innumerable"). Walter Weyrauch has suggested that elite American law schools teach law as gray, whereas less prestigious law schools teach law as black and white. See Ekkehard Klausa, review of *Hierarchie der Ausbildungsstätten, Rechtsstudium und Recht in den Vereinigten Staaten,* by Walter Weyrauch, *American Journal of Comparative Law* 25 (1977): 167.

2. In fact, Russian peasants have traditionally employed this metaphor for the criminal. See Harold Berman, *Justice in the U.S.S.R.* (Cambridge, Mass.: Harvard University Press, 1963), 248. Cf. John Maynard, *The Russian Peasant* (London: V. Gollancz, 1943), 189 ("the Russian people . . . pities the condemned criminal").

3. Aristotle used this example in discussing the importance of metaphor: "So we may speak of the wrong-doer as 'making a mistake,' or the erring man as 'guilty of a wrong.' We may say that the thief has merely 'taken,' or that he has 'plundered.' " *The Rhetoric of Aristotle,* trans. Richard C. Jebb, ed. John E. Sandys (Cambridge, England: Cambridge University Press, 1909), 150.

4. Lewis, "Bluspels and Flalansferes," 153.

5. Aristotle attributes three distinctive tenets to Socrates: "(a) virtue, *moral* excellence, is identical with knowledge . . . ; (b) vice, bad moral conduct, is therefore in all cases ignorance. . . ; (c) wrong-doing is therefore always involuntary, and there is really no such state of soul as . . . 'moral weakness' (*acrasia*), 'knowing

the good and yet doing the evil.' " A. E. Taylor, *Socrates: The Man and His Thought* (Garden City, N.Y.: Doubleday, 1953), 140–41.

NOTES TO THE CONCLUSION

1. Juliet Mitchell, *Psychoanalysis and Feminism* (New York: Pantheon, 1974), 12.

2. Friedrich Schiller, *Naive and Sentimental Poetry*, in *Naive and Sentimental Poetry and On the Sublime: Two Essays*, trans. Julius A. Elias (New York: Frederick Ungar, 1966), 87, as quoted in *Great Treasury of Western Thought*, ed. Mortimer J. Adler and Charles Van Doren (New York: R. R. Bowker, 1977), 49.

3. Irena Grudzinska Gross, *The Scar of Revolution: Custine, Tocqueville, and the Romantic Imagination* (Berkeley: University of California Press, 1991).

4. Mortimer Collins, *Sweet Anne Page* (London: Hurst and Blackett, 1868), 1:232 (describing an island as "romance-empurpled Monte Cristo").

5. Harper Lee, *To Kill a Mockingbird* (New York: Warner Brothers, 1982), epigraph (quoting Charles Lamb).

6. Charles Dickens, *Great Expectations* (New York: Heritage Press, 1939), 138.

7. For a psychoanalytic discussion of the concepts of "everything" and "nothing," see Leonard Shengold, *"Father Don't You See I'm Burning?" Reflections on Sex, Narcissism, Symbolism, and Murder: From Everything to Nothing* (New Haven: Yale University Press, 1991).

8. Wordsworth, "Ode: Intimations of Immortality from Recollections of Early Childhood," in *Poems by William Wordsworth*, st. 58.

9. Frances Hodgson Burnett, *A Little Princess* (Boston: David R. Godine, 1989), 81.

Bibliography

Books and Articles

Abraham, Karl. "Contributions to the Theory of the Anal Character." In *Selected Papers of Karl Abraham*, 370–92. London: Hogarth Press, 1948.

Aeschylus. *Prometheus Bound*. In *World Drama*, edited by Barrett H. Clark, vol. 1, 1–19. New York: Dover Publications, 1933.

Aichhorn, August. *Wayward Youth*. 1925. Reprint. Evanston, Ill.: Northwestern University Press, 1983.

Alexander, Franz, and William Healy. *Roots of Crime: Psychoanalytic Studies*. 1935. Reprint. Montclair, N.J.: Patterson Smith, 1969.

Allen, Francis A. "The Decline of the Rehabilitative Ideal in American Criminal Justice." *Cleveland State Law Review* 27 (1978): 147–56.

Allen, Trevor. "Crooks Are So 'Romantic.' " *Contemporary Review* 210 (April 1967): 213–15.

Andenaes, Johannes. *Punishment and Deterrence*. Ann Arbor: University of Michigan Press, 1974.

Angiolillo, Paul. *A Criminal as Hero: Angelo Duca*. Lawrence: Regents Press of Kansas, 1979.

Aries, Philippe. *The Hour of Our Death*. Translated by Helen Weaver. New York: Alfred Knopf, 1981.

Aristotle. *The Rhetoric of Aristotle*. Translated by Richard C. Jebb and edited by John E. Sandys. Cambridge, England: Cambridge University Press, 1909.

"Arthur Penn as Director." In *The Bonnie and Clyde Book*, edited by Sandra Wake and Nicola Hayden, 182–94. London: Lorrimer, 1972.

Auden, W. H. "The Guilty Vicarage: Notes on the Detective Story, by an Addict." *Harper's Magazine* 196 (May 1948): 406–12.

Auerbach, Erich. *Mimesis: The Representation of Reality in Western Literature*. New York: Doubleday, 1953.

Aydelotte, Frank. *Elizabethan Rogues and Vagabonds*. Oxford: Clarendon Press, 1913.

Bakan, David. *Slaughter of the Innocents*. Boston: Beacon Press, 1971.

Bald, R. C. "Introduction." In *The First Part of Henry the Fourth*, by William Shakespeare. Edited by R. C. Bald, iii-vi. New York: Appleton-Century-Crofts, 1946.

Ball, Milner S. *Lying Down Together: Law, Metaphor and Theology.* Madison: University of Wisconsin Press, 1985.

Bao, Ruo-Wang, and Rudolph Chelminski. *Prisoner of Mao.* New York: Coward McCann and Geoghegan, 1973.

Barfield, Owen. "Poetic Diction and Legal Fiction." In *The Rediscovery of Meaning and Other Essays,* 44–64. Middletown, Conn.: Wesleyan University Press, 1977.

Barnes, Harry. *The Evolution of Penology in Pennsylvania.* 1927. Reprint. Montclair, N.J.: Patterson Smith, 1968.

Barnes, Harry E., and Negley K. Teeters. *New Horizons in Criminology.* Rev. ed. New York: Prentice Hall, 1945.

Barrett, William. *Irrational Man: A Study in Existentialist Philosophy.* Westport, Conn.: Greenwood Press, 1977.

Barry, John Vincent. *Alexander Maconochie of Norfolk Island: A Study of a Pioneer in Penal Reform.* With a foreword by Sheldon Glueck. Melbourne: Oxford University Press, 1958.

Bartlett, John. *Familiar Quotations.* 14th ed. Boston: Little, Brown, 1968.

Beck, Julian. "Thoughts on the Theater from Jail: Three Letters to a Friend." In *Getting Busted: Personal Experiences of Arrest, Trial, and Prison,* edited by Ross Firestone, 319–23. N.p.: Douglas Book Corp., 1970.

Becker, Gary S. "Crime and Punishment: An Economic Approach." *Journal of Political Economy* 76 (1968): 169–217.

Becker, Lucille Frackman. *Georges Simenon.* Boston: Twayne Publishers, 1977.

Behan, Brendan. *Borstal Boy.* Boston: David Godine, 1959.

Bender, John B. *Imagining the Penitentiary: Fiction and the Architecture of Mind in Eighteenth-Century England.* Chicago: University of Chicago Press, 1987.

Bentham, Jeremy. "Panopticon versus New South Wales." In *The Works of Jeremy Bentham,* edited by John Bowring, vol. 4, 173–248. Edinburgh: William Tate, 1843.

Berger, Joseph. "Goetz Case: Commentary on Nature of Urban Life." *New York Times,* 18 June 1987, sec. B, p. 6.

Berlin, Sir Isaiah. "Two Concepts of Liberty." In *Political Philosophy,* edited by Anthony Quinton, 141–52. New York: Oxford University Press, 1967.

Berman, Harold J. *Justice in the U.S.S.R.* Cambridge, Mass.: Harvard University Press, 1963.

———. *Law and Revolution.* Cambridge, Mass.: Harvard University Press, 1983.

Berns, Jordan. "Is There Something Suspicious about the Constitutionality of Loitering Laws?" *Ohio State Law Journal* 50 (1989): 717–36.

Bettelheim, Bruno. *The Uses of Enchantment: The Meaning and Importance of Fairy Tales.* New York: Vintage Books, 1989.

Bienfeld, Franz Rudolf. "Prolegomena to a Psychoanalysis of Law and Justice." *California Law Review* 53 (October 1965): 957–1028.

Bizet, Georges. *Carmen.* Translated by Ellen H. Bleiler. New York: Dover Publications, 1970.

Blackstone, William. *Commentaries on the Laws of England.* 3d ed. Oxford: Clarendon Press, 1768.

Blainey, Geoffrey. *The Tyranny of Distance.* South Melbourne: Macmillan, 1982.

Blake, James. *The Joint.* Garden City, N.Y.: Doubleday, 1971.

Blamires, Harry. *Milton's Creation: A Guide through "Paradise Lost."* London: Methuen, 1971.

Blau, Eleanor. "Poet Rebuilds Life in U.S. after Soviet Prison Term." *New York Times,* 24 March 1987, sec. C, p. 13.

Blecker, Robert. "Haven or Hell? Inside Lorton Central Prison: Experiences of Punishment Justified." *Stanford Law Review* 42 (May 1990): 1149–1249.

Blok, Anton. "The Peasant and the Brigand: Social Banditry Reconsidered." *Comparative Studies in Society and History* 14 (September 1972): 494–503.

Boethius. *The Consolation of Philosophy.* With the English translation of "I.T." revised by H. F. Stewart. In *The Theological Tractates and the Consolation of Philosophy.* Cambridge, Mass.: Harvard University Press, 1918.

Bollinger, Lee C. "The Homer of the Pacific: Melville's Art and the Ambiguities of Judging Evil." *Michigan Law Review* 75 (1977): 823–44.

Bolt, Robert. *A Man for All Seasons.* New York: Vintage Books, 1960.

The Book of Common Prayer. New York: The Church Hymnal Corp., 1979.

The Book of J. Translated by David Rosenberg and edited by Harold Bloom. New York: Vintage Books, 1991.

Boudin, Michael. "Antitrust Doctrine and the Sway of Metaphor." *Georgetown Law Journal* 75 (December 1986): 395–422.

Bowen, Zack R. "Synge: The Playboy of the Western World." In *A J.M. Synge Literary Companion,* edited by Edward A. Kopper, Jr., 69–86. New York: Greenwood Press, 1988.

Brain, Robert. *Friends and Lovers.* New York: Basic Books, 1976.

Braly, Malcolm. *False Starts: A Memoir of San Quentin and Other Prisons.* Boston: Little, Brown, 1976.

———. *It's Cold Out There.* New York: Pocket Books, 1966.

Brenner, Charles. *An Elementary Textbook of Psychoanalysis.* Rev. ed. New York: International Universities Press, 1973.

———. *The Mind in Conflict.* New York: International Universities Press, 1982.

Brochier, J. "Prison Talk: An Interview with Michel Foucault." *Radical Philosophy* 16 (1977): 10–15.

Brombert, Victor. *The Romantic Prison: The French Tradition.* Princeton, N.J.: Princeton University Press, 1978.

———. *Victor Hugo and the Visionary Novel.* Cambridge, Mass.: Harvard University Press, 1984.

Brown, Claude, and Arthur Dunmeyer. "A Way of Life in the Ghetto." In *Problems in Political Economy*. 2d ed., edited by David Gordon, 362–64. Lexington, Mass.: D. C. Heath, 1977.

Brown, Norman O. *Life against Death: The Psychoanalytical Meaning of History*. Middletown, Conn.: Wesleyan University Press, 1959.

Brown, Rosellen. *Before and After*. New York: Farrar, Straus, Giroux, 1992.

Browning, Robert. *The Pied Piper of Hamelin*. In *The Poems*, vol. 1. New Haven: Yale University Press, 1981.

Bunyan, John. *The Pilgrim's Progress*. Nashville: Cokesbury Press, n.d.

Burke, Kenneth. *Permanence and Change*. Rev. ed. Indianapolis: Bobbs-Merrill, 1965.

Burnett, Frances Hodgson. *A Little Princess*. Boston: David R. Godine, 1989.

Bushinski, Leonard, and J. T. Nelis. "Gehenna." In *Encyclopedic Dictionary of the Bible*, edited by Louis F. Hartman, 847–48. New York: McGraw-Hill, 1963.

Butterfield, Fox. "Are American Jails Becoming Shelters from the Storm?" *New York Times*, 19 July 1992, sec. E, p. 4.

Byron, George Gordon, Lord. *The Prisoner of Chillon*. In *The Complete Poetical Works of Lord Byron*, 457–63. New York: Macmillan, 1927.

Campbell, Joseph. *The Hero with a Thousand Faces*. Princeton, N.J.: Princeton University Press, 1968.

Camus, Albert. *The Stranger*. New York: Vintage Books, 1954.

Castro, Josue de. *Death in the Northeast*. New York: Vintage Books, 1966.

Chasseguet-Smirgel, Janine. *Creativity and Perversion*. New York: W. W. Norton, 1984.

Cheever, John. *Falconer*. New York: Ballantine Books, 1977.

Christina, Diana, and Pat Carlen. "Christina: In Her Own Time." In *Criminal Women*, edited by Pat Carlen, 59–103. Cambridge, England: Polity Press, 1985.

Clark, C. M. H. *A History of Australia*. Parkville, Victoria: Melbourne University Press, 1962.

———, ed. *Sources of Australian History*. London: Oxford University Press, 1957.

Cleaver, Eldridge. *Soul on Ice*. New York: Dell, 1968.

Cockshut, A. O. J. *The Imagination of Charles Dickens*. New York: New York University Press, 1962.

Coles, Robert. *Children of Crisis*. Boston: Little, Brown, 1967.

Collins, Mortimer. *Sweet Anne Page*, vol. 1. London: Hurst and Blackett, 1868.

Collins, Philip. *Dickens and Crime*. London: Macmillan, 1962.

Collins, Wilkie. *The Woman in White*. London: Oxford University Press, 1975.

Colson, Charles. *Born Again*. Old Tappan, N.J.: Chosen Books, 1976.

Conrad, Joseph. *Heart of Darkness.* New York: W. W. Norton, 1971.

Crockett, Busby. "The Prison Trip." In *Getting Busted: Personal Experiences of Arrest, Trial, and Prison,* edited by Ross Firestone, 259–63. N.p.: Douglas Book Corp., 1970.

Dalton, Emmett. *When the Daltons Rode.* Garden City, N.Y.: Doubleday, Doran, 1931.

Davis, Jennifer. "The London Garotting Panic of 1862: A Moral Panic and the Creation of a Criminal Class in Mid-Victorian England." In *Crime and the Law: The Social History of Crime in Western Europe since 1500,* edited by V. A. C. Gatrell, Bruce Lenman, and Geoffrey Parker, 190–213. London: Europa Publications, 1980.

D'Eaubonne, Françoise. "Jean Genet, Or, The Inclement Thief." In *Genet: A Collection of Critical Essays,* edited by Peter Brooks and Joseph Halpern, 47–67. Englewood Cliffs, N.J.: Prentice Hall, 1979.

De Beaumont, Gustave, and Alexis de Toqueville. *On the Penitentiary System in the United States and Its Application in France.* Translated by Francis Lieber. New York: A. M. Kelley, 1970.

Defoe, Daniel. *The History of the Devil.* East Ardsley, England: E. P. Pub., 1972.

———. *Moll Flanders.* Norton Critical Edition. New York: W. W. Norton, 1973.

De Maupassant, Guy. *Ball-of-Fat.* In *The Great Short Stories of Guy de Maupassant,* 200–251. New York: Pocket Books, 1955.

Dickens, Charles. *Bleak House.* Boston: Houghton Mifflin, 1956.

———. *Great Expectations.* New York: Heritage Press, 1939.

———. *Little Dorrit.* Edition De Luxe. 2 vols. New York: Nottingham Society, n.d.

———. *Oliver Twist.* New York: New American Library, 1980.

———. *A Tale of Two Cities.* New York: New American Library, 1936.

Didion, Joan. *The White Album.* London: Flamingo, 1979.

Doctorow, E. L. *Billy Bathgate.* New York: Random House, 1987.

Dostoyevsky, Fyodor. *The Brothers Karamazov.* Translated by Richard Pevear and Larissa Volokhonsky. San Francisco: North Point Press, 1990.

———. *Crime and Punishment.* Translated by Jessie Coulson. Norton Critical Edition. New York: W. W. Norton, 1975.

———. *Notes from a Dead House.* Translated by L. Navrozov and Y. Guralsky. Moscow: Foreign Languages Publishing House, 1950.

Douglas, Mary. "Pollution." *International Encyclopedia of Social Sciences* 12 (1968): 336–42.

———. *Purity and Danger.* London: Frederick A. Praeger, 1966.

———. "Taboo." *New Society* 3 (1964): 24–25.

Doyle, Arthur Conan. "The Adventure of the Final Problem." In *The Illustrated Sherlock Holmes Treasury*, 315–26. New York: Avenel Books, 1976.

———. "The Adventure of the Missing Three Quarter." In *The Illustrated Sherlock Holmes Treasury*, 483–511. New York: Avenel Books, 1976.

———. "The Adventure of the Norwood Builder." In *The Illustrated Sherlock Holmes Treasury*, 354–67. New York: Avenel Books, 1976.

———. *The Hound of the Baskervilles*. In *The Illustrated Sherlock Holmes Treasury*, 529–631. New York: Avenel Books, 1976.

Drabble, Margaret. *The Ice Age*. New York: Alfred A. Knopf, 1977.

Drijvers, J. W. "Ablutions." In *Encyclopedia of Religion*, vol. 1, edited by Mircea Eliade and Charles J. Adams, 9–13. New York: Macmillan, 1987.

Dubin, Gary V., and Richard H. Robinson. "The Vagrancy Concept Reconsidered: Problems and Abuses of Status Criminality." *New York University Law Review* 37 (1962): 102–36.

du Maurier, Daphne. *Jamaica Inn*. New York: Sun Dial Press, 1937.

Durkheim, Emile. *The Division of Labor in Society*. 1893. Reprint. New York: Free Press, 1933.

———. *The Rules of Sociological Method*. 1895. Reprint. Glencoe, Ill.: The Free Press, 1958.

Ehrenzweig, Albert A. "Psychoanalytic Jurisprudence: A Common Language for Babylon." *Columbia Law Review* 65 (1965): 1331–60.

Eidelberg, Ludwig, ed. *Encyclopedia of Psychoanalysis*. New York: Free Press, 1968.

Eissler, Ruth. "Scapegoats of Society." In *Searchlights on Delinquency*, edited by K. Eissler, 288–305. New York: International Universities Press, 1949.

Eliot, George. *Middlemarch*. New York: W. W. Norton, 1977.

Erikson, Erik. *Childhood and Society*. New York: W. W. Norton, 1963.

———. *Young Man Luther*. New York: W. W. Norton, 1962.

Erikson, Kai. "On the Sociology of Deviance." In *Crime, Law and Society*, edited by Abraham Goldstein and Joseph Goldstein, 87–97. New York: Free Press, 1971.

Euripides. *Iphigenia at Taurus*. In *The Complete Greek Tragedies*, edited by David Grene and Richard Lattimore. Chicago: University of Chicago Press, 1959.

Evans, J. Martin. "Topics: Book X." In *Paradise Lost: Books IX-X*, by John Milton. Cambridge, England: Cambridge University Press, 1973.

Evans, Lloyd, and Paul Nichols, eds. *Convicts and Colonial Society*. Stanmore, N.S.W.: Cassell Australia, 1976.

Everingham, John. "Children of the First Fleet." *National Geographic* 173 (February 1988): 233–45.

Faust, Frederick, and Paul Brantingham. *Juvenile Justice Philosophy*. St. Paul, Minn.: West Publishing Co., 1979.

Feinburg, Joel. *Doing and Deserving*. Princeton, N.J.: Princeton University Press, 1970.

Fenichel, Otto. *The Psychoanalytic Theory of Neurosis*. New York: W. W. Norton, 1945.

Figner, Vera. *Memoirs of a Revolutionist*. New York: Greenwood Press, 1968.

Fitzgerald, F. Scott. *The Great Gatsby*. New York: Charles Scribner's Sons, 1925.

Fitzgerald, Tamsin. *Tamsin*. New York: Dial Press, 1973.

Fletcher, George. *A Crime of Self-Defense: Bernhard Goetz and the Law on Trial*. New York: Free Press, 1988.

Flugel, J. C. *Man, Morals and Society*. New York: International Universities Press, 1945.

Flynn, Thomas. *Tales for My Brothers' Keepers*. New York: W. W. Norton, 1976.

Foote, Caleb. "Vagrancy-Type Law and Its Administration." *University of Pennsylvania Law Review* 104 (March 1956): 603–50.

Forster, John. *The Life of Charles Dickens*. London: Dent, 1966.

Foucault, Michel. *Discipline and Punish: The Birth of the Prison*. Translated by Alan Sheridan. New York: Vintage Books, 1979.

Fowles, John. Foreword to *The Hound of the Baskervilles*, by Arthur Conan Doyle, 7–11. London: John Murray and Jonathan Cape, 1974.

Frank, Jerome. *Law and the Modern Mind*. New York: Brentano's, 1930.

Frantz, Douglas, and Robert L. Jackson. "The Spooks, the Kooks, and the Dictator: If Noriega Goes Down, He's Threatening to Take the CIA, the DEA, and the White House with Him." *Los Angeles Times*, 21 July 1991, magazine sec., p. 8.

Franz, M. L. von. "The Process of Individuation." In *Man and His Symbols*, edited by Carl G. Jung, 158–229. Garden City, N.Y.: Doubleday, 1964.

Frazer, James. *The Golden Bough*. New York: Macmillan, 1950.

Freud, Anna. *The Ego and the Mechanisms of Defense*. Rev. ed. New York: International Universities Press, 1976.

Freud, Sigmund. "Character and Anal Erotism." In *The Standard Edition of the Complete Psychological Works of Sigmund Freud*, edited by James Strachey. London: The Hogarth Press and the Institute of Psycho-analysis, 1953–74, vol. 9, 167–75.

———. "Civilization and Its Discontents." In *The Standard Edition*, vol. 21, 57–145.

———. "Dostoevsky and Parricide." In *The Standard Edition*, vol. 21, 173–94.

———. "Negation." In *The Standard Edition*, vol. 19, 233–39.

———. "On Transformations of Instincts As Exemplified in Anal Erotism." In *The Standard Edition*, vol. 17, 125–33.

———. "Some Character-Types Met with In Psycho-Analytic Work." In *The Standard Edition*, vol. 14, 309–33.

Freud, Sigmund. "Three Essays on the Theory of Sexuality." In *The Standard Edition*, vol. 7, 123–245.

Fromm, Erich. *Escape from Freedom*. New York: H. Holt, 1941.

Frost, Alan. *Convicts and Empire*. Melbourne and New York: Oxford University Press, 1980.

Frye, Northrup. *The Great Code: The Bible and Literature*. New York: Harcourt Brace Jovanovich, 1982.

Gaddis, Thomas. *Birdman of Alcatraz: The Story of Robert Stroud*. New York: Random House, 1955.

Gass, William H. "Paul Valéry: Crisis and Resolution." *New York Times Book Review*, 20 August 1972, p. 6.

Gibian, George. "Traditional Symbolism in *Crime and Punishment*." In *Crime and Punishment* by Feodor Dostoevsky, edited by George Gibian. 2d ed., 519–36. New York: W. W. Norton, 1975.

Ginzburg, Eugenia Semyonovna. *Journey into the Whirlwind*. Translated by Paul Stevenson and Max Hayward. New York: Harcourt, Brace and World, 1967.

———. *Within the Whirlwind*. Translated by Ian Boland. New York: Harcourt Brace Jovanovich, 1981.

Glaser, Daniel. "Capital Punishment—Deterrent or Stimulus to Murder? Our Unexamined Deaths and Penalties." *University of Toledo Law Review* 10 (Winter 1979): 317–33.

Glueck, Sheldon. Introduction to *Alexander Maconochie of Norfolk Island: A Study of a Pioneer in Penal Reform*, by John Vincent Barry. Melbourne: Oxford University Press, 1958.

Gluzman, Semyon. "Fear of Freedom: Psychological Decompensation or Existentialist Phenomenon." *American Journal of Psychiatry* 139 (January 1982): 57–61.

Goffman, Erving. *Asylums*. Garden City, N.Y.: Anchor Books, 1961.

Goldfarb, Ronald L. "Violence, Vigilantism and Justice." *Criminal Justice Ethics* 6 (Summer/Fall 1987): 2, 72.

Goldstein, Joseph. "Psychoanalysis and Jurisprudence." *Yale Law Journal* 77 (1968): 1053–77.

Goldstein, Joseph, Anna Freud, and Albert Solnit. *Beyond the Best Interests of the Child*. New York: Free Press, 1979.

Gorski, I. H. "Gehenna." In *New Catholic Encyclopedia*, edited by the Catholic University of America, Vol. 6, 312–13. New York: McGraw-Hill, 1967.

Greene, Donald. *The Age of Exuberance: Backgrounds to Eighteenth-Century English Literature*. New York: Random House, 1970.

Greene, Graham. *The Power and the Glory*. New York: Viking Press, 1970.

Grinstein, Alexander. "Vacations: A Psycho-Analytic Study." *International Journal of Psychoanalysis* 36 (1955): 177–86.

Gross, Irena Grudzinska. *The Scar of Revolution: Custine, Tocqueville, and the Romantic Imagination.* Berkeley: University of California Press, 1991.

Grupp, Stanley. *Theories of Punishment.* Bloomington: Indiana University Press, 1971.

Hamilton, Edith. *The Greek Way to Western Civilization.* New York: New American Library, 1942.

"Hansel and Gretel." In *The Complete Grimm's Fairy Tales*, 86–94. New York: Pantheon, 1944.

Hapgood, Robert. "Falstaff's Vocation." *Shakespeare Quarterly* 16 (1965): 91–98.

Harsin, Jill. *Policing Prostitution in Nineteenth-Century Paris.* Princeton, N.J.: Princeton University Press, 1985.

Hart, H. L. A. *Punishment and Responsibility.* New York: Oxford University Press, 1968.

Hellman, John. *American Myth and the Legacy of Vietnam.* New York: Columbia University Press, 1986.

Henderson, Joseph L. "Ancient Myths and Modern Man." In *Man and His Symbols*, edited by Carl J. Jung, 104–57. Garden City, N.Y.: Doubleday, 1964.

Henly, Burr. "'Penumbra': The Roots of a Legal Metaphor." *Hastings Constitutional Law Quarterly* 15 (Fall 1987): 81–100.

Herbert, Christopher. "Rat Worship and Taboo in Mayhew's London." *Representations* 23 (Summer 1988): 1–24.

Hibbert, Christopher. *Highwaymen.* London: Weidenfeld and Nicholson, 1967.

———. *The Roots of Evil.* 1963. Reprint. Westport, Conn.: Greenwood Press, 1978.

Himmelfarb, Martha. *Tours of Hell.* Philadelphia: University of Pennsylvania Press, 1983.

Hirsch, Adam J. "From Pillory to Penitentiary: The Rise of Criminal Incarceration in Early Massachusetts." *Michigan Law Review* 80 (1982): 1179–1269.

Hirsch, Edward. "The Gallous Story and the Dirty Deed: The Two Playboys." *Modern Drama* 26 (March 1983): 85–102.

Hobsbawm, Eric J. *Bandits.* New York: Delacorte Press, 1969.

———. *Primitive Rebels: Studies in Archaic Forms of Social Movement in the Nineteenth and Twentieth Centuries.* New York: W. W. Norton, 1959.

Hogarth, William. *A Harlot's Progress* (1732), plate 3. Reproduced in John Bender, *Imagining the Penitentiary: Fiction and the Architecture of Mind in Eighteenth-Century England*, 117. Chicago: University of Chicago Press, 1987.

Holt, Marilyn I. *The Orphan Trains: Placing Out in America.* Lincoln: University of Nebraska Press, 1992.

Hughes, Robert. *The Fatal Shore.* New York: Alfred A. Knopf, 1987.

Hugo, Victor. *Les Miserables.* Translated by Charles E. Wilbour. New York: Modern Library, 1938.

Hutheesing, Krishna Nehru. *Shadows on the Wall.* New York: J. Day, 1948.

Ignatieff, Michael. *A Just Measure of Pain: The Penitentiary in the Industrial Revolution, 1750–1850.* New York: Pantheon Books, 1978.

Ives, George. *A History of Penal Methods.* 1914. Reprint. Montclair, N.J.: Patterson Smith, 1970.

Jacobson, Edith. "Observations on the Psychological Effect of Imprisonment on Female Political Prisoners." In *Searchlights on Delinquency,* edited by K. Eissler, 341–68. New York: International Universities Press, 1949.

James, P. D. *Devices and Desires.* New York: Alfred A. Knopf, 1990.

Johnson, Adelaide. "Sanctions for Superego Lacunae of Adolescents." In *Searchlights on Delinquency,* edited by K. Eissler, 225–45. New York: International Universities Press, 1949.

Jonas, Hans. *The Gnostic Religion: The Message of the Alien God and the Beginnings of Christianity.* 2d ed. rev. Boston: Beacon Press, 1963.

Joyce, James. *A Portrait of the Artist as a Young Man.* In *The Portable James Joyce,* edited by Harry Levin, 243–525. New York: The Viking Press, 1947.

Jung, Carl G. "Approaching the Unconscious." In *Man and His Symbols,* edited by Carl G. Jung, 18–103. Garden City, N.Y.: Doubleday, 1964.

Kadish, Sanford, and Monrad Paulsen. *Criminal Law and Its Processes.* 3d ed. Boston: Little, Brown, 1975.

Kadish, Sanford, and Stephen Schulhofer. *Criminal Law and Its Processes.* 5th ed. Boston: Little, Brown, 1989.

Kaplan, Fred. *Dickens: A Biography.* New York: William Morrow, 1988.

Katz, Jay, Joseph Goldstein, and Alan Dershowitz. *Psychoanalysis, Psychiatry and Law.* New York: Free Press, 1967.

Keen, Maurice Hugh. *The Outlaws of Medieval Legend.* London: Routlege and Kegan Paul, 1961.

Kernberg, Otto. *Borderline Conditions and Pathological Narcissism.* New York: Aronson, 1975.

Kettle, Arnold. "In Defense of Moll Flanders." In *Moll Flanders,* by Daniel Defoe, 385–96. Norton Critical Edition. New York: W. W. Norton, 1973.

Kirschenbaum, Carol. "Women: The New White Collar Criminals." *Glamour* 306 (March 1987).

Klausa, Ekkehard. Review of *Hierarchie der Ausbildungsstätten, Rechtsstudium und Recht in den Vereinigten Staaten,* by Walter Weyrauch. *American Journal of Comparative Law* 25 (1977): 164–68.

Kohn, Jaakov. "Time: Two Interviews." In *Getting Busted: Personal Experiences of Arrest, Trial, and Prison,* edited by Ross Firestone, 246–57. N.p.: Douglas Book Corp., 1970.

Kohut, Heinz. *The Analysis of the Self.* New York: International Universities Press, 1971.

Kroll, Michael A. "Counsel behind Bars." *California Lawyer* (June 1987): 34–38, 99.

Kubie, Lawrence. "The Fantasy of Dirt." *Psychoanalytic Quarterly* 6 (1937): 388–425.

Lamott, Kenneth. Review of *False Starts: A Memoir of San Quentin and Other Prisons*, by Malcolm Braly. *New York Times Book Review*, 29 February 1976, 7.

Lane, Robert. *Political Ideology: Why the American Common Man Believes What He Does*. New York: Free Press, 1962.

Lansbury, Coral. *Arcady in Australia*. Carlton, Victoria: Melbourne University Press, 1970.

Lapham, Lewis. "Notebook: City Lights." *Harper's Magazine* 4 (1992): 4.

Leventhal, Harold. "Law and Literature: A Preface." *Rutgers Law Review* 32 (March/April 1979): 603–7.

Lewin, Linda. "The Oligarchical Limitations of Social Banditry in Brazil: The Case of the 'Good' Thief Antonio Silvino." In *Bandidos: The Varieties of Latin American Banditry*, edited by Richard Slatta, 67–96. New York: Greenwood Press, 1987.

Lewis, C. S. "Bluspels and Flalansferes: A Semantic Nightmare." In *Rehabilitations*, 135–58. Freeport, N.Y.: Books for Libraries Press, 1972.

Lichtenstein, Allen. "Polls, Public Opinion, Pre-trial Publicity and the Prosecution of Bernhard H. Goetz." *Social Action and Law* 10 (1985): 95–103.

Lifton, Robert. *Thought Reform and the Psychology of Totalism*. New York: W. W. Norton, 1969.

Linebaugh, Peter. "(Marxist) Social History and (Conservative) Legal History: A Reply to Professor Langbein." *New York University Law Review* 60 (1985): 212–43.

Low, Peter, John Jeffries, and Richard Bonnie. *Criminal Law*. 2d ed. Mineola, N.Y.: Foundation Press, 1986.

MacDowell, Douglas. *Athenian Homicide*. New York: Barnes and Noble, 1963.

MacInnes, Colin. *Mr. Love and Justice*. London: MacGibbon and Kee, 1960.

Mackay, David. *A Place of Exile*. Melbourne and New York: Oxford University Press, 1985.

MacKinnon, Roger, and Robert Michels. *The Psychiatric Interview in Clinical Practice*. Philadelphia: Saunders, 1971.

Mahler, Margaret, Fred Pine, and Anni Bergman. *The Psychological Birth of the Human Infant: Symbiosis and Individuation*. New York: Basic Books, 1975.

Mandelstam, Nadezhda. *Hope against Hope: A Memoir*. Translated by Max Hayward. New York: Atheneum, 1970.

Martin, Douglas. "At a Violent Jail, Warden Strives to Ease Tension." *New York Times*, 4 May 1987, sec. B, p. 1.

Massaro, Toni M. "Peremptories or Peers?—Rethinking Sixth Amendment Doctrine, Images, and Procedures." *North Carolina Law Review* 64 (March 1986): 501–64.

Maturin, Charles. *Melmoth the Wanderer.* London: Oxford University Press, 1968.

Maynard, John. *The Russian Peasant.* London: V. Gollancz, 1943.

McCarthy, Francis B., and James G. Carr. *Juvenile Law and Its Processes.* Charlottesville, Va.: Michie, 1989.

Melville, Samuel. *Letters from Attica.* New York: Morrow, 1972.

Merimee, Prosper. *Colomba and Carmen.* New York: D. Appleton, 1901.

Merton, Robert K. "Social Structure and Anomie." In *Social Theory and Social Structure.* New York: Free Press, 1968.

Meslin, Michael. "Baptism." In *Encyclopedia of Religion,* edited by Mircea Eliade and Charles J. Adams, Vol. 2, 59–63. New York: Macmillan, 1987.

Milton, John. *Paradise Lost.* In *Great Books of the Western World.* 2d ed., edited by Mortimer J. Adler, Vol. 29, 93–319. Chicago: Encyclopaedia Britannica, 1990.

Mitchell, Juliet. *Psychoanalysis and Feminism.* New York: Pantheon Books, 1974.

Moore, Barrington. *Social Origins of Dictatorship and Democracy.* Boston: Beacon Press, 1966.

Moore, Brian. Review of *Brendan,* by Ulick O'Connor. *New York Times Book Review,* 25 April 1971, 35.

Moore, Burness E., and Bernard D. Fine, eds. *A Glossary of Psychoanalytic Terms and Concepts.* 2d ed. New York: American Psychoanalytic Association, 1968.

Moore, David William. *The End of Long John Silver.* New York: Thomas Y. Cromwell, 1946.

Morgenstern, Joseph. "Bonnie and Clyde: Two Reviews by Joseph Morgenstern." In *The Bonnie and Clyde Book,* edited by Sandra Wake and Nicola Hayden, 218–19. London: Lorrimer, 1972.

Morrell, William Parker. *British Colonial Policy in the Age of Peel and Russell.* Oxford: The Clarendon Press, 1930.

Morris, Norval. "The Best Interests of the Child." *University of Chicago Law Review* 51 (Spring 1984): 447–516.

———. *The Future of Imprisonment.* Chicago: University of Chicago Press, 1973.

———. *Madness and Criminal Law.* Chicago: University of Chicago Press, 1982.

———. "The Watching Brief." *University of Chicago Law Review* 54 (1987): 1215–92.

Morris, Norval, and Michael Tonry. *Between Prison and Probation.* New York: Oxford University Press, 1990.

Morson, Gary S. "Verbal Pollution in *The Brothers Karamazov.*" In *Critical Essays on Dostoevsky,* edited by Robin F. Miller, 234–42. Boston: G. K. Hall, 1986.

Moynahan, Julian. "The Hero's Guilt: The Case of *Great Expectations.*" *Essays in Criticism* 10 (January 1960): 60–79.

Mulvaney, D. J., and J. Peter White, eds. *Australians: A Historical Library.* Cambridge, England: Cambridge University Press, 1987.

Mundy, Godfrey. *Our Antipodes.* 3 vols. London: R. Bentley, 1852.

Munroe, Ruth. *Schools of Psychoanalytic Thought: An Exposition, Critique and Attempt at Integration.* New York: Holt, Rinehart and Winston, 1955.

Murry, John M. "Metaphor." In *Countries of the Mind.* London: Oxford University Press, 1931.

Nehru, Jawaharlal. *Toward Freedom: The Autobiography of Jawaharlal Nehru.* Boston: Beacon Press, 1963.

Newman, David, and Robert Benton. "Lightning in a Bottle." In *The Bonnie and Clyde Book,* edited by Sandra Wake and Nicola Hayden, 13–30. London: Lorrimer, 1972.

Novick, Jack, and Kerry Kelly. "Projection and Externalization." *The Psychoanalytic Study of the Child* 25 (1970): 69–95.

Noyes, Alfred. *The Highwayman.* In *Collected Poems.* London: J. Murray, 1963.

Oberkirch, Ann. "Psychotherapy of a Murderer: Excerpts." *American Journal of Psychotherapy* 39 (1985): 499–514.

O'Dwyer, Josie, and Pat Carlen. "Josie: Surviving Holloway . . . and Other Women's Prisons." In *Criminal Women,* edited by Pat Carlen, 139–81. Cambridge, England: Polity Press, 1985.

The Official Icky-Poo Book. Palo Alto: Klutz Press, 1990.

Oppenheimer, Heinrich. *The Rationale of Punishment.* 1913. Reprint. Montclair, N.J.: Patterson Smith, 1975.

Osborne, Thomas Mott. *Within Prison Walls.* 1914. Reprint. Montclair, N.J.: Patterson Smith, 1969.

Payne, Robert. Introduction to *The Island: A Journey to Sakhalin,* by Anton Chekhov, xi–xxxvii. New York: Washington Square Press, 1967.

Perry, Bruce. "Escape from Freedom, Criminal Style: The Hidden Advantages of Being in Jail." *Journal of Psychiatry and Law* 12 (Summer 1984): 215–30.

Posner, Richard A. *Law and Literature.* Cambridge, Mass.: Harvard University Press, 1988.

———. "Retribution and Related Concepts of Punishment." *Journal of Legal Studies* 9 (January 1980): 71–92.

———. Review of *Hitler's Justice: The Courts of the Third Reich,* by Ingo Müller. *New Republic* 204 (June 1991): 36–42.

Puig, Manuel. *Kiss of the Spider Woman.* Translated by Thomas Colchie. New York: Vintage Books, 1978.

Punter, David. "Fictional Representation of the Law in the Eighteenth Century." *Eighteenth Century Studies* 16 (Fall 1982): 47–74.

Pyle, Howard. *The Merry Adventures of Robin Hood.* New York: New American Library, 1985.

Radzinowicz, Leon. *Ideology and Crime.* New York: Columbia University Press, 1966.

Reich, William. *Character Analysis.* 3d ed. New York: Simon and Schuster, 1972.

Renault, Mary. *The King Must Die.* London: Sceptre, 1958.

Richards, Bill. "As Legend Has It: He Used Pepper to Elude the Law. *Wall Street Journal,* 17 June 1989, sec. 1, p. 1.

Richmond, Susan. *Treasure Island: A Play in Six Scenes.* London: H. W. Deane, 1946.

Rickard, John. "Psychohistory: An Australian Perspective." *History Today* 31 (May 1981): 10–13.

Rieff, Philip. *Freud: The Mind of the Moralist.* Garden City, N.Y.: Doubleday, 1961.

Rochlin, Gregory. "The Dread of Abandonment." *The Psychoanalytic Study of the Child* 16 (1961): 451–70.

Rosenberg, Sidney. "Black Sheep and Golden Fleece: A Study of Nineteenth-Century English Attitudes toward Australian Colonials." Ph.D. diss., Columbia University, 1954.

Rothman, David J. *The Discovery of the Asylum.* Boston: Little, Brown, 1971.

Rothstein, Arnold. *The Narcissistic Pursuit of Perfection.* New York: International Universities Press, 1984.

Rycroft, Charles. "A Detective Story: Psychoanalytic Observations." *Psychoanalytic Quarterly* 26 (1957): 229–45.

Sabine, George. *A History of Political Theory.* 3d ed. New York: Holt, Rinehart and Winston, 1961.

Sachs, Albie. *The Jail Diary of Albie Sachs.* New York: McGraw-Hill, 1966.

Said, Edward. "The Mind of Winter: Reflections on Life in Exile." *Harper's Magazine* 269 (September 1984): 49–55.

Saleilles, Raymond. *The Individualization of Punishment.* 1911. Reprint. Montclair, N.J.: Patterson Smith, 1968.

Sands, Bill. *My Shadow Ran Fast.* New York: New American Library, 1964.

Schafer, Roy. "Narration in the Psychoanalytic Dialogue." *Critical Inquiry* 7 (1980): 29–53.

———. *Narrative Actions in Psychoanalysis.* Worcester, Mass.: Clark University Press, 1981.

Schiller, Frederich. *Naive and Sentimental Poetry.* In *Naive and Sentimental Poetry and On the Sublime: Two Essays.* Translated by Julias A. Elias. New York: Frederick Ungar, 1966.

———. Preface to the First Edition of *The Robbers.* In *The Works of Frederich Schiller.* Vol. 2, *Romances and Dramas,* 133–37. New York: John W. Lovell, n.d.

Schlossman, Steven L. *Love and the American Delinquent*. Chicago: University of Chicago Press, 1977.

Schoenfeld, C. G. "Law and Unconscious Motivation." *Howard Law Journal* 8 (1962): 15–26.

——. *Psychoanalysis and the Law*. Springfield, Ill.: Thomas, 1973.

Scott, Sir Walter. *Rob Roy*. Boston: Houghton Mifflin, 1923.

Shaffer, Peter. *Equus*. New York: Avon Books, 1974.

Shakespeare, William. *The Tragedy of Hamlet*. In *William Shakespeare: The Complete Works*, edited by Stanley Wells and Gary Taylor, 735–77. Oxford: Clarendon Press, 1986.

——. *I Henry IV*. In *The Complete Works*, 509–41.

——. *The Tragedy of King Lear. The Folio Text*. In *The Complete Works*, 1063–98.

——. *The Tragedy of Macbeth*. In *The Complete Works*, 1099–1126.

——. *The Tragedy of Othello*. In *The Complete Works*, 925–64.

——. *Two Gentlemen of Verona*. In *The Complete Works*, 1–27.

Shapiro, David. *Neurotic Styles*. New York: Basic Books, 1965.

Shaw, A. G. L. *Convicts and the Colonies*. 1966. Reprint. Melbourne: Melbourne University Press, 1978.

Shengold, Leonard. *"Father, Don't You See I'm Burning?" Reflections on Sex, Narcissism, Symbolism, and Murder: From Everything to Nothing*. New Haven: Yale University Press, 1991.

——. *Halo in the Sky: Observations on Anality and Defense*. New York: Guilford Press, 1988.

——. *Soul Murder: The Effects of Childhood Abuse and Deprivation*. New Haven: Yale University Press, 1989.

Sherry, Arthur H. "Vagrants, Rogues, and Vagabonds—Old Concepts in Need of Revision." *California Law Review* 48 (October 1960): 557–73.

Shipley, Joseph. *The Origins of English Words: A Discursive Dictionary of Indo-European Roots*. Baltimore: Johns Hopkins University Press, 1984.

Simmel, Georg. *Conflict*. In *Conflict and the Web of Group Affiliations*, translated by Kurt H. Wolff and Reinhard Bendix, 11–123. New York: Free Press, 1955.

——. "The Stranger." In *The Sociology of Georg Simmel*, translated and edited by Kurt H. Wolff, 402–8. New York: Free Press, 1950.

Simon, Harry. "Town without Pity: A Constitutional and Historical Analysis of Official Efforts to Drive Homeless Persons from American Cities." *Tulane Law Review* 66 (March 1992): 631–76.

Skura, Meredith Anne. *The Literary Uses of the Psychoanalytic Process*. New Haven: Yale University Press, 1981.

Slote, Walter. "Case Analysis of A Revolutionary." In *A Strategy for Research on Social Policy*, edited by Frank Bonilla and José Silva Michelena, 241–311. Cambridge, Mass.: MIT Press, 1967.

Smith, Alexander. *A Complete History of the Lives and Robberies of the Most Notorious Highwaymen*. Edited by Arthur L. Hayward. London: G. Routledge, 1933.

Smith, Edgar. "Life in the Death House." In *Getting Busted: Personal Experiences of Arrest, Trial, and Prison*, edited by Ross Firestone, 339–46. N.p.: Douglas Book Corp., 1970.

Smith, Langdon. *Evolution: A Fantasy*. Boston: J. W. Luce, 1909.

Sobell, Morton. *On Doing Time*. New York: Charles Scribner's Sons, 1974.

Solzhenitsyn, Aleksandr. *The Cancer Ward*. Translated by Rebecca Frank. New York: Dial Press, 1968.

———. *The First Circle*. Translated by Thomas P. Whitney. New York: Bantam Books, 1969.

———. *The Gulag Archipelago*. Translated by H. Willetts. New York: Harper and Row, 1978.

———. *One Day in the Life of Ivan Denisovich*. Translated by Ronald Hingley and Max Hayward. New York: Bantam Books, 1963.

Sophocles. *Antigone*. In *World Drama*, edited by Barrett H. Clark, vol. 13, 20–42. New York: Dover Publications, 1933.

———. *Oedipus Tyrannus*. New York: W. W. Norton, 1970.

Spence, Donald. *Narrative Truth and Historical Truth*. New York: W. W. Norton, 1982.

Spurgeon, Caroline F. E. *Shakespeare's Imagery and What It Tells Us*. 1935. Reprint. New York: Cambridge University Press, 1968.

Stallybrass, Peter, and Allon White. *The Politics and Poetics of Transgression*. Ithaca, N.Y.: Cornell University Press, 1986.

Steckmesser, Kent L. "Robin Hood and the American Outlaw." *Journal of American Folklore* 79 (1966): 348–55.

Steffan, Thomas Guy, ed. *Lord Byron's Cain*. Austin: University of Texas Press, 1968.

Steinbeck, John. *The Grapes of Wrath*. 1939. Reprint. New York: The Viking Press, 1958.

Stendhal. *The Charterhouse of Parma*. Translated by C. K. Scott Moncrieff. 2 vols. New York: Boni and Liveright, 1925.

Stevenson, Robert Louis. *The Black Arrow*. New York: Airmont Books, 1963.

———. *Kidnapped*. New York: New American Library, 1987.

———. *Treasure Island*. New York: Charles Scribner's Sons, 1911.

———. *Treasure Island*. New York: Bantam Books, 1981.

Strauss, Erwin W. *On Obsession: A Clinical and Methodological Study*. Nervous and Mental Disease Monographs, no. 73. 1948. Reprint. New York: Johnson Reprint Corp., 1968.

Sturma, Michael. *Vice in a Vicious Society*. St. Lucia, Queensland: University of Queensland Press, 1983.

Sullivan, Richard F. "The Economics of Crime: An Introduction to the Orthodox Literature." In *Problems in Political Economy*. 2d ed. Edited by David Gordon, 374–78. Lexington, Mass.: D. C. Heath, 1977.

Suro, Roberto. "A Model and a Murder: Italy's High Life on Trial." *New York Times*, 16 June 1986, sec. A, p. 5.

Swinburne, Algernon Charles. *The Triumph of Time*. In *The Complete Works of Algernon Charles Swinburne*. New York: Russel and Russel, 1925.

Symons, Julian. *Mortal Consequences*. New York: Harper and Row, 1972.

Synge, John Millington. *The Playboy of the Western World*. London: Benn, 1975.

Tannenbaum, Frank. *Osborne of Sing Sing*. Chapel Hill: University of North Carolina Press, 1933.

Tatum, Stephen. *Inventing Billy the Kid: Visions of the Outlaw in America, 1881–1981*. Albuquerque: University of New Mexico Press, 1982.

Taylor, A. E. *Socrates: The Man and His Thought*. Garden City, N.Y.: Doubleday, 1953.

Tchaikovsky, Chris. "Looking for Trouble." In *Criminal Women*, edited by Pat Carlen, 14–58. Cambridge, U.K.: Polity Press, 1985.

Teeters, Negley K., and John D. Shearer. *The Prison at Philadelphia*. New York: Published for Temple University Publications by Columbia University Press, 1957.

Terry, Don. "More Familiar, Life in Cell Seems Less Terrible." *New York Times*, 13 September 1992, sec. A, p. 1.

Thomas, Dylan. "Fern Hill." In *Selected Writings*. New York: New Directions, 1946.

Thomas, Mason P. "Child Abuse and Neglect, Part I: Historical Overview, Legal Matrix, and Social Perspectives." *North Carolina Law Review* 50 (1972): 293–349.

Thoreau, Henry David. *Walden*. Philadelphia: Courage Books, 1987.

Tiedeman, Christopher. *Limitations of Police Power*. St. Louis: F. H. Thomas Law Book Co., 1886.

Tolkien, J. R. R. "On Fairy Stories." In *Tree and Leaf*, 9–73. London: Unwin Hyman, 1988.

Tolstoi, Lev. *Resurrection*. Translated by Louise Maude. Moscow: Foreign Languages Publishing House, 1899.

———. *War and Peace*. Translated by Louise and Alymer Maude. New York: W. W. Norton, 1966.

Treaster, Joseph. "Two U.S. Judges, Protesting Policies, Are Declining to Take Drug Cases." *New York Times*, 17 April 1993, p. 7.

U.S. Department of Justice. *Correctional Populations in the United States: 1991.* Washington, D.C.: U.S. Department of Justice, 1993.

———. *Criminal Victimization in the United States, 1990.* Washington, D.C.: U.S. Department of Justice, 1992.

Ullathorne, William. *The Catholic Mission in Australasia.* Liverpool: Rockliff and Duckworth, 1837.

Van den Haag, Ernest. *Punishing Criminals: Concerning a Very Old and Painful Question.* New York: Basic Books, 1975.

Viard, A. "Gehenna." In *Encyclopedic Dictionary of Religion,* edited by Paul Meagher, Thomas O'Brien, and Sister Consuelo Maria Aherne, vol. F-N, 1457. Washington, D.C.: Corpus Publications, 1979.

"Vigilante Justice." *National Law Journal* 7 (1985): 12.

von Gebsattel, V. E. "The World of the Compulsive." In *Existence,* edited by Rollo May, Ernest Angel, and Henri F. Ellenberger, 170–87. New York: Basic Books, 1958.

Von Hentig, Hans. *Punishment: Its Origin, Purpose and Psychology.* 1937. Reprint. Montclair, N.J.: Patterson Smith, 1973.

Von Hirsch, Andrew. *Doing Justice.* New York: Hill and Wang, 1976.

Wake, Sandra, and Nicola Hayden, eds. *The Bonnie and Clyde Book.* London: Lorrimer, 1972.

Walker, Nigel. *Punishment, Danger and Stigma.* Oxford: Basil Blackwell, 1980.

Wallach, Erica. *Light at Midnight.* Garden City, N.Y.: Doubleday, 1967.

Warren, Jennifer. "A Modern-Day Dungeon." *Los Angeles Times,* 7 September 1993, sec. A, p. 3.

Warren, Robert Penn. *All the King's Men.* New York: Modern Library, 1953.

Weisberg, Richard H. "Comparative Law in Comparative Literature: The Figure of the 'Examining Magistrate' in Dostoevski and Camus." *Rutgers Law Review* 29 (1976): 237–58.

———. *The Failure of the Word.* New Haven, Conn.: Yale University Press, 1984.

———. "Wigmore's 'Legal Novels' Revisited: New Resources for the Expansive Lawyer." *Northwestern University Law Review* 71 (1976): 17–28.

Wertenbaker, Timberlake. *Our Country's Good.* Royal Court Writers Series. London: Methuen in Association with the Royal Court Theatre, 1988.

Wesley, John. "On Dress." In *Sermons on Several Occasions,* 3:417. Nashville, Tenn.: Southern Methodist Publishing House, 1879.

West, Robin. "Authority, Autonomy and Choice: The Role of Consent in the Moral and Political Visions of Franz Kafka and Richard Posner." *Harvard Law Review* 99 (1985): 384–428.

Wexler, Richard. *Wounded Innocents.* Buffalo, N.Y.: Prometheus Books, 1990.

Weyrauch, Walter O., and Maureen A. Bell. "Autonomous Lawmaking: The Case of the Gypsies." *Yale Law Journal* 103 (1993): 323–99.

Wheelwright, Philip. *The Burning Fountain: A Study in the Language of Symbolism.* Rev. ed. Bloomington: Indiana University Press, 1968.

———. *Metaphor and Reality.* Bloomington: Indiana University Press, 1962.

White, James Boyd. *The Legal Imagination: Studies in the Nature of Legal Thought and Expression.* Boston: Little, Brown, 1973.

———. *When Words Lose Their Meaning.* Chicago: University of Chicago Press, 1984.

White, Richard. "Outlaw Gangs of the Middle Border: American Social Bandits." *The Western Historical Quarterly* 12 (October 1981): 387–408.

Wideman, John Edgar. *Brothers and Keepers.* New York: Holt, Rinehart and Winston, 1984.

Williams, Patricia. *The Alchemy of Race and Rights.* Cambridge, Mass.: Harvard University Press, 1991.

Winnicott, D. W. *Deprivation and Delinquency.* London: Tavistock Publications, 1984.

Winter, Steven L. "The Metaphor of Standing and the Problem of Self-Governance." *Stanford Law Review* 40 (July 1988): 1371–1516.

Wolin, Sheldon. *Politics and Vision: Continuity and Innovation in Western Political Thought.* Boston: Little, Brown, 1960.

Wood, F. L. W. "Jeremy Bentham versus New South Wales." *Royal Australian Historical Society: Journal and Proceedings* 19 (1933): 329–51.

Woolf, Virginia. "Defoe." In *Moll Flanders*, by Daniel Defoe, 377–43. Norton Critical Edition. New York: W. W. Norton, 1973.

Wordsworth, William. "Ode: Intimations of Immortality from Recollections of Early Childhood." In *Poems by William Wordsworth*, edited by Edward Dowden. Boston: Ginn, 1897.

Wright, Judith. *Preoccupations in Australian Poetry.* Melbourne: Oxford University Press, 1965.

X, Malcolm, and Alex Haley. *The Autobiography of Malcolm X.* New York: Ballantine Books, 1965.

York, Michael. "Judge Rejects Federal Sentencing Guidelines: Mandatory 30-Year Imprisonment for Repeat Drug Offender Called Unconstitutional." *The Washington Post*, 30 April 1993, sec. D, p. 5.

Zamyatin, Yevgeny. "Backstage." In *A Soviet Heretic: Essays by Yevgeny Zamyatin*, 190–201. Translated by Mirra Ginsburg. Chicago: University of Chicago Press, 1970.

Zilboorg, Gregory. *The Psychology of the Criminal Act and Punishment.* New York: Harcourt, Brace, 1954.

Zimring, Franklin, and Gordon Hawkins. *Deterrence: The Legal Threat in Crime Control.* Chicago: University of Chicago Press, 1973.

FILMS AND TELEVISION SHOWS

"Gangsters: A Golden Age" (WVEU television broadcast, 28 September 1989).

The Grapes of Wrath. Produced by Darryl F. Zanuck. Twentieth Century-Fox Film Corp., 1940.

"Jessye Norman Sings *Carmen*" (WPBA television broadcast, 20 November 1989).

Modern Times. Produced by Charles Chaplin. United Artists, 1936.

Murder by Decree. Produced by Bob Clark and Rene Dupont. Embassy Pictures, 1978.

Otello. Produced by Menahem Golan and Yoram Globus. Cannon Films, Inc., and Cannon International, B.V., 1986. Videocassette.

Peter Pan (NBC television broadcast, 8 December 1960).

The Princess Comes Across. Produced by Arthur Hornblow, Jr. Paramount Pictures, 1936.

Psycho. Produced by Alfred Hitchcock. Paramount Pictures, 1960.

60 Minutes (CBS television broadcast, 12 September 1993).

To Catch a Thief. Produced by Alfred Hitchcock. Paramount Pictures, 1954.

Treasure Island. Produced by Perce Pearce. Disney, 1950.

Treasure Island. Produced by Hunt Stromberg. Metro-Goldwyn-Mayer, 1934.

Index